PRACTICALLY

RADICAL

"Practically Radical is the most powerful and instructive change manual you'll ever read."
—Daniel H. Pink, bestselling author of *A Whole New Mind* and *Drive*

NOT-SO-CRAZY WAYS TO TRANSFORM YOUR COMPANY, SHAKE UP YOUR INDUSTRY, AND CHALLENGE YOURSELF

WILLIAM C. TAYLOR

COFOUNDER, FAST COMPANY MAGAZINE

Named a
Best Book of the Year
by

Best Books for Entrepreneurs
Inc. magazine

Best Leadership Books
Leadership Now

Great Education Reads
Huffington Post

Best Business Books
American Express Open Forum

Praise for *Practically Radical*

"*Practically Radical* inspires leaders to aim higher—to produce lasting change by advancing deeply held values. The ideas are fresh, the advice is stuff you can actually use, and the results will be tangible. Read this book—then roll up your sleeves and get to work!"

—Arianna Huffington, cofounder and editor in chief, Huffington Post

"*Practically Radical* can rightly be seen as a successor to Jim Collins's seminal book, *Good to Great* . . . with an enthusiasm that shines through and becomes infectious—the type of enthusiasm that makes a reader devour the book and then return for seconds."

—Logan Lo, *New York Journal of Books*

"*Practically Radical* is the most powerful and instructive change manual you'll ever read. It will persuade and inspire you to change your business, your work, and maybe your life."

—Daniel H. Pink, bestselling author of *A Whole New Mind* and *Drive*

"Average is no longer an option for those that want to be successful. Bill Taylor lives that idea every day and on every page."

—Seth Godin, bestselling author of *Linchpin*

"An eye-opening joy . . . a dynamic tutorial that anyone who works for a living and who wants his company to succeed can benefit from. As a bonus, Mr. Taylor is a natural storyteller."
—Carol Herman, *Washington Times*

"Bill Taylor has a cult following in workplace and management circles."
—Christine Romans, CNN, *Your Bottom Line*

"*Practically Radical* is a radically practical book, chock-full of instantly applicable ideas and lessons."   —Jack Covert, founder, 800-CEORead

"Taylor has created a lens through which leaders can look at an emerging reality and thus ask better questions and get better answers. The ideas and stories are compelling."   —David K. Hurst, *Strategy+Business*

"An engaging and briskly written read that will captivate and benefit businesspeople interested in change and innovation."
—*Publishers Weekly*

"An up-close look at some of the most fascinating and successful organizations in the world. . . . If you are looking for unique ways to tackle the biggest and thorniest of your strategic challenges, *Practically Radical* is a good book to have on your desk to guide you."
—Steve Cunningham, *National Post* (California)

"*Practically Radical* is just the catalyst we need to foment the reinvention of companies and leadership for the next decade. Bill Taylor offers provocative ideas and real-world wisdom for executives in any field who want to energize themselves and their people."
—Arkadi Kuhlmann, President and CEO,
ING Direct USA; author of *The Orange Code*

"*Practically Radical* is a must-read for organizations that want to stay energized and relevant in today's changing markets. The book challenges leaders to think differently in order to renew their companies, while staying true to their core mission."
—Gail McGovern, President and CEO, American Red Cross

"Bill Taylor's timing is ideal. After staring into the abyss of the financial crisis, it's human nature to become risk-averse. *Practically Radical* reminds us that this is not the time to downsize your dreams or stop taking chances. These times demand ideas and actions to capitalize on crisis and change the competitive landscape. Whether you are with a startup or trying to transition a legacy business, there are important lessons to be learned from this book."

—Sir Martin Sorrell, Chief Executive, WPP

"We all understand the need for change and transformation in the business world. Rarely do we address the implications of implementing change in organizations. *Practically Radical* takes on this challenge as a handbook for successful transformation. A great tutorial for implementing your change agenda."

—Anne Mulcahy, former chairman and CEO, Xerox Corporation

"*Practically Radical* is packed with big ideas, hands-on advice, and inspiring case studies to help you succeed. It's a game plan for entrepreneurs and executives who want to change the world for the better."

—Guy Kawasaki, cofounder of Alltop.com
and former Apple chief evangelist

"I haven't had a book this marked-up, underlined, starred, and dog-eared in quite a while." —Mark Howell, StrategyCentral.org

"Lively and eloquent. . . . The book provides a wealth of information about the behind-the-scenes efforts of change agents in the real world."

—Robert Morris, Employee Engagement Network

Praise for *Mavericks at Work*

"A pivotal work in the tradition of *In Search of Excellence* and *Good to Great*." —*The Economist*

"Thinking differently is one thing, but what about actually doing differently? That's precisely the key to success for each of the three dozen companies profiled by veteran business journalists Taylor and LaBarre. Eschewing the platitudes that mar many 'visionary' business tomes, the authors instead use concrete examples from firms big and small, old and new to show what's possible for those smart and bold enough to follow their own drummers."
                                                    —John Sparks, *Newsweek*

"In the introduction, Taylor and LaBarre say they will consider the book a success if it 'opens your eyes, engages your imagination, and encourages you to think bigger and aim higher.' On that level, with many readers managing in a business world plagued by risk-aversion, conformity, and copycat benchmarking, *Mavericks* is likely to succeed."
                                              —Jena McGregor, *BusinessWeek*

"The mavericks described in *Mavericks at Work* are to be admired and imitated. . . . Example after example tumbles out of these pages in a seemingly inexhaustible supply. The energy of the narrative never slackens. . . . In a sense the book is also a defiant act, a bold and idealistic declaration of faith in the principles of the 'new economy', five years on."
                                               —Stefan Stern, *Financial Times*

"You're fed up with business as usual. You've got a bundle of fresh ideas and bottomless ambition. You're determined to shake up your company and make a difference. But do you have the moxie, smarts, and staying power to be a great innovator? To find out, compare yourself with some of the most restless and creative business minds at work today: thirty-two remarkable entrepreneurs who have battled bureaucracy and stasis, and won, while redefining success in their industries. In their stories, captured in *Mavericks at Work: Why the Most Original Minds in Business Win*, some common traits emerge. . . . *U.S. News* has distilled this insightful book's key lessons into five maxims of mavericks."
                                       —Rick Newman, *U.S. News & World Report*

"*Mavericks at Work* profiles nonconformists who have turned quixotic ideas into great companies. By the time you reach the end of this very readable set of profiles, you may just be itching to set aside the blinders of conventional wisdom and embark on a quixotic quest of your own."
                                              —Amy Joyce, *Washington Post*

"If this book does not leave you inspired to change, I'm not sure what will."
—Management Today

"If *Mavericks at Work* had come out before I started TheStreet.com, I could have saved my investors (and myself) $100 million—because I would have applied its lessons every day to my company. If you own a business, or want to own a business, this one's for you!"
—James J. Cramer, cofounder, TheStreet.com and host of CNBC's "Mad Money with Jim Cramer"

"Just below the surface in today's plodding environment, a new crop of business upstarts has been challenging incumbents in industry after industry. These 'mavericks,' celebrated in a new book by *Fast Company* magazine alums William C. Taylor and Polly LaBarre, are defined less by their use of technology than by what the authors term their 'strategic originality' in approaching the market. The roster of mavericks presented by Taylor and LaBarre is remarkably diverse, from Craigslist to Cirque du Soleil, but the common thread is energy, imagination, and an anti-establishment bent."
—Robert Weisman, *Boston Globe*

"It's a nice change of pace to read a business book that's exceptionally well written. . . . Nicely constructed and a welcome relief to anyone who regularly slogs through the underbrush of financial or marketing tomes or too-cute parables. . . . William Taylor's and Polly LaBarre's palpable enthusiasm . . . and the selection of companies and people they examine in their book make the whole add up to much more than the sum of its parts. . . . Stimulating thinking to help all employees—not just owners and managers—transcend constraints to make their organizations successful and meaningful. . . . Good book!"
—Richard Pachter, *Miami Herald*

"I've read [*Mavericks at Work*] and find it a multi-splendored information engine about innovative business approaches so much so that when you get over its exciting, fluid prose, you are left with more questions than the book answers. Which means, given its genre, that it is a very good book indeed, steering you, as it does, to explore your own 'maverick' territory."
—Ralph Nader

ALSO BY WILLIAM C. TAYLOR

*Mavericks at Work: Why the Most Original
Minds in Business Win* (with Polly LaBarre)

*Going Global: Four Entrepreneurs Map the
New World Marketplace* (with Alan M. Webber)

*No-Excuses Management: Proven Systems for Starting
Fast, Growing Quickly, and Surviving Hard Times*
(with T. J. Rodgers and Rick Foreman)

The Big Boys: Power and Position in American Business
(with Ralph Nader)

PRACTICALLY RADICAL

NOT-SO-CRAZY WAYS TO TRANSFORM YOUR COMPANY, SHAKE UP YOUR INDUSTRY, AND CHALLENGE YOURSELF

WILLIAM C. TAYLOR

WILLIAM MORROW
An Imprint of HarperCollinsPublishers

HarperCollins books may be purchased for educational, business, or sales promotional use. For information please write: Special Markets Department, HarperCollins Publishers, 10 East 53rd Street, New York, NY 10022.

A hardcover edition of this book was published in 2011 by William Morrow, an imprint of HarperCollins Publishers.

FIRST WILLIAM MORROW PAPERBACK EDITION PUBLISHED 2012.

Designed by Jamie Lynn Kerner

Library of Congress Cataloging-in-Publication Data
Taylor, William C. (William Charles), 1959–
    Practically radical : not-so-crazy ways to transform your company, shake up your industry, and challenge yourself / William C. Taylor. —1st ed.
        p. cm.
Includes bibliographical references and index.
    ISBN: 978-0-06-173461-8
    1. Organizational change. 2. Leadership. I. Title.
HD58.8.T394 2011
658.4'06—dc22   2010028021

ISBN 978-0-06-173468-7 (pbk.)

12 13 14 15 16 OV/RRD 10 9 8 7 6 5 4 3 2 1

CONTENTS

A GAME PLAN FOR GAME CHANGERS

Problems cannot be solved at the same level of awareness that created them.

—ALBERT EINSTEIN

If all you ever do is all you've ever done, then all you'll ever get is all you ever got.

—UNKNOWN TEXAS GENIUS

THIS BOOK IS MEANT AS a guide for leaders in all walks of life who aspire to fix what's wrong with their organizations, to launch new initiatives with the best chance to succeed, and to rethink the logic of leadership itself as they work to rally their colleagues around an agenda for renewal. In other words, it is a manifesto for change and a manual for achieving it—at a moment when change is the name of the game.

Full disclosure: A few years ago, when I first had the idea for *Practically Radical*, I had no inkling that America and the global economy were about to experience the worst dislocation since the Great Depression. And, truth be told, my mind-set in the early stages of this work, as stock markets slid and panic spread, was a self-centered mix of doubt and despair: How could I develop a game plan for game changers when everything was changing right before my eyes—and in the wrong direction? How could I provide a set of insights and answers to help leaders transform their organizations when many of the economy's leading organizations seemed to be on the brink of disaster—and almost everything about leadership seemed to be open to question? How could I produce a work of energy and optimism when the spirit of the times was marked by fear, confusion, and division?

Then something eye-opening happened. I put aside my anxieties, set aside the grim headlines, and immersed myself in the struggles and triumphs of more than twenty-five organizations that are achieving dramatic results under some of the most trying conditions imaginable. Like most business thinkers, I read widely about the ever-changing dynamics of competition, work, and success: media accounts, scholarly articles, books, blogs, business-school cases. But the way I truly change my mind about business and organizational life is to see it for myself, up close and personal: to spend time with executives and frontline employees; walk the halls of their companies and factories; visit labs, warehouses, and stores; sit in on closed-door meetings; and hang out in training sessions. I learn the most when I encounter organizations whose strategy, culture, and day-to-day ways of working are the least like what passes for established thinking and conventional wisdom.

The more places I visited, and the closer I looked, the more convinced I became that turbulent times were precisely the *right* time to explore the hard work of making big change. I was privy to the strategies and tactics of a diverse collection of business innovators in a wide variety of fields: a high-profile Internet company that reinvented customer service for the digital age and invented an iconic brand in the process; a ninety-five-year-old hospital company, based in one of America's most distressed cities, that has redesigned how a hospital works and what patients experience; the irrepressible billionaire who rescued the Swiss watch industry from near oblivion and transformed it into a global juggernaut; an upstart Brazilian retailer that figured out how to deliver rich shopping experiences to the country's poorest shoppers and used its unique business model to hold its own against bigger rivals; a health-care company that recovered from near bankruptcy to thrive in a punishing field by unleashing an energetic and highly engaged workforce whose enthusiasm has to be seen to be believed.

I also made it a point to search beyond the traditional boundaries of business, to explore the hard work of making big change in areas where organizations play for high stakes, but where success is not defined by profit and loss. So I studied the strategies and tactics of a diverse collection of governmental, social, even cultural innovators in a wide variety of fields: the leader of one of the world's most famous crime-fighting organizations, who has visited 125 countries in a crusade to transform how police respond to the most dangerous threats of the twenty-first century; the chief of one of the oldest police departments in the United States, who has remade a force that was once notorious for corruption and cronyism into a model of excellence and innovation; a world-class chamber orchestra that dazzles audiences around the world with its daring and precise live performances, despite the fact that it plays without the ultimate symbol of leadership in the classical-music world, the all-powerful conductor; the CEO of one of the most iconic and ubiquitous membership organizations in the United States, who has led a truly all-American case study in how to make a nearly one-hundred-year-old brand meaningful and relevant again.

These innovators were not paralyzed by the degree of difficulty associated with their agenda for renewal. In fact, they were *energized* by it. They were making big things happen in new ways—unleashing improvements and driving transformations that will shape the fortunes of their organizations and the future of their fields for years to come. They were mastering a set of challenges that define the work of leaders in every field—challenges that the global economic crisis and its aftermath make more urgent than ever.

Paul Romer, the influential economist, is celebrated within the profession for his vital (albeit highly technical) contributions to our understanding of the relationship between new ideas, technological change, and growth. To us civilians, though, he may be best known for a passing quip that he made to *New York Times* columnist Thomas L. Friedman, a one-liner that has become the mantra of the moment from the White House to Silicon Valley: "A crisis," Romer famously said, "is a terrible thing to waste."[1]

We are all struggling to make sense of the fallout from a once-in-a-lifetime crisis that promises to shape the economy and the business culture for years to come, to learn lessons that will guide us as we recover and rebuild. My worry is that too many leaders will learn the *wrong* lessons, that they will become conservative and risk averse, that they will resist deep-seated change rather than embrace it as the only way to emerge from the depths of their (and our) despair. That would be a huge mistake—and a terrible way to let a crisis go to waste.

In *Reset*, a meltdown-inspired treatise that argues for a sweeping reevaluation of American politics, culture, and society, novelist and radio host Kurt Andersen offers a reform agenda for business as well. It is urgent, he says, for executives to question their priorities and retool their strategies. At the same time, "We must not start behaving now like overcautious, unambitious scaredy-cats," he warns. "We cannot just hunker down, cross our fingers, hysterically pinch our pennies, wait for the crisis to pass, and expect to go back to business as usual. . . . This *is* the end of the world as we've known it. But it isn't the end of the world." It is, in fact, "the moment for businesspeople to think different and think big."[2]

I like how Andersen thinks. To be sure, at some level, corporate conservatism—cut costs first, worry about the costs of those cuts later—is a natural reaction to decades of creativity run amok. Who are the geniuses who invented subprime loans and collateralized debt obligations, and can't we exile them to Elba for the next ten years? (Seems fair; Napoleon stayed for only three hundred days.) Weren't we all better off before the creation of the vast worldwide market in derivatives, the impossible-to-understand financial contracts that were at the root of so much of what went wrong in the capital markets? Shouldn't we concede, once and for all, that our fascination with "disruptive" technologies and "breakthrough" business models has done more harm than good?

> **Novelist Kurt Andersen puts it well: This is "the moment for businesspeople to think different and think big."**

Leave it to Warren Buffett, one of the world's richest men, to offer a thoughtful perspective that's worth its weight in gold. In a memorable, hour-long PBS interview with Charlie Rose, Buffett gave a master class in how the world got into this economic mess and what we can learn from it.

At one point, Rose asked the question that scholars, pundits, and plaintiff's attorneys will be debating for years: "Should wise people have known better?" Of course they should have, Buffett replied, but there's a "natural progression" to how good new ideas go badly wrong. He called this progression the "three Is." First come the *innovators*, who see opportunities that others don't and champion new ideas that create genuine value. Then come the *imitators*, who copy what the innovators have done. Sometimes they improve on the original idea; often they tarnish it. Last come the *idiots*, whose avarice undermines the very innovations they are trying to exploit.

The problem, in other words, isn't with innovation itself—it's with the imitation and idiocy that follow. "People don't get smarter about things as basic as greed," Warren Buffett warned Charlie Rose. He's right. But there's no reason we can't be reasonably intelligent about what we learn from the idiocy of the last decade and how we move beyond it.[3]

On this score, the past is an illuminating guide to the future. What history shows is that economic trauma and its lingering aftershocks are as much about psychology as about GNP, as much about withering confidence as about shriveling demand. As leaders, we have no control over how fast markets grow or how wisely Wall Street gambles with other people's money. But we do control our own mind-sets and "animal spirits"—the memorable phrase coined by a thinker even more influential than Paul Romer or Warren Buffett.

Here's how John Maynard Keynes, in the depths of the Great Depression, explained what he meant: "A large proportion of our positive activities depend on spontaneous optimism rather than mathematical expectations, whether moral or hedonistic or economic. Most, probably, of our decisions to do something positive . . . can only be taken as the result of animal spirits—a spontaneous urge to action rather than inaction, and not as the outcome of a weighted average of quantitative benefits multiplied by quantitative probabilities."

In 2009, in the middle of the worst economic conditions since when Keynes wrote, two highly regarded economists published a book about "how human psychology drives the economy, and why it matters for global capitalism." In a nod to the master, Professors George A. Akerlof and Robert J. Shiller called their book *Animal Spirits* and restated and updated Keynes's forgotten message from the 1930s. "To understand how economies work and how we can manage them and prosper," they write, "we must pay attention to the thought patterns that animate people's ideas and feelings, their *animal spirits*. We will never really understand important economic events unless we confront the fact that their causes are largely mental in nature."[4]

Modern economists like Akerlof and Shiller have begun to turn to behavioral analysis to explain why markets, technologies, and industries first overshoot and then tumble to earth. But the ideas that explain why certain fields fly too high during boom times also explain why so many executives shoot so low during tougher times. If all you've got is a spreadsheet filled with red ink and dire forecasts, it's easy to be paralyzed by fear and resistant to change. But if you've got some leadership nerve, if you can summon the "animal spirits" of which Keynes and his modern disciples write, then hard times can be a great time to separate yourself from the pack and build advantages for years to come.

In part this is a matter of faith—in Keynes's words, "a spontaneous urge to action rather than inaction." But it's also a matter of record. The Great Depression itself was a springboard to a number of enduring product and business innovations that delivered great rewards to those with the courage to unleash them. For example, in a well-researched essay titled "Design Loves a Depression," Michael Cannell chronicled how the dark days of the 1930s became a golden age of design. For the best designers, the uniquely difficult circumstances were a spur to unprecedented creativity. They used new materials, new forms, and new styles to create products and looks that were relevant to a new era and culture.[5]

> If all you've got is a spreadsheet filled with red ink, it's easy to be paralyzed by fear. But if you can summon some leadership nerve, then hard times can be a great time to separate yourself and build advantages for years to come.

A case in point: designer Russel Wright, who, according to Cannell, "acted as the Depression's Martha Stewart," creating cheap and beautiful furniture that addressed a more frugal and informal consumer sensibility. His American Modern dinnerware still ranks as the bestselling dinnerware in U.S. history, and his signature, on the bottom of his mass-produced creations, was the first time a designer's name came to be a recognized brand in the mass market—a precursor of sorts to Martha Stewart and Ralph Lauren. Wright's official biography describes his legacy this way: "Russel Wright revolutionized the American home and the way people lived there. His inexpensive, mass produced dinnerware, furniture, appliances, and textiles were not only visually and technically innovative, but were also the tools to achieve his concept of 'easier living,' a unique American lifestyle that was gracious yet contemporary and informal."[6]

Cannell also highlights the legendary husband-and-wife team of Charles and Ray Eames (Ray's full name was Ray-Bernice Alexandra Kaiser Eames), who, "in the scarcity of the 1940s," produced "furniture and other products of enduring appeal from cheap materials like plastic, resin, and plywood." During an era of limited resources and unlimited anxiety, the creativity of Charles and Ray Eames, in the words of the Library of Congress, "gave shape to America's twentieth century. Their lives and work represented the nation's defining social movements: the West Coast's coming-of-age, the economy's shift from making goods to producing information, and the global expansion of American culture. The Eameses embraced the era's visionary concept of modern design as an agent of social change, elevating it to a national agenda."[7]

Cannell's ultimate conclusion: "Design tends to thrive in hard times." And it's not just design. A fascinating white paper by Bradley Johnson, director of data analytics with *Advertising Age*, makes the connection between dark times and bright opportunities in so many fields. Johnson looked at the lowest point of the Great Depression (August 1929–March 1933), the Great Stagflation of 1973–1975, and the Carter/Reagan recession of 1980–1982. What's remarkable about these three periods of economic trauma, he reminds us, is that the problems they posed inspired creative responses that reshaped markets for decades to come.[8]

One representative example from the Depression: General Motors had to figure out how to maintain its upscale Buick brand in a sinking economy. The solution? Persuade consumers to buy a used Buick rather than a cheaper new car—a way to keep struggling dealers afloat and hold back the encroachment of rival brands. It was a daring idea at the time, and it reshaped dealer economics and marketing priorities. (If only GM's modern-day leaders could have summoned such creativity amid crisis.)

Johnson also reminds us that it was the upheaval in the airline business during the early 1980s—a frightening combination of severe recession and industry deregulation—that inspired American Airlines to introduce the exotic concept of the "frequent-flyer" program in May 1981. Sure, it was a creative short-term move to promote brand loyalty. But it forever changed the dynamics of competition in the airline business.

There are so many other examples of the power of "animal spirits" in a dispirited and uncertain environment. Henry Luce launched the lavish and superexpensive ($10 per year!) *Fortune* magazine in February 1930, just months after the Crash of '29. It was a counterintuitive move that became an immediate success—and went on to become a publishing icon. Luce's successors at Time Inc. launched the intentionally escapist *People* magazine in March 1974, into the teeth of the worst media recession since the Great Depression. It too was a hit—and remains a leading magazine as measured by ad pages and total revenues.

Or consider this reminder from Johnson: "A deep recession can be a perfectly good time to launch an innovative company, putting the startup in a position to move when the economy recovers. Frederick Smith launched Federal Express in 1973 even as jet fuel prices were rocketing. Re/Max, now a major force in residential real estate, began in 1973, just as the housing market was entering a severe downturn. . . . Bill Gates and Paul Allen started Microsoft Corp. in [the recession of] 1975."

I don't mean to minimize the risks, pressures, and potential setbacks that are a necessary part of unleashing big change in tough times. In a wonderful *New Yorker* column, James Surowiecki, much like Bradley Johnson, chronicled bold strategic moves that repositioned companies and redefined industries during periods of turmoil. He compared how Post and Kellogg, two giants in the packaged-cereal industry, responded to the Great Depression. Post, he wrote— "did the predictable thing" when it "reined in expenses and cut back on advertising." Kellogg, on the other hand, "doubled its ad budget, moved aggressively into radio advertising, and heavily pushed its new cereal, Rice Krispies." As a result, Kellogg leaped ahead of its rival and became (and remains) the industry's dominant player.

It's also worth remembering that Texas Instruments introduced the revolutionary transistor radio during a recession in 1954, and that Apple launched the iPod six weeks after the September 11 terrorist attacks—hardly the best time to start a pop-culture phenomenon. All told, Surowiecki argues, periods of economic turmoil "create more opportunities for challengers, not less. . . . That may be why during the 1990–91 recession, according to a Bain & Company study, twice as many companies leaped from the bottom of their industries to the top as did so in the years before and after."

So why, he wonders, given all the evidence of the chance to gain ground during periods of economic upheaval, "are companies so quick to cut back when trouble hits?" One answer, he speculates, involves a distinction about risk made by two business professors nearly twenty-five years ago. In a paper published by the *Journal of Marketing*, Peter Dickson and Joseph Giglierano argue that executives and entrepreneurs face two very different sorts of risks. One is that their organization will make a bold move that fails—a risk they call "sinking the boat." The other is that their organization will fail to make a bold move that would have succeeded—a risk they call "missing the boat." Naturally, most executives worry more about sinking the boat than missing the boat, which is why so many organizations, even in flush times, are so cautious and conservative. To me, though, the opportunity for executives and entrepreneurs is to recognize the power of *rocking the boat*—searching for big ideas and small wrinkles, inside and outside the organization, that help you make waves and change course.[9]

That's the call to action that animates all of the arguments, advice, and case studies in this book: don't use the long shadow of economic crisis and slow recovery as an excuse to downsize your dreams or stop taking chances. The challenge for leaders in every field is to emerge from turbulent times with closer connections to their customers, with more energy and creativity from their people, and with greater distance between them and their rivals. The organizations that opened my eyes and captured my imagination did so because they offered a compelling alternative to a demoralizing status quo—as the only way to create a compelling future for themselves.

It is for these leaders, and for those who aim to match their commitment to unleashing big change in tough times, that I have written *Practically Radical.* I'm convinced that more and more executives, deep down, are beginning to appreciate that caution and conservatism—doing more of the same, but with less confidence and conviction—is a formula for disaster, not a source of stability or shelter from the economic storm. For these aspiring game changers, the book explores *radical shifts* that represent a direct challenge to convention and a break with the status quo. At the same time, most leaders are realists of the first order. They may get energized by new ideas, but they recognize the limitations within their companies, among their colleagues, even inside themselves, to bring these new ideas to life. In that spirit, the book offers next steps and ready-to-go techniques— *practical steps* they can apply right away.

> The challenge for leaders in every field is to emerge from turbulent times with closer connections to their customers, with more energy and creativity from their people, and with greater distance between them and their rivals.

These radical shifts and practical steps are meant to apply to readers in their varied roles—as change agents, builders, and individuals determined to take charge of their own success and legacy. Some leaders are responsible for the hard work of driving improvements within established organizations. Others are charged with launching something new—a start-up, a new business unit within an existing enterprise. All leaders worry about themselves as individuals: How can they handle the stress, demands, and pressures to both embrace the new and deliver day-to-day results?

That's why *Practically Radical* is built around three distinct (but related) modules: transforming your company, shaking up your industry, and challenging yourself. These are the defining issues for leaders today. So feel free to treat the material as if it were three books in one. If big-company change is your first order of business, then begin with the material in Chapters 1 through 3 and move ahead from there. But if the challenges of launching something new (inside an established organization or with a blank-sheet-of-paper start-up) are what keep you up at night, then begin with the material in Chapters 4 through 6 and move around at your discretion. (My guess is that nearly all readers will turn at some point to the material on "Challenging Yourself" that begins with Chapter 7.) In the spirit of maximum utility, each of the three modules ends with a hands-on section called Radically Practical. The book ends with a Practically Radical Primer, ten make-or-break questions that every aspiring game changer must ask of themselves and their colleagues.

The focus and format of the book reflect my desire to be as relevant as possible to as wide a range of leaders as possible—and to be as realistic as possible given the gravity of the challenges we face. My aim is to equip leaders with both provocative ideas and useful practices, a blend of thought and action that supports progress in the real world. That means writing a book steeped in the real world—telling stories that take readers deep inside a variety of organizations working on problems we all can recognize, teasing out lessons from those stories that we all can put to work in our organizations. I can't offer simple answers, quick fixes, or other comforting bromides that make positive change seem easier to achieve than it really is. What I can offer is a set of ideas, a collection of case studies, and a group of questions to help you do the hard work of making a real difference in your company, in your industry, and with your colleagues.

Samuel Johnson, the eighteenth-century poet, essayist, and all-around man of letters, famously warned that second marriages represent "the triumph of hope over experience." My hope is that the turmoil of the early twenty-first century will give leaders a second chance to think more deeply about their organizations—and that the experiences of the leaders I've studied will help other leaders triumph as they pursue the radical shifts and take the practical steps that fuel progress and growth.

PART I

TRANSFORMING YOUR COMPANY

CHAPTER ONE

WHAT YOU SEE SHAPES HOW YOU CHANGE—THE VIRTUES OF VUJA DÉ

Crime is for the most part not about strangers. Most crime is intimate and personal. A lot of criminals rarely travel outside their neighborhood; they certainly don't travel outside their city. That's why so much crime goes unreported. You call who you know—and people don't know the police. Over two generations, we have moved from the "cop on the beat" to anonymous blue soldiers. We are strangers in your midst. That's why we have to wear a number on our badge and a name on our chest. That's been the model of policing, and that's what we are changing.

—COLONEL DEAN ESSERMAN, CHIEF OF
POLICE, PROVIDENCE, RHODE ISLAND

IT'S 8:30 A.M. ON A Tuesday in downtown Providence, and the only thing colder than the January air is the chill in the economy. On this frosty morning, America's most compact state can lay claim to a wide range of problems: the country's second-highest rate of unemployment, the lowest high school graduation rate in the Northeast, a sky-high rate of mortgage foreclosures, and a reputation for corruption that rates among the most notorious anywhere. Who says good things come in small packages? When two reporters from the *New York Times* took a hard look at the "oversize problems" facing Little Rhody, many of the experts and officials they talked to worried that the state and its capital city were trapped in "parochialism, insecurity and outdated traditions that block change at every turn."[1]

Yet despite the winter temperatures and frigid social conditions, the atmosphere inside the Providence Public Safety Complex is white hot. A third-floor conference room is bustling with people, some in crisply pressed uniforms, some in expensive suits, some in jeans and T-shirts. There's small talk and laughter, handshakes and pats on the back, colleagues catching up and busting chops. Once the session comes to order, though, the chatter stops and the intensity level rises. This is one of Chief of Police Dean Esserman's first weekly command meetings of the New Year, and everyone recognizes that the eroding climate in both the state and its largest city has created the perfect conditions for challenges to law and order. It's up to the people in this room to demonstrate, no matter the conditions, that crime does not pay.

Computer-generated data, neighborhood maps, and photos of suspects get displayed on a big screen. There's a rapid-fire, district-by-district review of new incidents, open cases, and worrisome trends, from nightclubs that seem to be on the edge of chaos to troublemakers from out of town. There is a special focus on guns and gangs, twin plagues of a city like Providence. In minutes, it becomes clear that escalating beefs between two gangs on the city's South Side—C-Block (for Congress Avenue) and M.O.P. (for "Members of Pine")—are creating big problems. When talk turns to a recent gunshot victim, and officers around the table inquire about his affiliation, Esserman himself weighs in: "I rolled on this. He seems like a decent kid. He lives with his mother. They shot him just because he was there."

That makes a bad situation worse—innocent victims are getting caught up in the cross fire, as a sergeant reminds his colleagues. "I talked with his mom yesterday," another participant says. "It's very busy for January," adds a worried voice from the back of the room. "I've been at the hospital more than I can remember. I agree with Sarge. We have to crush this now." (The warning would prove to be prophetic. Two months after this command meeting, a seventeen-year-old "known associate" of the M.O.P gang was shot dead at a backyard party. Five days later, a seventeen-year-old associate of C-Block was shot in retribution for the killing.)[2]

The serious tone gets broken up a few times by funny stories. In his district, a local commander notes, one of the week's more colorful crimes was "an eighty-five-year-old guy who got assaulted by his fifty-year-old girlfriend." The other cops, impressed by the man's apparent romantic prowess, ask about his condition. "She hit him on the head with an ashtray," the commander says. "His main concern was getting his ashtray back." The room explodes in laughter.

On the surface, then, the meeting looks much like what you'd expect from an urban police department—the sort of computer-aided strategy session that William Bratton made famous when he ran the NYPD (the legendary CompStat reviews), complete with all the human drama and gallows humor that gets celebrated on TV shows like *The District*, the melodramatic CBS series that was modeled on the take-charge style of Bratton and his deputy commissioner, the late Jack Maple. "Is this guy known to us? I don't know him—is he in the system?" asks one frustrated detective about a suspect in one of his cases. "I can't believe we can't find this car!" exclaims the chief in frustration as a different detective runs down another case.

Look more closely, though, and what you see represents a sharp challenge to business as usual in this gritty city. One sign that there's something different going on is who's in the room. It's not just police brass. There's Richard Rose, the federal prosecutor who sent Providence's disgraced former mayor, the infamous Vincent "Buddy"

Cianci, to jail for five years on a racketeering charge. (The under-cover FBI investigation went by the made-for-the-movies name Op-eration Plunder Dome.) There are social workers from Family Service of Rhode Island; Teny Gross, executive director of the Institute for the Study and Practice of Nonviolence, which trains ex-gang members as "street workers" to intervene in tough neighborhoods; and the Rever-end Dr. Jeffrey Williams, founder of the Cathedral of Life Christian Assembly, one of the city's largest Protestant congregations. There are even half a dozen nervously fascinated students from Brown Univer-sity, who are getting an up-close-and-personal look at life outside the ivory tower.

Why is this unlikely group of civilians sitting in on the command session of a big-city police department? Because Chief Esserman has opened his mission-critical meetings to anyone who wants to attend: government officials, high-powered community leaders, grassroots activists, ordinary citizens, even members of the press. Virtually any-thing and everything about crime in this troubled city is open to the public and on the record every Tuesday morning at 8:30 sharp. In return, virtually anyone and everyone who wants to play a role in reducing crime has a seat at the table. Rhode Island may have a repu-tation, as the *Times* noted, for "parochialism" and "insecurity"—but there is nothing parochial about these gatherings, and most of the participants are secure enough to speak their mind.

One hard-boiled local reporter, who was sentenced to six months of home confinement for refusing to divulge his sources for a series of all-too-accurate reports on the Cianci investigation, sat in on a com-mand session and was struck by the changes it represented in how most institutions in Providence have worked for most of the city's his-tory. This was the first time ever that civilians were welcomed "into the inner sanctum" of the police department, he wrote, and the chief presided with "a sometimes combustible mixture of Donald Trump's candor and the probing questions of Socrates."[3]

After the meeting adjourns, Esserman returns to his office, which is filled with books, reports, white papers, framed photos, and mementoes of his years in law enforcement, and explains what just took place and why. "I love John Wayne," he says with gusto. "I have seen every John Wayne movie. I have been to his birthplace in Iowa, *twice*. Last summer I drove across country with my son, and we sang 'The Ballad of the Green Berets' together—in John Wayne's house! I could sing it now and it would bring a tear to my eye.

"But even I have to admit that the lone cowboy is dead," he continues. "Tough guys say, 'Cops shouldn't be social workers.' We patrol with social workers in the cars! Ministers used to march against us. Now they come to these meetings. Street workers are crucial partners in fighting violence. But the only way to get a job as a street worker is if we have put you away for heavy time. Late one night, I took some cops and some street workers out for lousy coffee and greasy fries. It felt tense, then I realized why. The guys on one side of the table had at some point arrested all the guys on the other side of the table! Now we're on the same side."

Esserman has been undeniably creative—indeed, downright unorthodox—in the resources he's tapped to change the climate in his city. He persuaded high school students to design some truly arresting posters (pun intended) that he displays in the department's holding cells, reminding their occupants that the city makes it a point to "federalize" weapons charges whenever possible, and that such a gun conviction means serious time in a federal prison (of which there are none in Rhode Island) without the possibility of parole. As I toured the lockup with the chief, he pointed to one poster, created by an eleventh grader, that featured mug shots of Rhode Island young people languishing in federal facilities far from home. The caption: "No Friends. No Family. No Freedom."

The tough-minded chief also has an unapologetic soft spot for the city's social workers—who literally have a seat at the table during his weekly command meetings, as well as in patrol cars with his beat cops. Family Service of Rhode Island has social workers who are available to police twenty-four hours a day and get called immediately whenever a child witnesses a crime. Social workers respond to every murder and to all cases of domestic violence. There are designated social workers who roll with the cops to intervene with and follow up on tough family issues. Margaret Holland McDuff, the CEO of Family Service of Rhode Island, explained it this way to *Governing* magazine, the go-to journal for state and local officials. "The [Providence] police have become brokers of service. They have their tool kit, and we're one of the tools in it."[4]

But it's the no-nonsense relationship between Dean Esserman's cops and Teny Gross's street workers—between law enforcers and former lawbreakers—that is the most vivid example of the unlikely partnerships that have been created in the interest of fighting crime. Jack McConnell, a high-powered Providence lawyer who was nominated by President Obama in March 2010 to become a U.S. District Court judge, put it succinctly in the profile of Esserman for *Governing*: "The relationship between Teny and the police chief should be a national model."

Gross, who runs the Institute for the Study and Practice of Nonviolence, is a truly intriguing character. Born in Israel, he served in the Israeli Army and patrolled the tense streets of the West Bank as a sergeant before he devoted himself to the mean streets of Providence. So he's studied at the school of hard knocks. But he's also quite the intellectual. After he moved from Israel to New England, he received a master's degree from the Harvard Divinity School, and then found himself in Rhode Island, where his wife teaches photography at the Rhode Island School of Design (RISD). When I met him at the weekly command meeting (he's the one who'd brought along the Brown students), he'd just finished reading Malcolm Gladwell's *Outliers* and was eager to discuss it. He also asked whether I'd ever sat in on Professor Michael Sandel's famous seminar on "Justice" at Harvard.

Gross's much-admired organization, which was established by a group of ministers in 2000, isn't exactly the stuff of the Ivy League.

It hires former gang members, convicted felons (including a few convicted of murder), and other recruits with deeply troubled pasts to walk and work the streets, deal with all kinds of tensions and social problems, organize after-school activities, intervene in fights and disagreements, and otherwise try to solve problems before they erupt into violence. In other words, his team of street workers will never be confused with civic-minded do-gooders or public-policy wonks. They are tough, gritty, complicated—which is precisely why they have such credibility among the kids (even the gangs) in the city's roughest neighborhoods, and why they are of such value to the cops.

This is not to suggest the day-to-day relationship between hard-nosed police officers and onetime lawbreakers is always smooth and effortless. Sometimes, cops resent it when street workers show up at the scene of a crime and inject themselves into the situation. They resent it even more when they believe street workers have information that might help to crack a case and choose not to share it right away. But more often than not, cops are quick to call in street workers before a crime takes place, to defuse a tense situation or straighten out a wayward kid. "Not long ago, the police were arresting these guys," Gross explained to a Rhode Island writer who chronicled his underappreciated work. "Now they're called peacekeepers. The cops are like, 'yea, right.' But street workers are a daily reminder to all those in power that people who have done wrong in the past can be among the most useful members of our society."

They are also, according to Esserman, his department's secret weapon in making the streets safer. "Teny is the single most important partnership we have to fight crime and violence," the chief told a writer from *Harvard Magazine* who profiled one of the university's more hard-to-pigeonhole alumni. "Everywhere I go—to every shooting, every ER, in classrooms, to every wake, every funeral—I see Teny, even if it's two o'clock in the morning. He and the street workers are about building sustained relationships of trust. The kids know that they love them—they don't get that from many adults."[5]

Esserman himself does not mince words about the loveless realities of life on the streets in Providence or any other American city. He carries the human and social cost of youth violence on his shoulders with a palpable sense of moral failing and personal loss. You can hear the tragedy in his voice. "I remember so clearly what Osama bin Laden said after September 11," he told me. "He said, 'I'm coming back and next time it will be one hundred thousand dead.' Well, just seven years after those horrible attacks, we had done his job for him. We had lost a hundred thousand Americans to murder. I grew up watching Walter Cronkite and the body count in Vietnam. But the American peacetime body count dwarfs the military body count. We approach fifty murders every day, sixteen thousand every year. And it's almost always the same story: a young man is dead, another young man is suspected or arrested, the instrument is a gun—all three elements of the crime are made in America. Immigration has nothing to do with this issue. As a father and a patriot, it is hard for me to accept the fact that we have become a land that buries its young, and with no moral outrage."

In Providence, at least, Chief Esserman's sweeping transformation in how his organization fights crime has changed the prospects for criminals—and not for the better. He took command of the Providence Police Department in January 2003. In the first five years of his tenure, total crime dropped by a head-spinning 30 percent. Murders were down by 39 percent, rapes by 64 percent, robberies by 30 percent, aggravated assaults by 17 percent. This dramatic progress, it should be noted, came during a period when police chiefs across the country were worried that crime was poised to make a comeback in many urban centers after widespread declines in the 1990s—a trend so pronounced that the Police Executive Research Forum issued a dire report on the "gathering storm" of violent crime in America.[6]

In 2009, as a result of a free fall in economic conditions and the always-unpredictable vagaries of human behavior, violent crime in

Providence (murder and rape) rose sharply over the year before, even though other crimes (burglary, larceny, motor-vehicle theft) continued their remarkable downward progression. Domestic violence often turned fatal, gang members shot and stabbed each other more, petty quarrels escalated into more serious confrontations—developments that shook a city that had grown accustomed to steady improvements. Esserman makes it a point to visit the hospital whenever a victim gets admitted with a serious gunshot wound, a sign that he is serious about recognizing the fallout from violence. He made more of those visits in 2009 than he expected. "There are too many shootings and too much violence," he told a local reporter. "It's hard to tell what we've prevented, but we haven't prevented enough."

Whatever the shorter-term flare-ups and statistical fluctuations, though, when it comes to public safety, there's no denying that Dean Esserman's crime-fighting strategy has had a dramatic impact on the streets of his city, and on the direction of crime fighting itself. In an exhaustive review of police innovations around the country, the authoritative Governing magazine offered this assessment of what's happened in Providence since 2003: "Esserman has taken a department that was widely seen as corrupt, only sporadically effective and isolated from the community it ostensibly served, and turned it into a nationally respected force for civil order." Even among reform-minded chiefs, Governing concluded, "Esserman stands out for an iron-willed determination to explore just how thoroughly a police department can enmesh itself in community life."

The chief, true to form, makes the point even more radically—and more practically. "My father was an old-time physician," he remarked at the end of one of our discussions. "If you asked anyone in the neighborhood, 'Who's your family doctor?' they'd say Paul Esserman. Ask most people today, 'Who's your family priest or rabbi?' and you'll get a name. But ask, 'Who's your family cop?' and you'll get a blank stare. In the postmodern era, with the technology revolution, policing became two cops in a car with a radio. We became strangers in our own communities. There has to be better way. We have to go back to what we were."

DISRUPTION DAYS—BACK TO THE FUTURE OF CHANGE

THERE'S NOTHING QUITE AS EXHILARATING AS watching a young organization change the game in its field—a hard-charging start-up that reshapes an industry (think FedEx, Google, Teach for America), a challenger brand that redefines a market (think Nike, Apple, Oprah). Alas, there's nothing quite as common as watching an established organization—a company that reached great heights in one era of technology, markets, and popular culture—struggle to regain its stature as a force for leadership in a new era. Despite millions of words of advice from gurus on organizational renewal, and despite billions of dollars budgeted for reengineering, Six Sigma, and other dogmas of transformation, the work of making deep-seated, sustainable change remains the hardest work there is.

No one appreciates this sobering reality more fully than John Kotter, the Harvard Business School professor who has literally written the book on making a big difference in big organizations. One of his most widely read books, *Leading Change*, offers a hopeful, eight-point program to maximize the chances that transformation programs will succeed. But haunting the book—indeed, haunting much of Kotter's work—is the specter of failure.

"Over the past decade, I have watched more than 100 companies try to remake themselves into significantly better competitors," he wrote in a high-profile essay that laid the groundwork for *Leading Change*. "A few of these corporate change efforts have been very successful. A few have been utter failures. Most fall somewhere in between, with a distinct tilt toward the lower end of the scale."

More recently, in *A Sense of Urgency*, Kotter revisited the track record of change programs and highlighted the same "appalling" results. "Incredibly," he wrote, "we found that in 70 percent of the situations where substantial changes were clearly needed, either they were not fully launched, or the change efforts failed, or changes were achieved but over budget, late, and with great frustration." Only 10 percent of the time, he declared, "people achieved more than would have been thought possible."[7]

What explains why so many blueprints for renewal achieve so little, while a few achieve "more than would have been thought possible"? That's one of the urgent questions at the heart of this book, of course, and I'll suggest all sorts of answers in the chapters that follow. But the answer at the heart of this chapter is the one I find most refreshing—and in a way, most reassuring. It begins with a strange term and an unlikely twist that capture the mind-set of leaders who are best equipped to make fundamental change.

Let's be clear: We are living in the age of disruption. You can't do big things anymore if you are content with doing things a little better than everyone else, or a little differently from how you've done them in the past. The most effective executives I've come to know don't just rally their colleagues to outrace the competition or outpace prior results. They strive to *redefine the terms* of competition by embracing one-of-a-kind ideas in a world filled with me-too thinking. That's a defining challenge in times of great dislocation: What do you see that other organizations don't see?

Or, to put it differently, the best leaders demonstrate a capacity for vuja dé. We've all experienced déjà vu—looking at an unfamiliar situation and feeling like you've seen it before. Vuja dé is the flip side of that—looking at a familiar situation (an industry you've worked in for decades, products you've worked on for years) *as if you've never seen it before*, and, with that fresh line of sight, developing a distinctive point of view on the future. If you believe, as I do, that what you see shapes how you change, then the question for change-minded leaders becomes: How do you look at your organization and your field as if you are seeing them for the first time?

Vuja dé may be a strange term, but it's become a strangely popular term among some of the brightest thinkers on creativity. Tom Kelley, general manager of IDEO, the legendary Silicon Valley design firm, uses vuja dé to describe the habits of mind of his most creative people. Kelley says he was introduced to vuja dé by Stanford University's Bob Sutton, a truly original thinker whose terrific book, *Weird Ideas That Work*, describes a set of offbeat practices to sustain innovation. Sutton, for his part, says he got the term from Jeff Miller, an accomplished sailor who also holds a PhD in biochemistry. For the best sailors, Miller told Sutton, "the same old stuff seems brand new" because it enables them "to keep learning small lessons from every race." Strangest of all, the term may in fact have originated with the late great comedian George Carlin, who used it in his routines and wrote about it in his book *Napalm and Silly Putty*.[8]

Ultimately, what matters is not whether a sailor, a professor, or a comedian coined the term. What matters is how leaders apply the vuja dé mind-set to the challenge of making big change in tough times. And that's where the unlikely twist comes in. The virtue of vuja dé is that it reframes how organizations make sense of their situations and build for the future. But that's different from a wholesale disavowal of the past. Sometimes, the very act of rediscovering and reinterpreting the past creates the clarity and confidence necessary to craft a distinctive game plan for the future.

> We are living in the age of disruption. You can't do big things if you are content with doing things a little better than everyone else.

There are, of course, many different ways to unlock vuja dé. In Chapter 2, I'll draw lessons from organizations that have searched far afield for ideas about how to compete in their own fields—a health-care innovator who looks to the women's movement and political campaigns for techniques to organize for reform, a hospital that found prescriptions for change in the practices of a luxury hotel company. But for even the most determined agents of change, history and tradition can be unrivaled sources of strength—as the foundation for an enduring sense of purpose that newcomers can't begin to copy; as a reservoir of professional wisdom that gets more valuable as times get more volatile; as an engine of expertise that competitors can't hope to match; as a reminder of certain founding principles that never go out of style, regardless of how styles change.

The cutting-edge marketers at TBWA Worldwide, the celebrated Madison Avenue agency, have learned to look hard at what's come before as inspiration for disruptive ideas about what comes next. As marketing specialists, TBWA personnel have designed memorable campaigns for some of the most glamorous brands of the last few decades, from Absolut to Adidas to Apple. As creative strategists, TBWA marketers have invented a blueprint for organizational renewal that the agency calls "Disruption Days"—wide-open, freewheeling, yet highly structured examinations of the assumptions, practices, and behaviors that stand in the way of progress for a brand, a company, or an industry.

TBWA chairman Jean-Marie Dru, the figure most closely associated with the disruption model, is adamant about the core changes it is designed to provoke. The process "is at once a method, a way of thinking, and a state of mind," he writes in *Disruption: Overturning Conventions and Shaking Up the Marketplace*, the first of his four excellent books on the subject. "It is a matter of questioning the way things are, of breaking with what has been done or seen before, of rejecting the conventional." All told, he argues, the methodology is "a system for those who hate systems, a method that encourages reversing perspectives."[9]

TBWA has conducted more than fifteen hundred Disruption Days for clients around the world (with nearly twenty-five thousand members of client organizations participating), and the methodology has improved and evolved over the years. But certain techniques remain central to the process. For example, TBWA has developed a list of sixty what-if questions to guide strategic rethinking. What if we stop focusing on the traditional competitors and focus instead on the source of business (often indirect competition)? What if we reconsider using strategies usually considered unsuccessful (or taboo) for this category? What if, instead of differentiating the brand, we redefine the category experience? What if we reverse the logic of things? The specific questions, of course, are less important than the general spirit, which is to challenge conventional wisdom.

In other words, Disruption Days lay the foundation for radical shifts in strategy, product development, and, of course, marketing. Yet one of the most revealing exercises in the process of shaping a brand's future is revisiting the past—often to identify practices that need to be discarded, sometimes, though, to uncover virtues that deserve to be reborn. Indeed, some of the agency's most newfangled marketing strategies can trace their inspiration to long-forgotten principles inside its client companies.

> Originality matters. But history matters too. The very act of rediscovering and reinterpreting the past creates the clarity and confidence necessary to craft a distinctive game plan for the future.

In 2004, for example, TBWA was charged with revitalizing Pedigree dog food, one of the most important brands for Mars Incorporated, the huge global company famous for Snickers (not to mention Mars bars, M&Ms, and Twix), Uncle Ben's rice, and other consumer staples. Pedigree was (and is) the most prominent dog-food brand in the world, with annual sales of some $2.5 billion. It was also under siege on all sides. High-priced "health" brands were getting more affordable; cheap "private-label" brands were improving quality. In other words, Pedigree, like so many established brands, was stuck in the middle. Its response, also like so many established brands, was to scrutinize the competition, improve at the margins (pack in nutrients to battle premium rivals, slash costs to fight the low end), and hope for the best.

Until, that is, the TBWA-sponsored Disruption Days, which were held in seven cities (including London, Warsaw, Shanghai, and Los Angeles) over two months. The point of the exercise, according to a TBWA write-up, was "to identify any and all conventions in the category," as "the first step in trying to find a way to disrupt those conventions." To that end, the participants "set out to completely immerse themselves in the images, the language, the packaging, the smells, the tastes (yes, even the tastes), and everything else associated with life in the world of dogs and their food."[10]

They also immersed themselves in the history of the company and the brand—a history that traces back to London in 1935, a few years after Forrest E. Mars Sr. set out for England to expand his father's fledgling empire. One of young Mars's first moves (after launching the Mars bar in the United Kingdom) was to buy Chappel Bros Ltd, a pioneer of the British pet-food market whose product line took shape in 1922 with canned food. (Talk about golden oldies: the company's American brand, Ken-L-Ration, was sold in cans whose labels featured images of dogs playing poker.)

Suzanne Powers, worldwide strategy director of TBWA, described the impact of this journey through time. "Everybody here is interested in the history of brands and companies," she told me. "So we build 'brand attics'—timelines of products, campaigns, artifacts—and then 'mine' the attics to see what we learn. We might uncover a treatise from 50 years ago, a product that got invented and discarded, nuggets that get to the 'guts' of the organization. The Mars family has been a passionate, pet-lover family for generations. In many parts of the world, Pedigree invented the market, and it had always been the brand endorsed by breeders. But in the quest to compete against a barrage of new entrants, Pedigree forgot why it was here. It had become a manufacturing company—'How do we make crunchier food that costs less?'—rather than a company that said, 'We are in this business because we love dogs.' There was a 'soul' that had gotten lost."

Rediscovering its "soul" allowed Pedigree to rejuvenate its culture—and infuse the brand with a renewed sense of purpose. "You don't buy or adopt a dog to feed it," Powers says. "Your primary purpose is to share your life with this other 'member of your family.' We realized that Pedigree couldn't just be about dog food. It had to be 'for the love of dogs'—dogs living the best lives they can." TBWA's Lee Clow, the creative genius behind Apple's "Think Different" ads, the Taco Bell Chihuahua, and the Energizer Bunny (and a dog lover himself), summed up the brand challenge this way: "If you can prove you love dogs as much as I do, I'll let you feed mine."

So that's what Pedigree set out to do. Mars CEO Paul Michaels (aka the company's "Top Dog") issued an eloquent statement of beliefs called *Dogma* that reminded his colleagues why Pedigree exists and how it should behave. ("We're for dogs," it begins. "Some people are for the whales. Some are for the trees. We're for dogs. The big ones and the little ones. The guardians and the comedians. The pure breeds and the mutts.") *Dogma* is a strikingly beautiful, surprisingly rich document that includes a dog-loving Manifesto, a Dog Bill of Rights, even an engaging description of Pedigree's target customers. ("People who stop to play with a stranger's puppy; people who dish out an extra belly rub on their way out the door; people who go out of their way to help a lost dog find his way home.")

The next step was to walk the canine talk, so Pedigree adopted all sorts of dog-centric innovations to recast its culture. Business cards and ID badges were redesigned to include pictures of each employee's dog. Employees were encouraged to bring their dogs to work, or, where that was not feasible, to put them in on-site day care. (Pedigree's Tokyo office actually relocated because its building was so unfriendly to dogs.) The company offered health insurance for employee pets and urged other companies to do the same. In some locations, salespeople brought their dogs to call on supermarket buyers. Simply put, you could no longer spend time inside the company without encountering dogs in all their glory. It was a cultural breath of fresh air—inspired by a purpose-driven blast from the past.

It was only then, after the dog-centric culture began to take hold inside the organization, that Pedigree took its message to customers. The marketing wasn't just about new ads, although TBWA designed a series of award-winning spots under the tagline "Dogs Rule." It was about a high-profile commitment to advocacy. Pedigree led public campaigns around the world to improve the lot of dogs. In Brazil, the focus was on getting stray dogs off the street and into shelters. In the United States, the focus was on adoption drives to get dogs out of shelters and into homes. During the 2008 Westminster Dog Show, Pedigree opened a "pop-up" store in Times Square that featured a dog-adoption center and sold "Dogs Rule" merchandise—gear that had been designed for employees but had become a hit with customers. When Pedigree ran its first-ever Super Bowl ad in 2009, the spot did not push product, it pushed dog adoption. "That's a big investment for an oblique message," the *Wall Street Journal* worried. "It's the right message to send out at this time," Pedigree's director of marketing replied.[11]

It's hard to overstate the transformation at Pedigree since those Disruption Days back in 2004. The culture is different, the marketing messages are different, the conversation with customers is different, even something as technical as how the company presents dogs on packaging and in ads is different. "There is a 'Pedigree Way' of doing things, right down to how we photograph dogs," says Suzanne Powers. "If you're a real dog lover, and you go to a park and meet a dog for the first time, you put your face up against that dog's face—'let me understand you eye-to-eye.' That's how we photograph all our dogs. It's a very distinctive visual point of view."

TBWA's Lee Clow believes that Pedigree's distinctive point of view about how to build for the future, based on a different way of making sense of its past, has met the brand challenge he set out in 2004. People at the company "used to come to work every day thinking they worked for a dog-food company," he noted in a TBWA report. "Now they come in thinking they work for a company that loves dogs."

WHY PAST IS PROLOGUE—THE POLICE DEPARTMENT THAT WENT "BEYOND 911"

PETER DRUCKER, THE GREATEST MANAGEMENT thinker ever, posed two of the most famous strategic questions ever to Jack Welch soon after Welch became CEO of General Electric. The new boss had been analyzing GE's wide-ranging portfolio of businesses, looking to develop his blueprint for the future. Drucker, with his unique capacity to distill even the most complex challenges to their essence, asked the new CEO to ponder two thoughts: "If you weren't already in a business, would you enter it today? And if the answer is no, what are you going to do about it?"[12]

Drucker's questions were meant to challenge the tunnel vision that history and tradition often impose on organizations—the assumption that the path to the future is a series of incremental steps from the past. Welch's answers, of course, led to one of the most heart-stopping, head-spinning campaigns to reinvent an enterprise the world has known. For all their virtues though, the questions run the risk of blinding leaders to what once made their organizations successful in the first place. So to Drucker's two questions I'd add a third: How can you rediscover and reinterpret what's come before as a way to develop an original and compelling line of sight into what comes next?

To me, that's the genius of Dean Esserman's blueprint for transforming how a troubled city fights crime. He is, to be sure, a demanding leader with an in-your-face style—a Jack Welch of policing. He arrived in Providence as an outsider, having worked alongside William Bratton when Bratton (who became chief of police in Los Angeles after his tenure in the Big Apple) ran the New York City Transit Police, then moving to two Connecticut cities. When Esserman took over in Stamford, according to *Governing*, he roused his staff with this call to arms: "I want you up all night thinking about this joint. I want you back in the morning before you need to be because you can't wait to get to work. I want you thinking about your job. I want you dreaming about it . . . I want it to be your obsession." After his arrival in Providence, Esserman left no doubt there was a new sheriff in town. He promised that he would show up at every shooting in the city, a vow he has maintained throughout his tenure. The unmistakable message: "If it's two o'clock in the morning, and it's raining, and there's a shooting, I'm coming. So you better be there already, *and you better be wet.*"

Like most hard-charging, change-minded bosses, Esserman is also unafraid to invite the wrath of powerful figures who disagree with him. He was, after all, brought in to clean up an organization that had been riddled with cronyism, favoritism, and flat-out corruption. So he showed little regard for what came before in terms of how the organization hired, promoted, or managed its officers. Here's how one profile described the early days: "When Esserman arrived in Providence . . . he found a dysfunctional department, riddled with corruption, without an organizational chart, where no one knew what anyone else was doing. Not long after he took over, he had to go to the payroll department to find out where his officers were."

Small wonder, then, that he drives the old guard in Providence crazy. The notorious Buddy Cianci, who completed his prison sentence in 2007, has a daily radio show on which he misses no opportunity to foment (and invent) opposition to Esserman as well as to David Cicilline, the ex-mayor's popular successor. Cicilline, who was elected and then reelected with more than 80 percent of the vote, is fiercely supportive of his chief. Cicilline likes to tout Esserman as "the best police chief in America." (Top cop Bill Bratton, the former chief in New York and L.A., echoes that assessment.) Cianci, though, likes to disparage Esserman as "Chief Shiny Badge"—and he encourages disgruntled cops and members of the old guard to leak e-mails or call into his program with stories that cast Esserman in an unflattering light. The *New York Times* described the Cianci show, quite accurately, as "taunts and half-truths, released into the radio air like toxic puffs."

Meanwhile, Cianci's former cronies on the city council and in city hall miss no opportunity to harass, embarrass, and otherwise insult Esserman and his reform-minded colleagues, going so far as to criticize him for traveling to Washington, D.C., and testifying before the Senate Judiciary Committee about strategies to reduce crime. "He has moved on in doing other and greater things, going across the country and talking about all the wonderful things he does," complained one narrow-minded city councilman. "It's clear he is not watching the shop. His personality has become greater than the role."

Esserman certainly feels the heat, even as he dismisses it as part of the job. In October 2009, the chief was asked to address a conference of business and technology innovators who had come to Providence to discuss the future of strategy, creativity, and social change. It was a pretty high-powered group, filled with scientists and product designers and marketing gurus. When the chair of the conference was lavish in his praise for Esserman, the chief couldn't resist an old joke. "Thanks for that wonderful introduction," he cracked. "As they say in my business, fix a ticket, make a friend for life." Then Esserman described his far-reaching work at the head of the department, the progress he and his colleagues had made, and the fierce old-guard resistance it had generated over the years. "I still have my wife start my car in the morning," he wisecracked to howls of laughter.[13]

So the backward-looking taunts come with the territory, as do the forward-looking advances. Shortly after taking office, Esserman dismantled and rebuilt the entire department, dividing the city into nine freestanding districts, each with its own "minichief"—a first for a force that was undisciplined and unaccountable. "When I got here there were no districts, no precincts, no nothing," Esserman marvels. "The city was divided into twenty-seven patrol-car beats. Do you know why? *No one knows why!* No one in the building could explain why we policed this way."

These freshly minted (and newly accountable) district commanders not only had to devise policing strategies that made sense for their neighborhoods, they also had to establish their own district headquarters and find a way to pay for them. Their boss provided no taxpayer dollars for rent, utilities, or operating costs. The new commanders had to "bootstrap" resources by getting businesses or universities to donate space and provide in-kind support: "I told the district commanders, 'I will do nothing for you.' They had to be complete entrepreneurs. This was created absolutely from nothing."

Esserman also initiated a fabulously creative program called "cops and docs." On a regular basis, detectives sit in with doctors at Brown University Medical School as they discuss tough cases. In turn, doctors sit in on the department's command meeting to learn how cops crack their cases. It's a one-of-a-kind way to open up an insular department to outside ideas, fresh perspectives, and new ways of thinking. In 2008, the chief took "cops and docs" even further. He announced that the Providence PD, once a source of community outrage and professional shame, would become the country's first "teaching police department"—modeled on teaching hospitals that train doctors and promote state-of-the-art medical practices. Esserman persuaded police chiefs in a consortium of cities to exchange ideas, swap personnel, and experiment in new techniques to battle guns, drugs, domestic violence, and other shared problems. "We want to become a place that embraces research, that figures out and spreads methodologies that work in the ways that medical schools do," he says. "Think of what it would mean to create that sort of institution and those types of values in a police department."

Yet despite the radical shifts associated with his tenure, there's a palpable throwback quality to Esserman as well. He never tires of celebrating his force as one of the oldest police departments in the United States, tracing its roots back to when night watchmen patrolled the streets before the American Revolution. These days, he spends one night a week on patrol with officers, and he expects his command staff to do the same. He also visits city classrooms and reads or talks to kids just about as often, a high-powered twist on Officer Friendly. (At a gathering of the city's middle-school students, Esserman asked kids to stand if they knew anyone who had been shot or killed. Nearly three-fourths of the assembly got to its feet.) Most important, he is a devoted student of the history of policing and has been an influential voice in the community-policing movement, which has shaped so much of how top officials think about their jobs. In a series of conversations, Esserman displayed an encyclopedic knowledge of the myriad conferences, white papers, academic studies, and arcane debates devoted to police reform over the last three decades, and he keeps a thick notebook of good ideas and memorable quotes he's picked up from criminologists, social scientists, and fellow chiefs.

In other words, Esserman's cutting-edge blueprint to reinvent his troubled organization is rooted in a clear understanding of the best of what has come before in his profession. It's another way that a sense of history can inspire a sense of vuja dé. It offers time-tested answers to contemporary problems and provides clear-eyed alternatives to standard practices and conventional wisdom. Seeing the future with fresh eyes doesn't mean turning a blind eye to history. What's past really can be prologue.

"To see police as mere enforcers of the law is to miss the point of how we spend our time," Esserman explains. "I've never shot anyone in my life, but I've delivered eight babies. That's what I was needed to do. There is a break between 'law enforcement' and police work. 'Law enforcement' is an American, postmodern term. Police work goes back to our nineteenth-century ancestry in London with Sir Robert

Peel and the bobbies, where police were there to keep the peace, but also to serve the community in ways the community needed. We're going back to what we were."

When I first met Esserman, he handed me his business card, which included not only his direct-dial phone number at headquarters but also a cell-phone number where he was reachable twenty-four hours a day. Every member of the Providence Police Department, from the most decorated major to the most junior officer on patrol, has such a card, with his or her 24/7 cell-phone number. Officers urge merchants, banks, doctors, clinics to display the cards on their walls, in waiting rooms, on cash registers. They want people to know them on sight, by name, and to have easy access to them.

"We are in the midst of a quiet revolution in how we do business," Esserman says. "What was our gift to policing in the 1960s and the 1970s? It was 911. We told America, 'Your job is to call, our job is to come.' That made us anonymous and distant. You don't meet us until you need us, and you don't know us when you meet us. We're not abandoning 911, but we want to go *beyond* 911. We want police officers to think more broadly about their jobs, to get reengaged in the life of their communities." In fact, to Esserman, one vital sign of change for his organization is that the volume of 911 calls keeps going down, even as problems keep piling up. Not because people make fewer calls to the police, but because, more and more, they call an officer they know or drop in on a district substation. "I'll be at a homicide scene, it's the middle of the night, and I'll hear something interesting," he says. "Cell phones are ringing, and they are the cell phones of patrolmen. People in the neighborhood are calling to tell us what they know! That is the sound of things changing."

As of June 2011, Esserman's role in Providence changed as well. He announced that after more than eight years in command of the force, he would step aside. His tenure was remarkable for its length among urban police chiefs. (The legendary Bill Bratton served as chief for only two years in New York and seven years in L.A.) More-over, his indispensable partner, Mayor David Cicilline, surprised the city when he decided not to stand for reelection, choosing instead to run for (and win) the congressional seat vacated by longtime incum-bent Patrick Kennedy.

So Esserman decided to turn in his badge—but stay in the mix. He accepted a role as "senior law-enforcement executive in-residence" at Roger Williams University, based in nearby Bristol, Rhode Island, which has a highly regarded criminal-justice program. Less than six months later though, Esserman was wooed away from his academic perch to pick up a new badge, this time as chief of police in New Haven, Connecticut—a city, much like Providence, with pressing social problems, a desperate need for police reform, and an Ivy League university in the midst of the turmoil. Although his platform is changing, his change agenda and his identity as a change agent are secure. It goes back to the ethos of the family cop. "The day you can ask someone to name their family cop," he concludes, "and that question resonates with people, that's the day American policing will have evolved to where we hope to take it."

TURN BACK THE HANDS OF TIME—HOW NICOLAS HAYEK SWATCHED THE WORLD

DEAN ESSERMAN IS NOT THE only innovator whose radical agenda for change draws heavily on practical insights from the past. Indeed, many of the most striking transformations I stud-ied were built on some version of a "back-to-the-future" game plan. I saw it in all sorts of settings: the most farsighted leaders could be as conservative as they were disruptive. Sure, they had a fresh-eyed per-spective on the shortcomings of their organizations and a far-reaching blueprint for reform. But they also had a deeply held appreciation for the insights and expertise that once made their organizations strong.

They were zealous advocates for shifts in strategy and structure—and careful stewards of history and tradition.

That's a hard-to-find combination, especially in a business culture that clamors for easy answers. Pundits love to excoriate companies because they don't have the guts to change. In fact, the problem with many organizations is that *all they do is change*. They lurch from one consulting firm to the next, from the last year's hot management fad to this year's model, from last year's hot market segment (luxury SUVs!) to what's in vogue now (eco-friendly hybrids!). But the more things change under these ever-changing conditions, the more they tend to stay the same. Management guru Jim Collins puts it this way: "The signature of mediocrity is not an unwillingness to change. The signature of mediocrity is chronic inconsistency."

I'm convinced that one of the big reasons for the failure of so many change programs is that by focusing almost solely on what's *wrong* with their organizations, and by importing *off-the-shelf* strategies devised by outside experts consumed with what's new, leaders undervalue what's *right* with their organizations and overlook *homegrown* strategies rooted in the wisdom of the past. In his first inaugural address, President Bill Clinton offered his perspective on national renewal. "There is nothing wrong with America," he argued, "that cannot be cured by what is right with America." That sentiment speaks to the renewal of companies as well as countries— it's a political insight with big implications for making change in business.

Nicolas G. Hayek, the outspoken billionaire who was the face of the Swiss watch industry for twenty-five years, personified this leadership mind-set. In North America, Hayek never really broke through as a public figure, although his company's brands are instantly recognizable to their passionate customers, from the colorful Swatch to the superelite Breguet, whose pieces can sell for hundreds of thousands of dollars. Throughout Europe, though, Hayek was a high-profile executive whose pronouncements made headline news, a celebrity whose friends included fashion models and the Hollywood elite. (George Clooney serves on the board of one of his ventures, and Cindy Crawford wrote the foreword to a collection of interviews that was published in French and German.) In a vote of his countrymen, Hayek was named one of the most notable figures in Swiss history, alongside Albert Einstein and Henry Dunant, who inspired the Red Cross and the Geneva Convention. He passed away in June 2010, at the age of eighty-two, doing what he loved—working at company headquarters.

Why did an executive with a company based in a small Swiss village attract such giant acclaim? Because he engineered one of the most spectacular comebacks in business history—the reinvention of an industry that was thought to be lost to the sands of time. I first got immersed in Hayek's work in the early 1990s, when his turnaround of the Swiss Corporation for Microelectronics and Watchmaking (SMH) was just starting to click. I visited him in Biel/Bienne, the small, bilingual city (hence the hybrid German/French name) thirty minutes from Berne, the Swiss capital. I toured factories and labs, and traveled to Zermatt, at the base of the Matterhorn, to join forty thousand guests celebrating the production of the one-hundred millionth Swatch. The event included a light show set to original music by French composer Jean Michel Jarre, and an over-the-top performance of the gathering's sweet (but goofy) theme song, which included the chorus, "Swatch Time, it's a helluva good time. Swatch Time, Swatch the world!"

Hayek had cause for celebration. He'd been hard at work since the mid-1980s, when he recommended that Switzerland's banks merge the country's two giant (and insolvent) watchmakers, which had collapsed under the triple whammy of competition from Asia, shifting consumer tastes, and new technologies that the Swiss had invented but ignored. Here's how one business-school case study described the situation: "The rise of quartz technology hastened the decline of the Swiss watch industry. Ironically, the Swiss had pioneered quartz technology; however, Swiss watchmakers had refused to embrace quartz based on the belief that electronic watches were unreliable, unsophisticated, and beneath Swiss quality standards. . . . As Japanese watchmakers saturated the global market with quartz watches at rock-bottom prices, Switzerland found itself unable to compete."[14]

> Not enough change? The problem with many organizations is that all they do is change. Management guru Jim Collins puts it this way: "The signature of mediocrity is not an unwillingness to change. The signature of mediocrity is chronic inconsistency."

Sound familiar? Indeed, the parallels between the plight of the Swiss watch industry and the crisis in U.S. automobile industry are downright eerie—except for how the story ends. After World War II, the Swiss built 80 percent of the world's watches. By 1970, with the rise of foreign competition, the Swiss share of the global watch market was down to 42 percent. In 1983, just before Hayek took charge, the industry was on its last legs. SMH (a watch-industry equivalent of General Motors and Ford put together) had sales of $1 billion, losses of $124 million, and a nervous workforce of fifteen thousand people. Then began the comeback. Ten years later, SMH was back on its feet, with sales of $2 billion, profits of $286 million, and, with Swatch, the bestselling new brand in history. In 2008, the company (renamed Swatch Group) stood tall as the undisputed giant of its field—the leading watchmaker on the planet, with nineteen brands, twenty-six thousand people, and profits of more than $720 million. Hayek himself had become one of the richest men in one of the richest countries in the world.

"Our sales are five billion dollars," he marveled when we reconnected in 2009 at a rollicking convention about a year before his death.

"We have five hundred shops worldwide, including a Swatch store in Times Square and an Omega store on Fifth Avenue. With Breguet, we have the highest-luxury watch brand ever. We sent a piece to the United States priced at $700,000 and it sold in a week, in a strong recession! The bestselling imported watch in China is Omega, number two is Longines, three is Rado—all our brands. I have been sending the same messages for years. Still, when I think back, I am amazed by what has happened."

What's more amazing than the company's performance over the last fifteen years is the plan its chairman devised to reverse its slide toward irrelevance. To be sure, Nicolas Hayek was a state-of-the-art product innovator with a keen eye for marketing. The ultra-affordable Swatch has been an endless source of sharp looks and funky features: the first see-through watch, the first scented watch, limited-edition models created by artists and film directors. Even at the highest end, Hayek bucked convention and attracted eyeballs. In 2008, after four years of top-secret work, he unveiled a perfect replica of a Breguet pocket watch completed in 1827 to honor Marie Antoinette. The original, considered the most valuable timepiece of all time, was stolen from a museum in Jerusalem in 1983. The Breguet replica sent watch historians into a frenzy of delight and generated frenzied attention for the brand, even after the original was recovered.

Still, at his core, Hayek was a deeply conservative leader who looked to Switzerland's 450-year watchmaking tradition as a source of strength rather than as a burden of history. He didn't reinvent a crisis-ridden organization by disavowing its legacy and reaching for solutions cooked up by turnaround specialists and finance wizards. Instead, he realized that the way to devise a game plan for the future was to draw on the compelling ideas around which the organization first took shape—ideas that had gotten lost or disfigured through decades of uninspired leadership, me-too growth strategies, and deadening bureaucratic practices. There was nothing wrong with the Swiss watch industry, he concluded, that could not be fixed by what was right with the Swiss watch industry.

The fall and rise of Omega is a case in point. When Hayek took control of the company, the Omega brand was, in his words, "near oblivion." For years, the leaders of the unit had been impatient for growth and unsure of how to respond to foreign competition. So they took the brand in all sorts of directions. Here's how Hayek explained it: "A jeweler would say, 'Omega is wonderful, but it is too expensive for my clients. How about giving me an Omega that is cheaper?' Now if you are crazy, or I guess if you are greedy, you agree. That was the kiss of death. Omega was everywhere: high price, medium price, precious metals, cheap gold plating. There were two thousand different models. No one knew what Omega stood for."

Some of his bankers urged Hayek to sell Omega to one of its Japanese rivals, who would pay dearly for it. Some of his executives pleaded that he move the brand further down-market, and use its prestige to go head-to-head with Citizen and Seiko. Hayek would have none of it. "That was absurd!" he thundered. "Omega is one of the Swiss watch industry's great brands. Its history goes back to 1848. You should visit the watchmaking museums and look at the pieces Omega made fifty or one hundred years ago. They are wonderful. Few brands had or have Omega's potential power."

So the strategy he devised was to remind Omega's bankers, executives, employees, and customers what had made the brand so distinctive for so many years, and to build an ultramodern game plan around those enduring qualities. He slashed the number of models to 130, ended all licensing agreements, eliminated showy designs that spoke to indulgence rather than achievement, and, in countless other ways, returned the brand to its roots. There were product launches, marketing twists, and manufacturing improvements. But these newfangled innovations were all in the service of reconnecting to a glorious past. The result? In 2008, Omega generated sales of more than $1 billion and profits of hundreds of millions of dollars. It is, simply put, one of the most valuable watch brands in the world.

In his first inaugural address, President Clinton offered his perspective on national renewal: "There is nothing wrong with America that cannot be cured by what is right with America." That sentiment speaks to the renewal of companies as well.

"Omega is an elite watch for people who achieve—in sports, the arts, business, the professions—and help shape the world," Hayek said. "The astronauts who landed on the moon achieved something. They wore Omega. So did the Soviet cosmonauts." By virtue of his plan, he continued, "Omega started making sense again. This is what an Omega looks like. This is what Omega stands for. We gave Omega its message back."

That message continues to resonate, years after Hayek refined it. In 2009, to commemorate the fortieth anniversary of the *Apollo* moon landing, Omega became the first commercial brand to receive permission to use the image of President John F. Kennedy in an advertisement. The campaign highlighted the Omega Speedmaster, the watch NASA chose for use in space ("the first and only watch worn on the moon"). According to the *New York Times*, the Kennedy-Omega connection stretches back to JFK's inauguration, when a photograph in *Life* magazine showed the new president wearing an Omega Ultra Thin. Comedian Jon Stewart couldn't help but comment on the audacity of using a beloved president's image in a commercial campaign. On *The Daily Show*, he ran clips from the spot and then identified JFK as "that guy from the Omega watch ad."[15]

But Hayek's plan didn't just apply to one of his company's brands. *It applied to the company itself.* His turnaround strategy violated almost every piece of standard-issue advice peddled by highly paid consultants and Wall Street titans—not because he was reluctant to break from the past, but because his radical changes were built on a genuine appreciation for the past. The business was in a shambles when Hayek took over. "A chaotic jungle," he called it, "an absolute mess." But buried inside the mess, he knew, was a treasure trove of skills and centuries of savvy just waiting to be unleashed: "We have hundreds of years of experience in the technologies and techniques of watchmaking. Families have spent generations in our factories. They have a feel for this business, a special touch."

This rich tradition gave Hayek the confidence to buck twenty-first-century convention. The first rule of global competition is to seek out low-cost production in every corner of the world. Yet the bulk of Swatch Group's 160-plus factories remain clustered in the towns and villages around the Jura Mountains on Switzerland's border with France, the traditional heart of Swiss watchmaking. The second rule is specialization—divest or outsource all activities that aren't crucial to success. Yet Swatch Group remains a vertically integrated fortress. It assembles all the watches it sells and builds nearly all of the components for the watches it assembles. That's hundreds of millions of finished products and tens of billions of parts every year. The third rule is niche marketing—identify the most profitable customer segments and ignore the rest. Yet Swatch Group's nineteen brands cover all geographic markets and every price point imaginable.

Why reject so many of the accepted ideas and familiar strategies that define "modern" management? Because, by insisting that his organization stay rooted in Switzerland, even as it competed everywhere in the world in every segment of the market against everyone in its field, Hayek imposed enormous pressures for breakthroughs in design, manufacturing, and overall performance—pressures far more intense (and useful) than those created by traditional financial reengineering. One of his most simple (and transformational) demands was that whenever his engineers designed a new product, direct labor had to account for less than 10 percent of total costs.

"CEOs must say to their people: 'We will build this product in our country at a lower cost and with higher quality than anywhere else in the world,'" he argued. "Then they have to figure out how to do it." With enough innovation in enough phases of the business, he insisted, "There is nothing to stop us from building a product in Switzerland, the most expensive country in the world. Nothing."

His company's namesake offering, the low-price, high-style Swatch, is the ultimate validation of this strategic calculation. Swatch has been a worldwide, mass-market phenomenon—the bestselling product in the history of the industry, the watch world's version of Apple's iPod. As a brand, it has set a standard for creative design, offbeat marketing, and distinctive retail environments. As a business, it has been the subject of countless case studies and in-depth academic research. By March 2008, the twenty-fifth anniversary of its launch, Swatch had released five thousand different models and produced more than 350 million watches.

"The Swatch is based on radical innovations in design, automation, and assembly, as well as in marketing and communications," Hayek told me. But those innovations grew out of the limitations his game plan imposed. "The people on the original Swatch team asked a crazy question," he said. "Why can't we design a striking, low-cost, high-quality watch and build it in Switzerland? The bankers were skeptical. A few suppliers refused to sell us parts. They said we would ruin the industry with this crazy product. But the team overcame the resistance and got the job done."

There is also a powerful marketing dividend to the commitment to design and build products where they've been designed and built for centuries. "We are offering our products to a sympathetic audience," Hayek argued. "The people who buy Swatches are proud of us. They root for us. They want us to win. Europeans and Americans are damn happy if you can show that their societies are not decadent—that every Japanese or Taiwanese worker is not ten times more productive or more intelligent than they are."

Back in the early 1990s, as Hayek's comeback strategy was ticking along, I asked if other big established organizations could learn from his game plan. "Everything we've done can be done by lots of companies in Switzerland, or France, or Germany, or America," he replied. "All it takes is the will to do it. Which is, I admit, no small matter." More than fifteen years after that initial encounter, with the Swatch Group widely recognized as one of the great turnarounds in business history, I asked how many CEOs had adopted his ideas. Hayek just laughed. "None of the big bosses think of me as a teacher," he said. "They like me, they respect me, but they refuse to accept that we have done better than any of them. The newspapers put me on the front page, but no one tries to copy what we've done."

WHAT WOULD JULIETTE DO?—MAKING CHANGE THE GIRL SCOUT WAY

TRUTH BE TOLD, IT'S EASY to understand why Nico-las Hayek was covered widely by the European press but copied rarely by his peers. He was a larger-than-life figure who engineered a once-in-a-lifetime comeback—a case study in change that is fascinating to analyze but daunting for others to replicate. Much the same can be said for Dean Esserman, although, as a leading figure in the commu-nity-policing movement over the last twenty-five years, he has devel-oped a powerful network of fellow innovators with whom to compare notes and exchange strategies. Still, in terms of substance and style, Esserman is edgy, headstrong, impatient—revealing to study, hard to copy.

Hayek and Esserman are alike in another way: both were called upon to unleash radical shifts in their organizations after the orga-nizations had arrived at the brink of disaster. For the Swiss watch in-dustry, the choice was to change or die. For the Providence Police Department, the choice was to reinvent its crime-fighting strategies or sentence an entire city to a life of crime. It's never easy to transform an organization filled with bad habits and obsolete practices—even if, buried deep inside, are all the ideas, skills, and sense of purpose required to mount a comeback. But the outlook improves when the alternative to making change is staring into the abyss.

Which raises an obvious question: Does meaningful transformation *require* a dance with death? Irving Wladawsky-Berger, one of the key figures in the still-underappreciated transformation of IBM since the early 1990s, has no doubt that the prospect of imminent demise fueled a new lease on life at the computer giant. Not long ago, I listened with fascination as this thirty-seven-year company veteran, a brilliant technologist and a beloved IBMer, reflected on the big changes at Big Blue over the last fifteen years—from its game-changing embrace of the Internet to its aggressive support of Linux and open-source software to a profound shift of its famously top-down culture. But Wladawsky-Berger wasn't interested in reveling in triumph. In fact, he was more interested in reckoning with tragedy.

"I wonder if a company can reinvent itself if it doesn't have a near-death experience," he fretted at an innovation summit that I cohosted with *Wall Street Journal* columnist Walt Mossberg. "The Greek playwrights wrote about this. The things that made you great will turn out to be your undoing. IBM became very, very successful [in the 1960s and 1970s] . . . and [in later years] management thought it was because of *their* brilliance that the business was doing so well. Of course, they were living off the brilliance of their predecessors. The near-death experience cleansed our brain. I don't know how else to say it. Once you go through a near-death experience, it reshapes your head and opens you up to new ideas."[16]

This thoughtful IBMer may be right about the impact of a near-death experience on his company—but it's a grim thought indeed if the only way to "reshape your head" is to face the prospect of a visit from the grim reaper. With apologies to the Greek playwrights, I believe the attributes that made you great once can make you great again—if you summon the "brilliance of your predecessors" as a call to action rather than a cause for complacency.

The transformation of the Girl Scouts of the USA under CEO

Kathy Cloninger is an all-American case in point. The Girl Scouts have long been considered a model of sound management. Back in 1989, in his landmark *Harvard Business Review* essay, "What Business Can Learn from Nonprofits," Peter Drucker paid homage to the group as one of "America's management leaders." More than fifteen years later, when Jim Collins published a supplement to *Good to Great* focused on the. social sectors, he praised former Girl Scouts CEO Frances Hesselbein as a classic Level 5 leader, a "master of getting things done within a diffuse power structure."

So unlike, say, IBM or the Swiss watch industry, Kathy Cloninger's organization was nowhere near death when she took charge in late 2003. It was, however, adrift and uncertain. Membership (roughly 2.8 million girls and 1 million adult volunteers) was stagnating, traditional programs felt out of sync with youth culture and demographic trends, the organizational structure was in need of an overhaul, and the brand, while ubiquitous, was uncool. In other words, based on the track records of most big organizations in most fields, conditions were in place for years of slow decline, or, at best, modest progress. Instead, the CEO and her colleagues devised one of the most ambitious, far-reaching, fast-paced change programs I have seen—an agenda for transformation that should be the envy of CEOs in *every* field.

It's hard to set out in a few paragraphs (or even a few chapters) the scale and scope of what's happened since 2003. Suffice it to say, this is not your mother's Girl Scouts. The organization has reimagined the signature elements of the experience, from the programs it offers to the volunteers it recruits to the uniforms that scouts wear. Adult volunteers don't have to be moms to be troop leaders, and girls don't have to be full-time members of troops to participate in big-time activities. There are troops for girls with mothers in prison ("Girl Scouts Beyond Bars") and all-Muslim troops for girls looking to maintain traditions as they assimilate into new surroundings.

The high-powered initiatives have attracted high-profile attention across the media landscape. When a *Boston Globe* reporter hung out with a group of thirteen-year-old girls from New Bedford, Massachusetts, her sense of surprise leaped off the front page: "These dues-paying Girl Scouts do not belong to a troop. They do not earn badges. They do not sell cookies. Instead, they represent the vanguard of efforts to revamp Girl Scouts for the 21st century." The *Washington Post* took a bigger-picture look at the group's change program. "Long associated with images of dorky vests and singalongs around the campfire," a front-page article blared, "the organization is experimenting with a total makeover of the Girl Scout experience." Few nonprofits, it concluded, "have gone as far as the Girl Scouts in attempting to keep up with the times."[17]

More important, these fun-to-describe changes in style don't begin to capture the hard-to-execute changes in strategy that made them possible. The core question for the Girl Scouts, CEO Cloninger says, is, "What is the most compelling reason to be the largest all-girls organization in the world?" The answer, she insists, is not to sell cookies or hand out badges, but to serve as "the premier leadership-development experience for girls."

To that end, in 2005, the organization rewrote its mission statement for the first time in fifty years. The new mission: "Girl Scouting builds girls of courage, confidence, and character, who make the world a better place." The old mission: "The Girl Scout organization is dedicated to helping girls develop as happy, resourceful individuals willing to share their abilities as citizens in their homes, their communities, their country and the world."

The new mission is simpler, crisper, and more assertive than what came before, but the process of agreeing upon it was delicate and intricate to say the least. Cloninger had to put the new statement, as well as the plan that turned the statement into a strategy, up for a vote at the group's fiftieth national convention—an exercise in democracy that would flummox most my-way-or-the-highway CEOs. Moreover, a big part of the new strategy was devising new metrics of success—fifteen "leadership outcomes" that describe how girls should change and grow as a result of their experiences. These outcomes are a long-term scorecard for the entire organization. Finally, even as Cloninger was expanding the group's horizons, she was rationalizing its operations—shrinking the number of local councils (the national network of affiliate organizations that actually delivers Girl Scout programs and services) from 315 to 109, a painful restructuring that cost jobs and carried risks for morale.

For all the risks, though, the rewards have been huge. An examination of the group's "massive transformation effort" by *The NonProfit Quarterly* offered this review: "Few nonprofits have taken on such a massive social experiment, and even fewer have done it in a planned and deliberate way." A profile of Cloninger in a leadership magazine aimed at Wall Street echoed that assessment. The CEO and her colleagues "have generated inspiring and instructive insights on what it means to be a winning leader today—and constructed a compelling model for radical change in any organization."[18]

How did the Girl Scouts experience so much change so quickly, without a near-death experience to concentrate the mind and cleanse the brain? When I posed this future-focused question to Kathy Cloninger, she immediately turned to the past. Sure, she and her colleagues relied on demographic surveys, competitive mapping, market research—all the tools of "modern" management. But some of their most inspiring insights came from getting reimmersed in the ideology, philosophy, and "business plans" of Juliette Gordon Low, the legendary social activist who started the Girl Scouts in 1912. The CEO and her colleagues came to understand what a firebrand, risk taker, and entrepreneur their founder was—and this appreciation for the group's hard-charging history created a sense of permission to push harder for far-reaching change.

Indeed, as Cloninger and her colleagues wrestled with an array of controversial decisions, one of their guiding mantras became WWJD—that is, What Would Juliette Do? "Even though we use the word 'transformation' it's not like we're breaking from our historical roots," the CEO explained. "Juliette Gordon Low was a revolutionary. She founded this movement at a time when women didn't have the right to vote. Her idea of what girls could and should be doing was way out on the cutting edge. Juliette's work was much more 'out there' than what this organization eventually became."

> How did the Girl Scouts experience so much change so quickly? By getting reimmersed in the ideology of Juliette Gordon Low, the social activist who started the group in 1912. An appreciation for its hard-charging history helped everyone push harder for change.

At the urging of several headquarters officials, I got a hold of the original Girl Scout handbook, written in 1913. In some respects, the 147-page manual, *How Girls Can Help Their Country*, is a quirky artifact of a bygone era, with arguments for the health benefits of breathing through your nose and instructions for the best way to polish floors and put away flannels. At the same time, it is a rousing call to action for girls to apply their unique skills to real-world problems and to develop those skills to exercise more power in the world. "Girls will do no good by trying to imitate boys," the founder writes in a section on how to be womanly. "You will only be a poor imitation. It is better to be a real girl such as no boy can possibly be." The ultimate value of scouting is that it "enables girls to better help in the great battle of life," she concludes.[19]

"I love that little book! It is so in sync with where we are trying to go now," exclaims Eileen Doyle, who, as vice president for programs, is responsible for translating the organization's timeless mission into offerings that speak to the times, from solar-science seminars to portfolio-management exercises to environmental activism. Talk about newly found relevance: in recent years, winners of the Girl Scout Gold Award (the group's highest honor) have included Connecticut sisters who helped rehabilitate a school in rural India; a Florida teen who built artificial reefs to protect coastal ecosystems; and an Ohio student who researched, selected, and installed a computerized composite-sketch system to help her town's police department identify criminals.

"This whole movement sprang from Juliette's vision that girls should get 'out of the parlor' and into the world," Doyle argues. "Girls have a yearning for a greater purpose in life, to leave their leadership imprint on the world. This has never been about girls sitting around and gluing things together. It's about girls getting out there and changing the world. Our work today is to reclaim the roots of the Girl Scouts movement."

CHAPTER TWO

WHERE YOU LOOK SHAPES WHAT YOU SEE—OF BIG DOTS, PIT STOPS, AND HOT SPOTS

Dr. Martin Bettes: How long has [your son] had the problem?
Carol Connelly: Since forever, six months old.
Dr. Bettes: Have they done blood tests on him?
Carol: Yes.
Dr. Bettes: Only in the emergency room or when he was well?
Carol: Emergency room only.
Dr. Bettes: How about skin testing for allergies?
Carol: No.
Dr. Bettes: No standard scratch test? They poke him with a needle . . .
Carol: No. I asked. They said my plan didn't cover it and that it wasn't necessary anyway. Why, should they have?
Dr. Bettes: Well . . .
Carol: Fucking HMO bastard pieces of shit! I'm sorry.
Dr. Bettes: It's okay. Actually, I think that's their technical name.

—HAROLD RAMIS AND HELEN HUNT,
AS GOOD AS IT GETS, 1997

I AM SITTING IN A CAVERNOUS ballroom at the Op-
ryland Hotel in Nashville, Tennessee. A sense of an-
ticipation fills the air. I am about to witness, along with six thousand
other members of the audience, the world premiere of a production by
theater icon Robert Brustein, former dean of the Yale Drama School
and founding director of the Yale Repertory Theater and the American Repertory Theater. The *Playbill* offers few details about the story,
but the cast is impressive: F. Murray Abraham, who won an Academy
Award for his role as Salieri, Mozart's archrival, in *Amadeus*; Emmy
winner Tony Shalhoub, best known for the long-running, hit television series *Monk*; and Brooke Adams, who has appeared in countless
stage productions, films such as *Gas Food Lodging*, and TV shows
such as *Thirtysomething* and *Lace*.

What makes the production so intriguing is that it's not some experimental performance at an arts festival or an out-of-town test of a
Broadway show. Rather, it's a keynote presentation at the 20th Annual
National Forum of the Institute for Healthcare Improvement (IHI)—
one of the most impressive professional gatherings I've seen, organized by one of the most unlikely forces for change the medical world
has known. Earlier in the day, Dr. Robert Waller, an ophthalmologist
who spent ten years as president and CEO of the famed Mayo Clinic,
described the summit as "the most super-charging, super-duper event
in the history of health care." He was having fun—but there was some
truth to the humorous hype.

Over the last two decades, IHI has shaped the agenda for health-
care reform around the world. Its six-point "No Needless List" has
become a to-do list for transforming medicine: no needless deaths, no
needless pain and suffering, no helplessness in those served, no un-
wanted waiting, no waste, no one left out. Among its many initiatives,
IHI has inspired, educated, and equipped hospitals to raise standards
for safety and reliability; waged two nationwide campaigns to eliminate deaths and harm due to medical errors and substandard care;
and reminded patients and politicians of the disconnect between the

highest-on-the-planet cost of care in the United States (16% of GDP) and the middle-of-the-pack results (29th in infant mortality, 48th in life expectancy) all that money buys. In a field riddled with confusing statistics (hospitals report some fifteen hundred different pieces of data to regulatory bodies), IHI's goal is to "move the big dots"—to make dramatic progress on scores (such as avoidable mortality) that change the game, focusing on measures of performance that have the biggest impact on cost, quality, and patient outcomes.

A few years ago, in one of his typically insightful *New Yorker* articles, Atul Gawande, a surgeon and bestselling author, noted that Donald Berwick, IHI's cofounder, president, and longtime CEO, had been named the third-most-powerful figure in health care. In Nashville at the IHI National Forum, with tongue in cheek, Robert Waller introduced the much-admired Berwick as the Lone Ranger, then as Superman, and finally as "His Holiness." But unlike the other power players, Gawande explained, Berwick mattered "not because of the position he holds." Instead, "he is powerful because of how he thinks." Actually, in July 2010, Berwick became powerful because of his position as well. After the passage of landmark health-reform legislation, President Obama named the CEO of IHI to run the Centers for Medicare and Medicaid Services, the single largest payer for health-care services in the United States. By virtue of the power of his ideas and the clout of this huge government agency, Berwick is in a unique position to shape the future of a system he's worked so hard to change.[1]

Much of how Berwick thinks, it's worth noting, draws on fields far outside the insular world of health care and hospital management. Berwick and his colleagues saw possibilities for change that most health-care professionals didn't see because they looked for ideas in places most of them didn't look: the unblinking metrics of the quality movement, the rabble-rousing strategies of political campaigns and social movements, the tools and techniques of grassroots organizing.

Berwick, a Harvard-trained pediatrician and son of a small-town doctor, began his journey as a medical change agent with a profound appreciation for the shortcomings of his profession as well as its obvious contributions. "I had a strong awareness of the degree to which medicine does harm, wastes money, and hurts people," he told me. "I understood the problems, but I had an impoverished view of how to make things better."

That's why, early in IHI's history, Berwick and his colleagues became devoted students of W. Edwards Deming, Joseph Juran, and other quality gurus whose insights shaped how so many companies organized work and reorganized their operations. The techniques they studied, while increasingly routine in the business world, were disruptive when applied to health care—and fueled a far-reaching agenda for change inside hospitals. "I was very much dislocated," Berwick said of his first encounters with Deming. "This guy had a theory of how complex human endeavors get better. Juran was a chess grandmaster and even more methodical. His handbook is fifteen hundred pages long—a very deep and challenging exploration of how things improve. They provided me with a theoretical foundation for our work."

Maureen Bisognano, IHI's high-energy chief operating officer (who became president and CEO after Berwick joined the Obama administration), was a hospital executive before she joined the institute to become a full-time advocate for reform. As a hospital CEO, she participated in a pre-IHI program (this was 1987) that paired executives like her with leaders from other industries that had adopted the principles of Deming and Juran. She was matched with executives from Florida Power & Light, a legend in the quality movement of the 1980s. "I flew to Miami," Bisognano told a Stanford researcher who wrote a case study of IHI. "I had no idea how to approach a quality problem. . . . When I sat down at the end of the day I said, 'How would I have approached this without the electrical people?' I would have approached the problem in a very different way. I would never have been able to accomplish the results we achieved."[2]

Thus began the formation of IHI and its efforts to immerse all kinds of hospital officials, at all levels of management, in the radical ideas and practical tools of the quality movement. Thousands of doctors, nurses, and administrators went to school on IHI's newfangled curriculum—yet the fervor produced as much resistance as results. "We attracted the zealots, the weirdos, the mavericks," Bisognano says with a smile. "We'd get them all worked up, they'd go back to their hospitals, and nothing would happen."

IHI adopted a slogan to describe the flaw in its original strategy: "It's a sin to send a changed man back to an unchanged organization." So it revised the strategy to fix the flaw: hospitals would enroll teams of doctors, nurses, or technicians who were eager to improve performance, and then work as a group to make change happen. This all-together model helped the once-isolated "zealots" to rally their organizations around dramatic improvement. At many hospitals across the country, rates of infections began to go down, medical errors were reduced, costs were cut, and lives were saved.

Years later, insights from a guru in a very different field inspired IHI to add to its change-the-game repertoire. Despite progress, Berwick and Bisognano were frustrated with the pace of improvement in health care. One much-cited study showed that it took seventeen years for a new practice that was documented to enhance quality or patient safety to become standard practice in all health care—*seventeen years!* Another of IHI's many slogans captured this reality: "We're excellent at everything, just not everywhere." (This mantra was coined by Dr. Louise Liang of Kaiser Permanente, former chairman of IHI's board, who was talking about Kaiser, but could have been talking about the entire system.) In other words, most of the solutions to the problems in health care were already being implemented in one hospital unit, or on one floor, or in one medical practice. The challenge was getting them adopted across an entire organization, and eventually the whole health-care system.

IHI was determined to accelerate the rate at which new ideas took hold and turned to Gloria Steinem and the women's movement for inspiration and strategies. Steinem, speaking at IHI's National Forum in 2002, urged the assembled health-care leaders to "name the problems" they were striving to solve (much like the term "date rape" reframed perceptions of an issue that was hard to describe and thus easy to ignore). She advised them to build coalitions for change around these well-named problems and to equip allies with ready-to-go solutions. She also urged them to use the media to raise the visibility of their agenda and to apply the tools of electoral politics to create grassroots pressures for its adoption.

After consulting with Steinem (plus veterans from presidential politics and field organizing), IHI launched its 100,000 Lives Campaign at the 2004 National Forum. The goal was as clear as it was ambitious—to convince hospitals to adopt six proven interventions that could, if they were embraced widely enough, eliminate a hundred thousand needless deaths. The timetable was just as specific: the campaign, unveiled on December 14, 2004, would end at 9:00 A.M. on June 14, 2006—eighteen months to the minute of when it was announced. "I'm losing my patience," Berwick declared. "Some is not a number, soon is not a time. . . . This isn't an event. It's a movement. . . . We are going to elect quality."

What followed was a march of progress unprecedented in modern health care. Surpassing expectations, some thirty-one hundred hospitals, representing 75 percent of the beds in the country, signed on to the campaign. Officials shared data, swapped ideas, and began implementing the six initiatives. In the fall of 2005, Joe McCannon, an IHI vice president who served as "campaign manager" for the program, hired a bus so that he and members of the campaign team could crisscross the country to spread the message and harvest success stories. "I went on the bus for some of the segments," Berwick recalled to the Stanford researcher. "You drive into these cities and at the campaign hospitals it would be like a [political] campaign. You had rallies and this outpouring of interest. We tapped this energy that no one knew was there." Hospitals in the campaign delivered on many life-saving improvements in patient care—and it became a much-analyzed case study of how to make big change fast.[3]

That's why six thousand doctors, nurses, hospital executives, and quality leaders have gathered this afternoon in Nashville. They want to know how IHI is thinking about what comes next—and what it means for the future of their organizations and the health-care system as a whole. That's also why we're about to watch a play. Berwick and his colleagues don't just draw on the techniques of management science or the tools of politics to agitate for reform. They also draw on the arts—poets, writers, and now, directors and actors—to change how health-care leaders make sense of the world and think about their jobs. Sometimes, the most bracing (and revealing) critiques of an industry can come from voices far outside that industry.

The house lights dim, the audience settles down, and the production, called *Dr. Hippocrates Is Out: Please Leave a Message*, begins. Robert Brustein describes the show as "an anthology of pathology." What it is, really, is a shock to the medical system—scenes from well-known plays and popular film that shine a light on the practice of medicine and the business of health care in all its tragedy, comedy, and occasional glory. Brustein knows that he is about to unsettle his audience—that's the point of the exercise—so he opens with a statement of intent.

"The risk we're taking this afternoon," he warns, "is to take a historical look at health care, not through the clear microscope of trained professionals like yourselves, but through the bloodshot eyes of often-cranky critics. It is a risk because most of these artists don't like what they see, and this means you may not like what they say. . . . You are the people who serve. These playwrights and filmmakers are the poetic spokesmen of the people *you* serve. And being passionate, they are sometimes intemperate. Indeed, some of these selections may make you angry, because, as in all roasts, the satire is exaggerated. But even distorting mirrors, especially in the hands of master writers and master actors, are capable of reflecting a piece of the truth."

One of the early selections is from Molière's *The Imaginary Invalid*, first performed in 1673. The original play, a comedy that featured the playwright himself as Argan, a miserly hypochondriac, had a bizarrely tragic twist. Molière collapsed after just the fourth performance and died soon thereafter of tuberculosis. Life, it seems, doesn't always imitate art.

"To be quite frank I've never found treating people of high rank very attractive," confesses the cynical Dr. Diafoirus (F. Murray Abraham) to Argan's maid, Toinette (Brooke Adams). "It's much better for us to practice among the general public. The trouble with people of high rank is that when they're sick, they absolutely insist on being cured!" Meanwhile, Argan (Tony Shalhoub) is desperate for advice on his latest phantom ailment. Diafoirus says the problem is his "disturbed" spleen. "The doctor says it's my liver that's no good," a puzzled Argan replies. Spleen, liver, it's all the same, Diafoirus reassures. "No doubt he urges you to eat a lot of roast beef," the pompous doctor adds. "No, no, only boiled beef," Argan replies. "Oh yes, roast or boiled, same thing. A very wise man, your doctor. You couldn't be in better hands."

A few scenes later, the mood turns from the gentle seventeenth-century comedy of Molière to the withering absurdism of Don DeLillo and *The Day Room*, first performed in 1986. The play is set in a psychiatric hospital where the doctors and nurses seem even more disturbed than the patients. "I don't like being the center of attention," complains a patient named Wyatt (Shalhoub). "But this is what hospitals are for. So a person can follow his disease into the ultra-violet light," insists Dr. Phelps (Abraham). "Disease itself is not unhealthy," says Nurse Walker (Adams). "We recover from disease." But "if the gravity of the disease is not reflected in the terminology, the patient feels cheated," she adds. "Sarcomas!" shouts Walker. "Blastomas!"

says Phelps. "I love the gleam of hospital corridors in the dead of night," the nurse muses as the scene winds down with a twisted meditation on mortality.

For all the power of live drama, though, it's a clip from the film *As Good as It Gets* (with which this chapter opens) that draws the most visceral reaction from the health-care professionals. When Carol, the worried-sick mother of an asthmatic son, delivers her kitchen-table tirade (*"fucking HMO bastard pieces of shit!"*), the audience gasps. When the sympathetic doctor validates her rage ("Actually, I think that's their technical name"), the room erupts with nervous laughter and a few shrieks.

This being Hollywood, the emotionally charged scene ends on an upbeat note. "Mrs. Connelly," says Dr. Bettes, "there's still a lot of tests I need to do, a lot of things I need to find out here. But look, whatever I find out, I promise you, at the very least, from now on, your son is going to feel a great deal better, okay?" Carol glows with hope. "Doc!" she cries, and hugs the embarrassed Bettes.

The audience breathes a sigh of relief, offers a round of applause, and the show goes on. Even the innovators in this change-minded crowd, as committed as any group of professionals anywhere to improving the state of the art in their field, could not help but be shaken by the barbs of voices from other fields, artists and critics with different life experiences and expectations. With a new point of view on their problems, the participants in the National Forum file out to work on solutions. Dr. Hippocrates would approve.

A "NEW AUDACITY OF IMAGINATION"—WHAT THE MAN FROM INTERPOL SAW IN GOOGLE

In Chapter 1, in settings as diverse as the Swiss watch industry and the Girl Scouts of the USA, we saw the power of history as a source of distinctive and disruptive ideas for the future.

Even in the most trying circumstances, organizations can refresh and reinterpret the best of what came before as a way to fashion what comes next. In the struggle to make fundamental change, leaders can reach deep into the past to rediscover what they and their colleagues have forgotten—a time-honored sense of purpose that can be made relevant to modern times, long-standing pockets of expertise that can drive excellence in a fast-moving marketplace.

But that's hardly the only way to unlock vuja dé. Leaders can also reach beyond the walls of their organizations and the boundaries of their industries to discover what they and their colleagues have been missing. One way to look at problems as if you're seeing them for the first time is to look at a wide array of fields for ideas that have been working for a long time. That's a key lesson behind IHI's unorthodox model for transforming health care. Who would have predicted that utility-company executives could teach a hospital CEO how to unravel quality issues? Or that strategies for social progress developed by the women's movement could translate into a campaign to eliminate preventable deaths in medical institutions? Some of the most powerful sources of new ideas are proven ideas from new places.

A classic example of this phenomenon, which I chronicled in a different context for a previous book, was the game-changing performance of Commerce Bank, one of the most colorful institutions in the history of retail banking. I first noticed Commerce back in 1997, when it was developing a reputation for creativity and had a stock-market value of $400 million. Ten years later, after a period of massive growth, the company sold itself to TD Bank in a stock transaction worth $8.5 billion—not a bad decade. Today, operating under the TD Bank umbrella, the outfit has nearly 1,300 branches up and down the East Coast, from Maine to Florida, and a well-earned reputation as "America's most convenient bank."

During its rise to prominence, the bank introduced one unheard-of innovation after another: seven-day-a-week service, free coin-counting machines that were hugely popular with customers and a raft of other unusual experiences crafted by the Wow! Department. The term it used to describe its strategy was "retailtainment"—making it fun for customers to do business in an industry that was devoid of personality. "The world didn't need another bank on the corner, and then we came along," said Dennis DiFlorio, who spent nearly twenty years in leadership positions, including chairman. "We created a cult brand in a dead business."[4]

Whenever I spent time with the bank's leadership team, they were adamant about their disdain for traditional approaches to "benchmarking" the competition as well as for traditional banks. They didn't evaluate themselves against Citigroup, Bank of America, or Wells Fargo. They looked to "power retailers" such as Starbucks, Target, and Best Buy. "Every great company has reinvented the industry it's in," founder Vernon Hill told me. "So we don't copy the stupid banks. We copy the great retailers." For example, the bank decided to open its branches for seventy to eighty hours a week, including Saturday and Sunday. "It's the simplest idea in the world," Hill said. "But to this day, it's heretical in banking. The first question bankers ask me is, 'How do you staff on Sunday?' I tell them: 'Wal-Mart stays open. The malls stay open. How hard can it be?'"

> One way to look at problems as if you're seeing them for the first time is to look at a wide array of fields for ideas that have been working for a long time. That's the real virtue of vuja dé.

Commerce was (and TD Bank remains) a unique outfit, but its blueprint for innovation was not an entirely new perspective on making change. In their definitive guide to organizational learning, *Benchmarking for Best Practices*, Christopher E. Bogan and Michael J. English tell a story that illustrates the long history of moving ideas between unrelated fields. "In 1912, a curious Henry Ford watched men cut meat during a tour of a Chicago slaughterhouse," Bogan and English write. "The carcasses were hanging on hooks mounted on a monorail. After each man performed his job, he would push the carcass to the next station. When the tour was over, the guide said, 'Well, sir, what do you think?' Mr. Ford turned to the man and said, 'Thanks, son, I think you may have given me a real good idea.' Less than six months later, the world's first assembly line started producing magnetos in the Ford Highland Park Plant."[5]

Or consider a more contemporary example—an illustrious British hospital that borrowed techniques from automobile racing to redesign how it transferred patients from one step of a complex medical procedure to the next. Fascinating articles in the *Daily Telegraph* and the *Wall Street Journal* described how London's Great Ormond Street Hospital for Children, renowned for its cardiac care, struggled with poorly designed "handoffs" that resulted in errors, complications, even deaths. So Dr. Martin Elliot, head of cardiac surgery, and Dr. Allan Goldman, head of pediatric intensive care, studied high-powered professionals who were better than anyone at organizing handoffs—the pit crew of Ferrari's Formula One racing team.

The doctors and the pit crew, the *Telegraph* reported, "worked together at [the team's] home base in Modena, Italy, in the pits of the British Grand Prix, and in the Great Ormond Street [operating room] and intensive-care ward." Members of the pit crew were struck by how clumsy the hospital's handoff process was—not to mention the fact that it often lacked a clear leader. (In Formula One races, a so-called lollipop man wields an easy-to-see paddle and calls the shots.) Moreover, they noted how *noisy* the process was. Ferrari pit crews operate largely in silence, despite (or because of) the roar of engines around them. As a result of "one of the more unlikely collaborations in modern medicine," the *Journal* reported, the hospital redesigned its handoff procedures and sharply reduced medical errors.[6]

Even mainstream companies and their leaders can learn to look for new ideas in unfamiliar places. Here's an easy-to-copy example: Maxine Clark, founder and CEO of (publicly traded) Build-A-Bear Workshop, switched companies for a day with Kip Tindell, cofounder and CEO of the (privately held) Container Store. Both outfits are big, fast-growing, passion brands in the ultracompetitive world of retail—although they have little in common in terms of target customers, in-store zeitgeist, or corporate missions. Yet those differences are precisely what made the CEO switcheroo so valuable: when the two leaders spent a day working on the front lines of each other's operations, they encountered all kinds of ideas about merchandising, employee motivation, and in-store communication that worked in one place, and might just work in the other if those ideas were exported to and adapted for the new environment.

To give credit where credit is due, neither Clark nor Tindell had the original idea for this clever exercise in idea swapping. In fact, credit goes to the editors of *Fortune* magazine, who were assembling their annual "Best Companies to Work For" issue. Build-A-Bear and Container Store both made the cut (Container Store is a perennial), and the editors thought it would be a neat trick if two CEOs on the list traded companies for a day. They were right; it was a neat trick. But it was more than that—it was yet another example of the power of a new mind-set about leadership, innovation, and change.[7]

Indra Nooyi, the change-minded CEO of PepsiCo, has her own language to capture the same phenomenon. She describes the new logic of innovation as "lift and shift." That is, search for great ideas in unrelated fields, lift them out of the context in which they took shape, and shift them into your company. Which is precisely what Tindell and Clark did. According to *Fortune*, the CEO of the Container Store was struck by the effectiveness of Build-A-Bear's "Strive for Five" sales technique—aiming to sell customers five items during their visit. The CEO of Build-A-Bear was impressed by how well the Container Store communicated with its frontline associates—lots of simple gestures that sent big signals through the ranks. Both CEOs vowed to apply these (and other) outside ideas inside their organizations.

Looking for ideas in unfamiliar fields, it is important to emphasize, is not just about relocating what works from one industry to another. It is also (and more significantly) about reimagining what's possible in an industry. "Every great advance in science," wrote the philosopher John Dewey in *The Quest for Certainty*, "has issued from a new audacity of imagination." That's true for leaders as well as scientists—and what better way to fuel your imagination than to look for inspiration beyond your field?[8]

Ron Noble, secretary general of Interpol, is a genuinely audacious thinker—and a fiercely determined change agent. As a leader, Noble breaks with convention on several levels. He is not only the first African American but the first American of any sort to run the organization, headquartered in Lyon, France, which has been dominated by Europeans for its sixty-plus-year history. (Interpol traces its origins to 1914, but it was disbanded during World War II and restarted from scratch.) What's more, the world's unofficial top cop isn't trained as a cop—he's a Stanford-trained lawyer who served in the U.S. Treasury under President Clinton as undersecretary for enforcement, where he oversaw the Customs Service, the Secret Service, and the Bureau of Alcohol, Tobacco, and Firearms. As for "renaissance tendencies," Noble speaks four languages and has studied Arabic during his tenure. When he met with Russia's Vladimir Putin after an Interpol gathering in St. Petersburg, he and Putin had a one-on-one session in German, which they both speak fluently.

I had my first interview session with Noble on November 3, 2008, at the Interpol offices across from the United Nations. That was eight years to the day after he took the helm of the crime-fighting organization, which was barely ten months before the September 11 terrorist attacks that remade the fields of national security and international law enforcement. It's hard to do justice to the depth and breadth of the changes Noble has unleashed at Interpol, or the pace he has maintained as secretary general. (As of March 2009, he had visited 125 countries in his quest to expand the agency's impact and enlist allies in his blueprint for renewal.) In just the last few years, Noble and his colleagues have conducted forensic examinations of computers seized from Colombian rebels; assisted Pakistan and India in their investigations of the terrorist attack in Mumbai; tracked down a vicious child abuser who was born in Canada, worked in Korea, and fled to Thailand to evade capture; and orchestrated a worldwide investigation of the Pink Panther thieves, a gang from the former Yugoslavia who had stolen more than $200 million worth of jewelry from 120 stores in twenty countries.

It sounds glamorous, dangerous, and cutting-edge—which is a big part of the problem Noble has had to overcome. When he took charge of Interpol, the legend surrounding the organization (the stuff of novels, TV series, and Hollywood movies) bore virtually no resemblance to how the organization worked. Fittingly, our second face-to-face conversation came just a few weeks after the release of *The International,* a Clive Owen thriller in which a dashing Interpol agent and a gorgeous Manhattan DA bring down a rogue bank. Had Noble seen the film? "Not yet." He smiled, although the headquarters staff in Lyon was scheduled to see it in a few days. "We've got a great brand name. We're trying to make Interpol more of what it should be like, more of what it's like in books and movies."

Looking for ideas in unfamiliar fields is not just about relocating what works from one industry to another. It is also about reimagining what's *possible* in an industry.

Over the years, for example, one of Interpol's main responsibilities has been to issue "red notices"—or international wanted-person notices to help law-enforcement agencies identify and arrest fugitives anywhere in the world. Before Noble arrived, it could take Interpol three to six months to issue a red notice. Here's how one magazine described the remarkably arcane process: "They [red notices] had to be reviewed for accuracy, translated into Interpol's four official languages (English, French, Spanish, and Noble's latest addition, Arabic), then printed, stuffed into envelopes, and mailed—third class, to cut costs. Email? Why bother? The previous secretary general never used it."[9]

Just as remarkably, Interpol headquarters was only open for business from 8:00 A.M. to 6:00 P.M., Monday through Friday. That's right: one of the world's most celebrated crime-fighting organizations worked bankers' hours during the week and shut down over the weekend. No wonder that *60 Minutes*, in an in-depth profile of Noble and his agenda for change, said that the agency "had the reputation of sort of being a retirement home for police officers"—a description the secretary general did not dispute. "If you had a request for assistance at five o'clock on Friday," he told the correspondent, "you'd have to wait until Monday morning for someone to respond to it."[10]

As soon as Noble took over, he devised a plan to create and run the agency's Command and Coordination Center twenty-four hours a day, 365 days a year—a plan that became operational the morning after September 11. It now takes less than seventy-two hours for Interpol to issue a standard red notice, and high-priority warrants go out in a matter of hours. More timely red notices have led to *more* red notices, as police come to believe that issuing warrants will actually lead to arrests. The number of red notices tripled between 2000 and 2007, and the number of criminals arrested as a result of these warrants and so-called diffusions increased tenfold. Interpol also launched I-24/7, the first secure communication systems to connect the world's police agencies. Today, cops from 188 countries (including such unlikely law-enforcement counterparts as Iran and Israel, Russia and Georgia, Cuba and Vatican City) can search and cross-check Interpol's information on terrorists, fugitives, fingerprints, and DNA profiles.

"We've transformed Interpol from an international organization, a place where you have meetings and move paper, to an international *police* organization that aspires to be a command center, a nerve center, for law enforcement worldwide," Noble told me. "Police are expected to be available 24/7; they are expected to prevent crime, to identify, locate, and apprehend bad guys, to improve the ways we keep society safe. To do that, to make ourselves relevant, we had to innovate."

But Noble's real challenge was more than just to make Interpol relevant in a changing world. It was to rethink and reimagine the agency's very role in the world. "Interpol had a 'monopoly' on alerting the world's police about people wanted for arrest," he told me. "But that's a pretty limited monopoly, we were slow to deliver on it, and there was so much more we could be doing. We had to figure out how to make Interpol's footprint larger, but to keep it recognizable to police officers in their work. What services could we offer such that every law-enforcement officer in the world would have an interest in it?"

There was little in the agency's history or traditions to answer that game-changing question. Noble couldn't look to the past for guiding principles or untapped expertise. So he looked outside the organization for clues about devising new services that could respond to twenty-first-century threats. Specifically, he looked to Google, and the immediacy with which people from all walks of life turn to the "search engine" as a part of their day. To what urgent problem might law-enforcement officers be searching for answers, and how could Interpol develop a search engine to respond?

His answer: the world's first database of lost or stolen travel documents. According to Noble, there were 850 million international arrivals in 2008, a figure that will increase to 1.4 billion by 2012. Among those arriving passengers are fugitives, war criminals, and terrorists— almost all of them traveling on forged or stolen passports, few of them subject to a passport check with truly worldwide reach. The mastermind of the first World Trade Center bombing, Noble reminded me, entered the United States on a stolen Iraqi passport. A stolen passport allowed the mastermind of the assassination of Serbian prime minister Zoran Djindjic to travel in and out of six different countries twenty-six times to plan his attack. One of the world's most wanted war criminals, Croatian general Ante Gotovina, used a stolen passport to travel through sixteen countries before he was arrested in 2005.

What if, Noble asked, his agency created a database of documents that would be as easy to search as Google—and, by virtue of the Interpol "brand name," reliable enough for government officials to trust? So that's what the agency did, with a small team, a limited budget, and no urgent demand from member countries, most of whom were oddly complacent about the flaws in their border-control procedures. Interpol launched the database in 2002 with 3,000 documents from 10 countries. As of mid-2009, it included 15 million documents from 140 countries. Border officials and law-enforcement agencies searched the database a few thousand times in 2002. The number of searches approached 100 million in 2009. China alone searched the database a million times in the run-up to the Beijing Olympics. The United States, which was decidedly unenthusiastic at the outset of the program, now checks the database millions of times each month.

I don't mean to overstate the current state of the art at Interpol. It's not as if Ron Noble has been able to take his outfit to a level of technological proficiency or organizational agility that defines what it means to be a twenty-first-century operation. In many respects, he and his colleagues are still catching up to best practices in global organizations such as IBM or General Electric. What *is* remarkable about Noble's tenure, though, is that he has been able to drive so much progress from such a tough starting point. Interpol, once such a laggard, truly is relevant to the great security threats facing the world and integral to fighting them, and Noble has made it so largely through the power of persuasion as opposed to the top-down tools available to CEOs of traditional organizations. In that sense, he has achieved greater progress, and has played for much higher stakes, than many of the innovators and change agents chronicled elsewhere in this book. Indeed, I'd argue that he has done more with less than most leaders of most organizations in most fields.

It's clear, by the way, that Noble understands the high-stakes position he is in. At the end of the 60 *Minutes* segment, which aired in October 2007, he opened up about his ongoing struggles to secure the level of funding he needs to pursue his agenda for innovation. As he described his frustrations, particularly with the limited levels of support from the United States, he lost his composure, began shedding a few tears, and asked interviewer Steve Kroft to stop the cameras. "What was it that triggered that" reaction? Kroft asked once the cameras started rolling again. "I keep thinking about September 11 and all the other terrorist attacks," Noble replied. "And I'm saying that I see the mistakes that are being made every day. And I think about one of these days it's going to happen again. And I've gotta be able to persuade people before it happens" again. "You're obviously very wrapped up in this," Kroft suggested. "Yeah," Noble said softly. "I realize I'm mortal and I'm not invincible. And I feel an urgency to communicate what I wanna communicate. My neck is out there with this interview."

Noble initiated the forged-or-stolen-passport database from a very personal sense of dread about a gaping hole in global security. "There was a void," he told me. "We go to the airport and surrender our shoes, belts, and water. But we're not checking passports against a database of documents that are known to be forged or stolen? This is the sort of thing, when people hear it, they say, 'It can't be true.' There was no entity in the world trying to gather this information."

Now, though, Noble is motivated by a sense of possibility. "I keep thinking about Google," he told me at the end of our second conversation. "If we were a private-sector company with a database that grew from three thousand units to fifteen million, with usage that grew from thousands of searches to a hundred million, our market value would be through the roof. But that's not our job. Our job is to build Interpol to the point that it becomes for law enforcement what Google and Yahoo have become in everyday life. It's not easy, but we're going to get there. We're going to change the world."

HOW TOYOTA TAUGHT VIRGINIA MASON TO SEE, AND LEXUS SAW THE GENIUS IN APPLE

I DON'T MEAN TO PORTRAY Ron Noble as a one-man band of imaginative thinking. He is quick to share credit for Interpol's transformation with a cast of innovators that has included Roraima Andriani, his Italian chief of staff; Dr. Rodolfo Ronconi, Interpol's vice president for Europe, who played a key role in the early days of the passport database; Stanley Morris, a veteran of the U.S. Marshals Service who led the creation of I-24/7; and Jean-Michel Louboutin, executive director of police services. ("I am a former federal law-enforcement officer, but never a police officer," Noble said. "I needed 'real police' out of central casting and Jean-Michel is that.")

Still, of necessity, change at Interpol has been a top-down process, which puts huge pressure on the people at the top. It's easier to see intractable problems with fresh eyes if lots of eyes are trained on those problems—and focused on solutions from new and unfamiliar fields. Game-changing strategies that evoke Dewey's "audacity of imagination" don't have to spring from the imaginations of a few senior leaders.

One audacious example of this phenomenon is the bottom-up transformation of Virginia Mason Medical Center (VMMC), a ninety-year-old hospital in Seattle, Washington, with four hundred doctors and nearly five thousand employees. For years, despite a rich history, Virginia Mason struggled with deteriorating finances, inefficient processes, and uneven quality—like so many other big, established hospital systems in the United States. Its CEO, Dr. Gary Kaplan, who took charge in February 2000, understood that merely trying to borrow ideas and techniques from the medical establishment might not have that great an impact on Virginia Mason's fortunes—best practices in the field, truth be told, weren't all that great. As they searched for new sources of ideas, he and some colleagues got exposed to, and became fascinated with, the most advanced practitioners of Japanese-style quality management in general, and the Toyota Production System in particular—the blend of "just-in-time" assembly techniques (*kanban*), continuous improvement (*kaizen*), and frontline employees who fixed problems in real time (*jikoda*). The legendary Eiji Toyoda had used the Toyota Production System to drive Japan's flagship company to global prominence—and Gary Kaplan came to believe that his organization could borrow methodologies from this rich tradition to fix its problems and advance the state of its practices.[11]

So he and the hospital's top executives began an intensive program of learning about the theory and practice of Japanese quality management, and the entire leadership team took its first trip to Japan in June 2002 to see for itself how the ideas worked on the ground. Ever since, literally hundreds of Virginia Mason staff members have made similar trips, with Kaplan leading all of them, in which doctors, nurses, and hospital staffers get exposed to the intricacies of how Toyota organizes work, tracks quality, and solves problems. Teams spend three months preparing for the learning journey. Each trip begins with a daylong tour of the Toyota Museum in Nagoya, which offers an eye-opening display of the ideas, technologies, and management techniques behind the company's rise. Virginia Mason employees visit the museum armed with sketchbooks, in which they are required to take visual notes of what catches their eye. "The museum is fundamental to the experience," Kaplan told me. "This is all about learning to see, and people see more when they draw."

There are plenty of classes and meetings, of course, but a defining piece of the experience is when doctors, nurses, and hospital staffers spend several days working eight-hour shifts in a factory. They are not playing shop—they staff the lines, do the work, and, like their

Japanese counterparts, are expected to use the Toyota Production System to solve problems as they arise. "This is a real eye-opener for the team," Kaplan explains. "We stick a bunch of doctors on an assembly line. We use the methods and tools we've learned, we come up with suggestions, and the Japanese put them into place! It's a very intense experience."

Very intense, and, early on, very controversial—as is often the case for leaders who break with standard operating procedure. Indeed, Virginia Mason was an organization steeped in tradition and stability. Gary Kaplan was only the seventh CEO in the organization's ninety-year history, and doctors actually elected him to the job. Some of those same doctors (along with others) voiced plenty of objections to the CEO's idea that well-trained and highly autonomous medical professionals could learn from a well-run and highly disciplined automobile company.

"We don't make cars, we treat patients" was the frequently voiced rallying cry. A bunch of doctors left the hospital, and some who stayed didn't rush to get with the program. "One of the hardest things for me to realize was that not everyone wanted or was able to come with us on this journey," Kaplan reflected in a Harvard Business School case study. "I recognized that you have to say good-bye, and this is a good thing. You can't keep everyone happy."

That includes the media. Back in 2002, right before Kaplan led the first delegation of thirty high-level staffers to Japan, the *Seattle Times* wrote a scathing article questioning the cost of the excursion, given the hospital's shaky financial condition. "Some employees are furious" about the trip, the newspaper reported, "calling the expense egregious from a company dedicated to a low operating budget. . . . 'Outraged is *not* an understatement,' said one employee who wished to remain anonymous. Said a former employee: 'This is the crème de le crème. This is what makes you think there is no decency left in the administration there.'"

Of course, just a few years later, as the impact of the trips on

Virginia Mason's financial results and quality performance became apparent, the media wrote exuberantly about the unique value of the very same excursions. In March 2008, for example, the *Seattle Post-Intelligencer* published a glowing account of the progress at Virginia Mason, with special emphasis on the learning journeys to Japan. "When you think of a hospital, what comes to mind?" the article asked. "Patients, emergency rooms, technology and medical advancement. Making the sick and injured well again. When officials at Virginia Mason think of hospitals, they think of cars. A car manufacturing plant, to be exact." Gary Kaplan explained to the newspaper why and how the trips had been such a game changer for the hospital. "We get so wrapped up in the seriousness and specialness of health care, but we also have to open our eyes to other industries," he said.[12]

It's easy to pick on the doubters-turned-supporters in the mainstream media, but it's important to remember that there were plenty of Virginia Mason doctors and executives who were doubters as well—and they only became supporters after they came face-to-face with the power of the ideas and the elegance of the execution they saw in Japan. It was then that they realized how much they had to learn about working more efficiently, more consistently, and thus more effectively, precisely because they were studying and actually working in a setting far removed from their own. In the Harvard case, Kaplan offered one small example of a conversion experience.

"When I asked one of our surgeons to go to Japan in 2003 he refused," the CEO said. "A year later he changed his mind because he'd heard that it was value-added time. So he is on the assembly line in Japan, and I send the team out to get measurements of their workers so that we can plot the work and find the waste. And he came running back and said, 'I can't clock it.' I asked, 'Why not?' And he answered, 'Because the operator does it differently every single time. There is no standard work!' And there was the teaching point right there: because this person did it differently each time, the surgeon couldn't properly measure the work; if you can't measure it, you can't improve it. That was very powerful."[13]

There's nothing like the zeal of a convert, of course, and the Virginia Mason Production System designed by Kaplan and his rank-and-file colleagues displays a near-religious devotion to the strategies, language, and practices of its Japanese mentors. There's a twenty-five-person Kaizen Promotion Office staffed with highly trained quality experts. Using Rapid Process Improvement Workshops (RPIW), modeled on Japanese problem-solving teams, groups of nurses, doctors, technicians, and many other staffers with varied job responsibilities, diagnose flaws in hospital operations and devise remedies. The Patient Safety Alert (PSA) system, borrowed from the emergency *andon* cord on Toyota's factory floor, allows employees to "stop the line" if they encounter a situation likely to harm a patient. (From 2002 through 2009, employees issued more than 14,600 safety alerts.)

Years of in-depth study of the Japanese quality movement have transformed Virginia Mason. Among its many achievements, the hospital eliminated millions of dollars of needless inventory, cut the time required to deliver lab results by 85 percent, and reduced staff walking distances by sixty miles per day. One rapid-improvement team redesigned how nurses interact with patients and with each other—allowing nurses to spend 90 percent of their time at the bedside, as opposed to 35 percent before. Another team figured out how to fit a new hyperbaric center within an existing space instead of in a new building. (Virginia Mason is renowned for hyperbaric medicine.) That innovation saved millions of dollars in construction costs, even as it increased treatment capacity from three patients at a time to as many as twenty patients.

The Harvard Business School case study described how the hospital's hematology and oncology unit applied ideas directly from the Toyota playbook to redesign how its department worked. The unit's doctors and nurses, working with patients as well, redesigned the treatment rooms, waiting rooms, and offices for maximum efficiency and patient comfort. Using the same amount of space, but a vastly different layout, the unit increased the number of daily patient visits it could handle by 57 percent, reduced patient walking distances by 76 percent per visit, and slashed waiting times for drug deliveries from two hours to thirty minutes, and for lab results from twenty minutes to one minute.

In other words, over the last decade, Virginia Mason became the ultimate learning organization. In recent years, it has also aspired to become the ultimate *teaching* organization. In October 2008, Kaplan and his colleagues created the Virginia Mason Institute and opened the doors of the hospital to the outside world. The Institute leads tours of the facilities and explains how they work, teaches classes in various management techniques, and otherwise shares what Virginia Mason knows with individual executives and entire health-care systems. The student has become the teacher.

Why bother? "First and foremost," Kaplan told me, "this is about our vision to be the quality leader in our field and to help transform the field as a whole. Part of our mission as a company is to help improve our industry. But the more we educate, the faster we move as well. This will spur us on and push us to keep getting better. Our credibility as a company is dependent on our ability to deliver results. By teaching others what we've learned, it forces us to keep learning."

Ultimately, though, the real impact of Virginia Mason's exposure to the theory and practice of Japanese quality management was as much about fueling imagination as it was about transferring methodologies. A story from Charles Kenney's book *The Best Practice*, an indispensable history of the quality movement in health care, makes the point well. When Dr. Robert Mecklenburg, the hospital's chief of medicine at the time, made his first pilgrimage to Toyota City, he worked closely with a *sensei*, or Japanese quality master. In one of his projects, Mecklenburg was looking for the most efficient way to add space for operating rooms at Virginia Mason. So he showed the *sensei* a layout of the hospital. The *sensei* asked about a particular room that caught his eye. Mecklenburg told him it was a waiting room. The average patient waits about forty-five minutes to see a doctor, he said.

The *sensei* asked if this was the only such room at the hospital. Not exactly, Mecklenburg replied, there were probably a hundred such rooms.

"It was as if the *sensei* had confronted an unexpected, deeply offensive cultural violation of some sort," Kenney wrote. "He lowered his gaze and looked steadily at Mecklenburg. 'You have a hundred waiting areas where patients wait an average of forty-five minutes for a doctor?' He paused and let the question hang in the air, then he asked: 'Aren't you ashamed?'" Suddenly, Mecklenburg *was* ashamed. As Kenney wrote, "The shame was in treating patients so shabbily as to make them wait; in wasting so much space throughout the medical center for waiting—an activity without any value added to patients at all. It was an activity that was wasteful in an almost pure form: It wasted space, wasted time for patients and family, and reduced the productivity of all the patients who were missing work or school."[14]

In other words, Dr. Mecklenburg's exposure to Toyota had not just taught him new management techniques. *It had inspired a whole new mind-set.* And that new mind-set, for him and so many doctors, nurses and administrators who eventually began to look at their hospital through Toyota's eyes, drove them to reimagine what was possible back in Seattle. What they saw in a completely unrelated field changed their point of view about their own field.

"Change is an affair of the head and of the heart," CEO Kaplan told me. "We have our share of devotees and skeptics when we start out on the trips. But almost everyone comes back believing it was a transformational experience. They did things they never thought they were capable of doing. It changes the way you think."

It's fitting that Toyota has been such an eye-opening teacher for aspiring innovators from the health-care industry, because Toyota has been such an eagle-eyed student of innovation in industries beyond automobiles. The company has always understood the power of looking for proven ideas in new fields, which helps to explain why it has remained such a powerful presence in its own field. To be sure, Toyota's legendary commitment to quality and efficiency couldn't keep it from veering sharply off the road to prosperity. In October 2009, in the face of two years of red ink, a high-profile recall of millions of cars, and a controversial decision to close its first factory in the United States, the company's new president and CEO, Akio Toyoda, a grandson of the company founder, issued a formal public apology for the company's disastrous performance, even as he prepared for more embarrassing front-page headlines and intense grillings from angry members of Congress. ("Customers bought our cars because they thought they were the safest," Toyoda declared. "But now we have given them cause for grave concern. I can't begin to express my remorse.") Still, despite these deep and damaging potholes, Toyota remains the largest car manufacturer on the planet—and its smartest.[15]

Consider, for example, how it launched Lexus, its game-changing entrant in one of the world's most competitive business arenas—the market for luxury automobiles in North America. Lexus was a radical departure for a company built on making slow-but-steady progress with solid-but-unspectacular products. Yet in less than two decades (the first LS 400 rolled off dealer lots in September 1989), Lexus was established as the bestselling luxury auto brand in the United States, outpacing BMW, Cadillac, and Mercedes. Its product-quality and customer-satisfaction numbers are consistently off the charts. J.D. Powers ranked Lexus as the most-dependable auto brand fourteen years in a row, and it has retained its allure for customers, despite high-profile safety problems at Toyota and even with some Lexus models. It is, quite simply, a crown jewel of the company that has reigned over the global auto industry.

How did Lexus get so much traction in such a short period of time? A big part of the explanation, of course, is the brand's first-rate fleet of sedans, performance cars, and SUVs. But the real genius behind the brand has been its capacity to imagine a one-of-a-kind customer experience. Lexus saw opportunities for innovation its established rivals didn't see, because it searched for ideas in places they had overlooked.

J. Davis (Dave) Illingworth, the brand's first vice president and general manager, was literally present at the creation of Lexus. To this day, he marvels at the painstaking attention to detail in the design of the early products. "I was in Japan with the chief engineer, and we were talking about the LS 400 key, which had no indentations," he told me when I visited U.S. headquarters in Torrance, California. "It was different from any key in the industry, and it cost more money to make. I asked him, 'Is this really necessary?' He came back with a box and emptied the contents onto a table. The box had every key for every car out there. He told me, 'Our key is the finest key in the world!' When I saw that intensity, the demands the engineers were putting on themselves to design the cars, I understood that we had to do the same thing with the customer experience."

To design a best-in-the-world customer experience, Lexus immersed itself in its customers' world. In the mid-1980s, a team of researchers took up residence in Laguna Beach to study the lifestyles, attitudes, and daily habits of affluent Americans. They tagged along as their research subjects shopped for groceries, went to the country club, and picked up the kids at school. A decade later, a so-called superaffluent team conducted in-depth interviews with well-to-do Americans about everything from how they chose their neighborhood to what sorts of experiences they found meaningful. Lexus didn't want to understand how Cadillac or BMW sold their cars. It wanted to understand how its target customers lived their lives.[16]

Lexus then made a larger-than-life commitment to its customers. Before the first car was sold, Dave Illingworth wrote the much-acclaimed "Lexus Covenant"—a statement of purpose that explained how the company would conduct itself. "Lexus will enter the most competitive, prestigious automobile race in the world," the covenant declared. It "will win the race because: Lexus will do it right from the start. Lexus will have the finest dealer network in the industry.

Lexus will treat each customer as we would a guest in our home." In its guiding principles, the company promised to provide an ownership experience "that is deeply satisfying to the senses;" that its service would "anticipate and seamlessly meet our customers' needs in every thought, word, and gesture;" and that it would "celebrate our customers' personal goals and achievements, and share in their passion for making the most of every moment."

This was not, needless to say, how most automakers talked about their business in the mid-1980s—which meant that Lexus could not look to other automakers for ideas about how to build its business. So it looked to high-end retailers and world-renowned service providers that had achieved the level of identification with customers that Lexus aimed to achieve. (It also looked beyond Toyota's existing base of retailers. Lexus required aspiring dealers to complete a grueling application process that focused on their track record of innovation, service, and customer satisfaction. Only eighty-one dealers out of the sixteen hundred that applied passed the test and got awarded a Lexus franchise.)

"Our customers don't compare us to other car brands," argues David Nordstrom, vice president of marketing at Lexus. "They compare us to other *luxury* brands. You have a certain experience with Tiffany or the Four Seasons. That's the experience you expect at Lexus. People don't say, 'Well, this is the car business, so our expectations should be different.' Customers are looking for companies whose beliefs align with theirs."

That's why, over the years, Lexus has gone to school on how many different companies operate. Back in 2005, it sent five hundred dealers and general managers for training at the Four Seasons Resort Aviara in Carlsbad, California. The visitors noted all sorts of little touches that added up to a big impression, and then put their own spin on them: flowers in the showrooms, marble floors in bathrooms, bottled water and chocolates when customers retrieved their cars from the service department (the Lexus version of a hotel turn-down service).

"It really made you open your eyes as far as the future of customer service and guest engagement," one dealer told a *Wall Street Journal* reporter who wrote an engaging account of the visit.[17]

Lexus was also struck by the excitement in Apple's retail stores generated by its Genius Bars, where customers with all sorts of questions (some advanced, some dumb) get answers from smart, friendly, well-trained employees. So dealers put their own spin on Genius Bars with so-called Answer Bars. Employees teach Lexus owners to program their Bluetooth phones, use their hard-to-navigate navigation systems, and, in general, tap into the powerful (but confusing) technology built into their vehicles.

For Lexus, though, as for Virginia Mason, the value in searching for ideas in unrelated fields isn't just about copying what works. It's about changing mind-sets, standards, and expectations. "For a long time, customers saw visiting a car dealer as the equivalent of visiting a dentist," says Al Smith, vice president of customer services at Lexus. "But our experience is an *enlightening* experience. Our dealers have putting greens, concierge services, workout facilities. When's the last time you were able to look through a plate-glass window as a technician worked on your car in a spotless environment? It's like going into a maternity ward and watching the babies behind the glass!

"But it's not just about the facilities," Smith continues. "It's about each customer being treated like someone who means something to us. I asked a doctor from Cincinnati, a really loyal customer, how he liked the new dealership in his city. He said he hasn't visited in ten years, because the dealer comes to him. He actually said to me, 'I like the guy because he makes house calls.' That's something a patient might say about a doctor, not something a doctor says about a car dealer! Does that matter to everyone? No. But for that customer, for ten years, it has had a huge impact."

THE PULL OF "ZERO-GRAVITY THINKERS"—HOW AN OLD HOSPITAL FOUND NEW WAYS TO HEAL

A HEALTH-CARE ORGANIZATION THAT BORROWED techniques for incremental improvement from a quality-obsessed car company. A car company that learned practices for memorable service from an iconic computer brand. Bankers who studied coffee shops and electronics stores. Surgeons who studied pit crews. The takeaway is as practical as the implications are radical: just as what you see shapes how you change, *where you look shapes what you see.* Ideas that are routine in one industry can be downright revolutionary when they migrate to another industry, especially when those ideas challenge the prevailing assumptions and conventional wisdom that have come to define so many industries.

In her underappreciated book, *The Innovation Killer*, Cynthia Barton Rabe, a former innovation strategist at Intel, explains how "what we know limits what we can imagine." Many organizations, she argues, struggle with a "paradox of expertise" in which deep knowledge of what exists in a marketplace or a product category makes it harder to consider what-if strategies that challenge long-held assumptions. "When it comes to innovation," she writes, "the same hard-won experience, best practice, and processes that are the cornerstones of an organization's success may be more like millstones that threaten to sink it."[18]

Her answer to the paradox is to populate organizations with "zero-gravity thinkers"—innovators "who are not weighed down by the expertise of a team, its politics, or 'the way things have always been done.'" In Rabe's formula, zero-gravity thinkers come from outside the corporate mainstream and work deep within the ranks of the organization. They are designers, ethnographers, anthropologists, and other creative types who get immersed in a project or a team, contribute their unique points of view, and then move on to the next change-the-game assignment. Ideal zero-gravity thinkers, she explains, have "psychological distance" from the setting in which they work, "renaissance tendencies" that draw on a range of interests and influences, and "related expertise" that allows them to find the points where blue-sky ideas intersect with real-world opportunities.

There's no reason why organizations as a whole can't demonstrate zero-gravity thinking, especially when they are so ripe for renewal that the pull of established practices loses its hold. For example, there hasn't been much good news coming from the business side of newspapers for a long time, and nowhere has the situation been grimmer than at the Tribune Company, which filed for bankruptcy protection in December 2008, sold the beloved Chicago Cubs in 2009, and continues to struggle with the faltering *Chicago Tribune* and *Los Angeles Times*. But the troubles at Tribune have inspired at least one intriguing approach to unleashing some inventive ideas for the future. The organization's top brass has turned to frontline employees to devise new ways to generate revenue, to conduct their own forms of R&D. At the Tribune, though, R&D doesn't stand for research and development. It stands for "rip off and duplicate." The theory? So many journalists and business-side employees are in touch with so many creative initiatives in other fields, why not look for revenue-generating ideas that are working elsewhere and figure out how to apply them inside the mainstream media?

Many organizations, argues innovation expert Cynthia Barton Rabe, struggle with a "paradox of expertise." Her answer is to populate organizations with "zero-gravity thinkers"—innovators "who are not weighed down by the expertise of a team, its politics, or 'the way things have always been done.'"

We'll see how this neat little initiative plays out in Chicago. In my search for organizations that achieved big change in tough times, though, ground zero for zero-gravity thinking was Detroit, Michigan, and the headquarters of the Henry Ford Health System. Its transformation under CEO Nancy Schlichting highlights every lesson we've learned in this chapter—and then some. Working with Donald Berwick and IHI, Schlichting and her colleagues borrowed ideas from outside fields and used them to make dramatic improvements in their biggest hospital. They displayed an "audacity of imagination" beyond even the best practices in health care to build a blank-sheet-of-paper hospital that reinvents the patient experience. And they persevered, even prospered, under the most trying conditions imaginable—conditions that would have been fatal were the organization not prepared to rethink the fundamentals of how it operated.

Consider first the circumstances under which the CEO and her colleagues work. Henry Ford created his namesake hospital back in 1915. He envisioned a "hotel for sick people" that would provide the best care in the most comfortable surroundings for a region that was poised to become the economic engine of the world. That was then, of course, and this is now. Detroit is a terminally ill city, with a third of its residents and nearly half its children living in poverty. The city has lost a quarter of its population since 2000, and business is fleeing even faster. As of January 2009, Detroit had no major grocery chains and only two movie theaters within the city limits. The median price of a home sold in December 2008—this is not a typo—was $7,500. Most relevant for our purposes, the city had forty-two hospitals in 1960, but only four were open for business in 2009.[19]

Schlichting, who joined Henry Ford Health System in 1998, was named CEO in June 2003, as the system was experiencing severe turmoil. It had lost some $100 million (on revenues of $2.5 billion) in 2001 and posted losses the next two years as well. Then the recovery began, with earnings of $112 million in 2005, $135 million in 2006, and continued profitability through 2008. Today, Henry Ford Health

System is a stable operation with seven hospitals in and around the city, more than a thousand doctors, twenty-one thousand employees, 3.1 million annual patients' visits, and revenues of $3.7 billion. Henry Ford Hospital, the huge, 903-bed downtown facility, generates $1 billion of annual revenue and continues to grow, adding two new floors even as the economy deteriorated. In spring 2009, with little fanfare, Henry Ford announced that it had retained its A1 bond rating—just as Chrysler and General Motors announced their Chapter 11 bankruptcy filings.

How did a ninety-five-year-old health-care organization emerge as an island of stability in a sea of despair? Part of the answer is savvy management: Schlichting upgraded the environment and improved morale at Henry Ford, even as she cut costs and rationalized operations. The downtown hospital "was a demoralized, underinvested-in place," she told me. "It was dark, dingy, the elevators didn't work. So we painted, we got new wheelchairs, we had 'planting parties' where volunteers put in flowers, we upgraded the uniforms our staff wore, we greeted folks with smiles when they came into the lobby. We did all sorts of little things that didn't cost much, but made a huge difference for our people and our patients."

A bigger part of the answer is the hospital's long-term commitment to improving quality, which had the benefit of cutting waste and bolstering financial results. In 2004, Henry Ford was one of the first organizations to join IHI's 100,000 Lives Campaign, and became a "mentor hospital" in the program. (The downtown facility has reduced its mortality rate by 25 percent since 2004, meaning that hundreds of people who would have died did not.) Schlichting herself leads a project devoted to moving one of IHI's "big dots"—reducing readmissions in the first thirty days after a patient is discharged. And Henry Ford doctors, even as they applied improvement techniques from other fields, pioneered techniques that influenced their field.

"We've adopted the whole IHI menu, plus a few things that we invented here," says Dr. William Conway, who has practiced at Henry

Ford since 1973 and is the organization's much-admired quality champion. (He is chief medical officer for Henry Ford Hospital and chief quality officer for the system.) For example, a "bundle" of procedures to combat sepsis, a deadly blood infection, has spread from Detroit to hospitals around the world. And the hospital's breakthroughs with suicide prevention have changed how other facilities treat this life-or-death challenge. When I checked in with Henry Ford in December 2009, a long time after my initial visit, Conway reported that the hospital had registered its ninth consecutive quarter (more than two full years) with no suicides among severely depressed patients—a truly off-the-charts performance.

"You can't get lower than zero," says Conway. "There was a debate: Could we promise severely depressed patients they would not commit suicide? Ultimately, we promised that we would work to get to zero. If our goal is not zero, what is the 'right' number of suicides? That kind of thinking, that culture of innovation, is going on in so many places here. We are reversing decades of neglect of quality. For five or six years, we've been asking: What would a 'perfect' health-care organization look like?"

Even as they worked to transform a long-established hospital, Schlichting and her colleagues began work on a related (and even more liberating) challenge: If they could begin anew, with no conventional wisdom or inherited behavior, what would the *ultimate* hospital look like? The answer is one of the most remarkable health-care facilities I've ever visited, the Henry Ford West Bloomfield Hospital in West Bloomfield, Michigan. The $360-million facility, roughly twenty-three miles northwest of the original Henry Ford Hospital, represents the biggest strategic bet by the organization since its founding. In many ways, West Bloomfield is to Henry Ford what Lexus was to Toyota—a chance for a highly respected organization, considered among the top class, to launch a one-of-a-kind innovation that remakes the sense of what's possible in its field.

"This was the first hospital we had built since 1915," says Schlichting. "Our other hospitals joined the system through acquisition. So we kept pushing: What is going to distinguish this hospital? What could we do that was unique and transformational? This had to be an exceptional place."

What's so exceptional about West Bloomfield? The hospital is built to resemble a northern Michigan lodge, on a 160-acre campus with rolling woods, scenic wetlands, and a pond. All 300 rooms (the first 191 of which opened in March 2009) are private and designed to accommodate family members who wish to stay overnight. All patients go to preassigned rooms when they arrive, rather than waste time in the lobby with forms. There is no overhead paging, and patients are guaranteed not to be disturbed, unless for emergencies, after 10:30 P.M. ("We won't wake you up to give you a sleeping pill," one official cracks.) There's a concierge to help with errands and a "tea sommelier" who touts the virtues of swimming marigold, tender lotus blossom, and other blends. There's a day spa (Vita) and an indoor farmer's market every Wednesday. The rooms are wired for Internet access and sound. The Detroit Symphony Orchestra even pipes live feeds into the hospital and has done two full-blown concerts in the atrium.

Oh, about that atrium. The beautiful indoor space looks nothing like a traditional hospital. More than two thousand live plants and trees line the curved "streets," which are decked out with various shops (selling products for sounder sleep, better diets, and so on) that feel like the world's healthiest vacation village. The food, by the way, is to die for (pun intended) and available via twenty-four-hour room service, which can be ordered off the interactive TV. Matt Prentice, a celebrity chef based in Bingham Farms, between Detroit and West Bloomfield, spent two years creating three thousand recipes so that patients can choose from items that are kosher, halal, organic, or gluten-free. (There are plans for some of the produce and herbs used in these recipes to be grown in an on-site greenhouse.) Indeed, the space is so striking and the food so appealing that the hospital is on track to generate millions of dollars a year hosting and catering functions for companies and community groups. In July 2010, the atrium at Henry Ford West Bloomfield hosted and catered its first wedding—with plans for many more in the future. For patients and visitors, the menu changes every two weeks, to create an unprecedented level of both quality and variety. "I'm going to revolutionize hospital food," Prentice has vowed.[20]

If the place sounds more like an elegant hotel than a traditional hospital, that's no accident. Gerard van Grinsven, West Bloomfield's CEO, joined Henry Ford in March 2006 (three years before his new facility opened its doors) after a long career with Ritz-Carlton, where he opened twenty properties around the world, served as vice president of food and beverage, and led a much-acclaimed turnaround of the Ritz-Carlton Dearborn, which, during his tenure as general manager, went from one of the company's lowest-rated locations to one of its highest. Talk about a commitment to zero-gravity thinking. Lexus dealers passed through the Four Seasons orbit and picked up all sorts of customer-friendly techniques. Henry Ford actually recruited a senior Ritz-Carlton executive to design, build, and staff a hospital that would take health care on a new trajectory.

"We've looked for opportunities to create 'hot spots'—memorable, signature moments in the customer experience that surprise and delight our patients and their families," CEO van Grinsven told me during a tour of West Bloomfield a few months before it opened. "It starts with how you're welcomed. You're worried, you're scared, the last thing you want is to step into noise and chaos. So we're going to escort you, offer an arm if you need it, get you right to your room. When you visit the café, or order from room service, we want you to say, 'I never thought hospital food could be like this.' When you're in your room, a concierge talks to you and your family: 'Do we need to do some shopping for you? Do we need to take care of any laundry?'

We have high tea in the atrium every afternoon. These hot spots cost almost nothing to create, yet they create a tremendous impression for everyone who encounters them."

How can you build and run a game-changing hospital with the same tired ideas about design, service, and quality? That's why the CEO of Henry Ford's new hospital is a former leader at the Ritz-Carlton hotel.

Questions of cost loom large for any hospital, of course, and many experts inside and outside the health-care field wondered how West Bloomfield could create its unique patient experience without busting budgets and creating all sorts of unsustainable financial pressures. In fact, van Grinsven insists, the hospital's change-the-game logic is to use these quality-enhancing innovations to bring down costs. "We don't have private rooms to be fancy," he argues. "We have private rooms because they significantly reduce rates of infection in the hospital and add to the personal privacy of patients. Over the long term, our focus on wellness and prevention will reduce overall health-care costs for the community, as people learn to take better care of themselves and avoid, or at least better manage, chronic diseases, which account for a huge portion of health-care spending in the country. This is a hospital designed to keep you well, and that design lowers costs for everyone."

Early on, not surprisingly, the new CEO's arrival was met with skepticism, even hostility, from the health-care establishment and the media: How can an executive move from hospitality to hospitals? What does someone from the Ritz-Carlton know about building, staffing, and running a medical facility? (One columnist went so far as to skewer the menu plans, arguing that hospital food *should* taste lousy.) But Henry Ford's leadership turned the question around: How can you build and run a game-changing hospital with the same ideas about design, service, and quality? If everyone agrees that there is a crisis in the health-care system, what better way to address the crisis than with a leader from outside the system?

Robert Riney, COO of Henry Ford Health System, explained the mind-set flip to a symposium of wide-eyed business leaders who gathered in Detroit in June 2010 to learn more about the hospital and its stunning innovations. The title of the gathering, "Going Radical," captured the spirit of the organization's leaders. "It's not radical to 'go radical,'" Riney argued. "It's *logical* to go radical. How can you look at the situation in our industry and say the answer is to make incremental change?"

Or to recruit traditional executives? "I had a fresh pair of eyes and no baggage when I arrived," Gerard van Grinsven explains. "In one sense I see this facility as a 'hotel for sick people' much like Henry Ford did. The challenge today is to deliver a level of service comparable to the best hotels in the world, to create a mystique that encourages people to seek us out. But the bigger challenge, the real opportunity for reinvention, is to rethink the role of a hospital. How do we position ourselves as a community center for well-being—as a destination that helps everyone to lead a healthier life?"

Which is why, in addition to the private rooms, the scrumptious menu, and the concierge service, the hospital is designed as much to be a teaching organization as a service organization. Its cobblestoned-paved atrium, designed to evoke an old-fashioned downtown, includes a ninety-seat demonstration kitchen where members of the community take classes on healthier cooking, and patients with cancer, heart disease, or diabetes can learn to prepare meals that are right for their conditions. The atrium also includes specialty retailers devoted to products for sounder sleep, healthier pregnancies, and more active lifestyles. Vita, the wellness center, offers acupuncture, therapeutic massage, yoga, and relaxation classes.

"We don't just want to be a place where sick people come," van Grinsven says. "We want to be a place where *healthy* people come to learn about diet and exercise. We want to be a place where people with chronic diseases come to meet with a health coach, try yoga, learn new recipes. We have hired all of our team members, including the doctors, based not just on their technical expertise, but on their natural talent to provide compassionate care and exceptional service. Our dream is to take health and healing beyond the boundaries of imagination."

It will be years before anyone can say whether the dream has come true, but the hospital is already registering patient-satisfaction scores in the 99th percentile of hospitals nationwide. And West Bloomfield has certainly captured the imagination of its community. As the hospital was being designed, van Grinsven spoke at schools, churches, neighborhood centers, and living-room parties to explain how it would reinvent health care and respond to the needs of specific populations. (His market has six major ethnic groups, including Japanese, Arab, and Chaldean.) As it was being built, he hosted tours for VIPs and rank-and-file residents to walk the halls and sample recipes. The result of this relentless, campaign-style barnstorming? With virtually no advertising, and still months to go before the opening, West Bloomfield had received twenty thousand job applications, and van Grinsven expected the final number to hit fifty thousand. A few months after the hospital opened, it had achieved 90 percent occupancy and won rave reviews from a once-skeptical press and the medical establishment.

Just as important, West Bloomfield has captured the imagination of the rest of the Henry Ford system. When I held my second conversation with van Grinsven, he had come from a ribbon-cutting ceremony. Henry Ford's ninety-five-year-old hospital was unveiling the first forty rooms in its new floors—and the rooms in downtown Detroit were faithful reproductions of the rooms in West Bloomfield. "This is not just a hospital," he argues. "It is a laboratory for innovation. We try ideas, show they make sense, and share them. That's how you get to the next level." Nancy Schlichting agrees. "This hospital is a game changer," she declares. "And the process of creating it has been life-changing for the people involved."

CHAPTER THREE

RADICALLY PRACTICAL (I)— FIVE TRUTHS OF CORPORATE TRANSFORMATION

AS THE COFOUNDER OF A magazine called *Fast Company*, I've always been struck by the slow-going rate of change inside most organizations. In the earliest days of the magazine, after we had a business plan but before we published the premiere issue, we convened a conference around the theme, "How Do You Overthrow a Successful Company?" It wasn't a gathering of hotshots eager to take on the corporate establishment. It was a gathering of big-picture thinkers and change agents from illustrious big companies who sensed that there were massive shifts on the horizon, but that there wasn't a commitment among their colleagues to reckon with what was coming.

It was a great conversation, ahead of its time in many ways (this was 1994), and the outlook was grim. Roger Martin, now dean of the Rotman School of Management at the University of Toronto, warned that "the role of big companies is to turn great people into mediocre organizations." Richard Pascale, a bestselling author and sought-after consultant, compared knowledge about how organizations renew themselves to the quality of medieval medicine. "We are," he said of people leading change programs inside big companies, "like earnest doctors with willing patients engaged in utter bullshit." Mort Meyerson, the much-admired CEO and philanthropist then at the helm of Perot Systems, compared leading an organization in fast-changing times to "floating in lava in a wooden boat." His plea to the group: "We need a new model to reach the future."

What a difference fifteen years *don't* make. Are those misgivings any less relevant today than they were back then—or the prospects for genuine transformation any less bleak? My goal in Chapters 1 and 2 has been to present a range of settings in which troubled organizations figured out how to learn from the past, and break from convention, to make creative changes. I hope you'll agree that these organizations are unleashing innovations that will shape their future, and the future of their fields, for years to come. But the real value of exploring stories of transformation at these organizations is that they can equip you to write a more compelling story for *your* organization.

If what you see shapes how you change, and where you look shapes what you see, then my hope is that seeing what these leaders have achieved will help you achieve your agenda for reform and renewal. Specifically, my hope is that it will allow you to reckon with the five truths of corporate transformation. Because the truth is, the work of making far-reaching change in long-established organizations is the hardest work there is.

I. MOST ORGANIZATIONS IN MOST FIELDS SUFFER FROM A KIND OF TUNNEL VISION, WHICH MAKES IT HARD TO ENVISION A MORE POSITIVE FUTURE.

THAT'S WHY THE FIRST CHALLENGE of change is originality—for leaders to see their organization and its problems as if they've never seen them before, and, with new eyes, to develop a distinctive point of view on how to solve them. All too often, especially in long-established companies, long-held expertise gets in the way of groundbreaking innovation. As Cynthia Barton Rabe warns, in her argument on behalf of zero-gravity thinkers, "What we know limits what we can imagine." But as we've seen time and again, whether the field is pet food or automobiles, global policing or local health care, it's the leaders and change agents who see a different game that produce the best results.

To me, that's the enduring lesson of the one-of-a-kind turnaround strategy developed by Nicolas Hayek. I remember my first trip to visit the Swatch titan. Here was a highly trained engineer steeped in the minutiae of quartz technology, advanced manufacturing, and global competition, who had launched one of the great comebacks in business history—a saga of innovation and creativity that defied the conventional wisdom of economists, consultants, and CEOs. Yet when I asked for the main lessons behind the Swatch story, Hayek didn't talk about technology or assembly lines. He talked about dreams and fantasy. He didn't respond to the rise of powerful Asian rivals by copying how they operated. He responded by rethinking and reinventing how his industry operated.

"You can build mass-market products in countries like Switzerland or the United States only if you embrace the fantasy and imagination of your childhood and youth," he told me. "Everywhere children believe in dreams. And they ask the same question: Why? Why does something work a certain way? Why do we behave in certain ways? We ask ourselves those questions every day. People may laugh—the [head] of a huge Swiss company talking about fantasy. But that's the real secret behind what we have done. It's an unnatural attitude for Switzerland—and for Europe. . . . We kill too many good ideas by rejecting them without thinking about them, by laughing at them." No one is laughing at Nicolas Hayek today—although few of his colleagues are copying from his playbook either.[1]

2. MOST LEADERS SEE THINGS THE SAME WAY EVERYONE ELSE SEES THEM BECAUSE THEY LOOK FOR IDEAS IN THE SAME PLACES EVERYONE ELSE LOOKS FOR THEM.

THAT'S WHY THE MOST EFFECTIVE leaders I know aren't big fans of "benchmarking" the competition—a commonplace exercise for inspiring change that often serves to reinforce the problem of tunnel vision I just discussed. How enlightening is it, really, to learn from the "best in class" in your industry, especially if best in class isn't all that great? So why not learn from innovators *outside* your industry as a way to shake things up and leapfrog your rivals? But looking for ideas in unfamiliar fields is not just about relocating what works from one industry to another. It is also (and more significantly) about reimagining what's possible in an industry.

Lexus, as we've seen, got some of its most powerful ideas for customer service by studying luxury hotels and Apple's retail environment. London's Great Ormond Street Hospital improved the quality of its medical performance by studying how Formula One racing teams ratcheted up their performance on the track. For two decades, Commerce Bank, a legendary innovator in financial-services, borrowed ideas from all kinds of different fields to fuel its growth. (Commerce did study it rivals, but only to discover "the stuff that drives customers at other banks crazy." These were called Competitor Rules and Practices—internal acronym, CRAP.)

In its Disruption Day methodology, TBWA uses what it calls the "CEO Hat" exercise to encourage organizations afflicted with tunnel vision to develop their peripheral vision. Participants search for out-of-the-box answers to important strategic questions by reaching into boxes filled with hats, shirts, and other paraphernalia from breakthrough organizations such as Apple, Virgin, Target, Southwest Airlines—and then adopt the mind-set of those free-thinking companies as they think about the questions with their clients. "We define possible strategies for companies through the eyes and values and under the leadership of a different CEO," explains Laurie Coots, TBWA's energetic chief marketing officer. "The sheer act of being free to think like somebody else gives you permission to generate ideas that you might not get to otherwise."

It's a fun way to make a serious point: there's no reason to gamble on untested strategies and ideas if you can identify and apply strategies and ideas that are already working elsewhere. Proven insights from one field can become a powerful force for innovation when they migrate to another field. "What better way to 'think different' than to think like somebody else, to wear someone else's hat?" writes TBWA chairman Jean-Marie Dru. "These hats are representative of powerful personalities or company cultures that have proven themselves in the business world. We use the hats to deliberately create a little theater, to get people out of their workaday personae and transport them to a totally new way of thinking."[2]

Wearing different hats can mess with your head (in the best sense of that phrase)—which is why TBWA, as it works with clients to reimagine how they approach their business, has also reimagined how it approaches *its own* business. In recent years, the agency has engaged in a searching reappraisal of what it means to be a Madison Avenue operation in the twenty-first century, going so far as to create a provocative (and slightly profane) manifesto called, "Who Wants to Be a F#@%ing Advertising Agency?"

The key to prospering in the future of the marketing business, the manifesto declares, is to embrace "the age of media arts"—to rethink the places, spaces, and experiences in which brands express themselves and communicate with customers. That means rethinking the technologies marketers have to master, redefining job descriptions on Madison Avenue, even inventing a new language to describe the work the firm does. TBWA has rethought and redefined the word *media* itself. It distinguishes among four different types of media and has different strategies for each. There are media you own: factories, offices, retail outlets, packaging. There are media you create: programs, events, contests, curriculum. There are media you earn: blog conversations, Twitter posts, your natural ranking in search engines. Finally, there are media you pay for—the bread-and-butter stuff that has defined life in advertising agencies since the days of Don Draper and his fellow Mad Men.

The manifesto even includes a "Media Arts Glossary" to introduce employees to a strange new strategic vocabulary, which, it argues, may be how everyone talks one day. Why learn a new language to describe a business that's been around for decades? "Because we live in a world where everything a brand does is media," explains TBWA's Lee Clow, "and media has become a huge part of the culture. So first we have to discover a brand's idea, its beliefs. Then we have to orchestrate the behavior of the brand so that every time it touches somebody, they are getting the kind of information and story, whether emotional or logical, that helps them like, trust, and respect that brand. Our business used to be pretty simple. It's not simple anymore."

3. IN TROUBLED ORGANIZATIONS RICH WITH TRADITION AND SUCCESS, HISTORY CAN BE A CURSE—AND A BLESSING. THE CHALLENGE IS TO BREAK FROM THE PAST WITHOUT DISAVOWING IT.

As we argued in Chapter 1, for even the most determined change agents, history and tradition can be unrivaled sources of strength—guides to enduring values, reservoirs of timeless expertise. Psychologist Jerome Bruner, in his collection of essays, *In Search of Mind*, has a pithy way to describe what happens when the best of the old informs the search for the new. The essence of creativity, he argues, is "figuring out how to use what you already know in order to go beyond what you already think." The most effective leaders I've met don't simply disavow the past. They reinterpret what's come before to develop a line of sight into what comes next.

That's why Dean Esserman, chief of police in Providence, Rhode Island, is such a keen student of history—even as he devises an ambitious blueprint for the future of a troubled department. The chief is an enthusiastic innovator when it comes to new technologies and experimental crime-fighting techniques—from "shot spotter" sensors that detect when and where handguns are fired and automatically notify police, to new approaches to gang intervention that aim to reshape how cops handle drug dealers. At the same time, he is a traditionalist who never tires of reminding his officers that the department's most effective crime-fighting weapon is the strength of their ties to the community. That's the heart of his "Beyond 911" strategy, a back-to-the-future approach to change that draws on the past as much as it breaks from it. "We are creating a people's police force again," he tells anyone who will listen. "We're going back into the neighborhoods."

This same learn-from-the-past mind-set ("What Would Juliette Do?") has inspired the transformation of the Girl Scouts of the USA since 2003. Laurel Richie, a former senior partner at Ogilvy & Mather who left to become the first-ever chief marketing officer for the Girl Scouts, works on many of the most visible elements of change within the organization. She's rethinking issues such as brand identity, public imagery, and social advocacy, and how they relate to the ever-changing culture of girls. "People have a 'false familiarity' with the Girl Scouts," she says. "They hear the name and a very short list of things comes to mind."

But she leaves no doubt about the relevance of the organization's founder to its future. "Juliette Gordon Low could hold her own with any leader today in business, philanthropy, politics," Richie argues. "She was well ahead of her time. We are mining our history for core truths, values, and beliefs, and just refreshing the manifestation of them in today's world. This is not about wanting to be something different. It's about wanting to be our best selves."[3]

Sometimes, the most rewarding path to the future is built on a return to first principles. "Over the last few decades, we got known as being nicer and nicer instead of being cutting-edge and revolutionary," concludes Kathy Cloninger, who retired as CEO in November 2011, and wrote a book of her own called *Tough Cookies: Leadership Lessons from 100 Years of the Girl Scouts*. "We got confused about who we were. In some sense, we are simply returning to the spirit of our founder."

4. THE JOB OF THE CHANGE AGENT IS NOT JUST TO SURFACE HIGH-MINDED IDEAS. IT IS TO SUMMON A SENSE OF URGENCY INSIDE AND OUTSIDE THE ORGANIZATION, AND TO TURN THAT URGENCY INTO ACTION.

IT'S ONE THING FOR LEADERS to use fresh eyes to devise a new line of sight into the future. It's quite another to muster the rank-and-file commitment to turn a compelling vision into a game-changing performance.

There's a reason Harvard Business School's John Kotter, whose ideas we explored earlier, titled one of his most recent books on change, *A Sense of Urgency*—that's the big missing ingredient. "It occurred to me how often I was being asked, 'What is the single biggest error people make when they try to change?'" he wrote. "After reflection, I decided the answer was that they did not create a high enough sense of urgency among enough people to set the stage for making a challenging leap in some new direction."

Even Interpol's Ron Noble, who sits in the middle of the urgent struggle against terrorism, has struggled to energize countries around the threat of lost, stolen, or forged travel documents. "There are times when I'm ecstatic," he told me, such as when he strategized with Vladimir Putin or with the prime minister of Pakistan—evidence that his border-security vision was finally getting traction with powerful allies. "There are times when I am disheartened too. That's when I think about the alternative, which is that we give up, that we wait for a biochemical or nuclear attack and everyone says, 'Why didn't we do it differently?' If we stop pushing, and something bad happens, I could never forgive myself."

That's why Noble has become such an accomplished storyteller. Indeed, after several in-depth conversations with the secretary-general, I was struck by how many of his answers to me, and how much of the content of his speeches around the world, drew on a deep well of well-told stories—stirring tales of cutting-edge Internet cases, chilling scenarios of potential security breaches, hopeful accounts of strategy sessions with important leaders. So I asked him why, as a communicator, he relied so heavily on storytelling, and why so many of his stories were of the nightmarish variety. The answer, he replied, was all about creating a sense of urgency. "If you look at history," he said, "governments and law-enforcement agencies respond with the greatest sense of urgency to failures of epic proportions, much more so than they rise to potential opportunities. So I have to give them hypotheticals: Can you imagine this scenario? Can you imagine this disaster? How could you justify it to your people? Then I have to tell them stories, show them cases of what Interpol has done that could prevent those disasters. I am in the persuasion business—persuading governments to act on future threats. Stories are a powerful way to persuade."

The determined change agents at IHI are never reluctant to tell stories about the shortcomings of hospitals and health-care systems. So when they rave about a system, and point to it as a model for others, it qualifies as high praise indeed. In this case, the object of IHI's affection is the health-care system of Jönköping County, Sweden, with 330,000 residents served by three hospitals and thirty-four primary-care centers. When it comes to cost, quality, consistency, and patient outcomes, Jönköping County is off the charts, whether it's compared to other parts of the world or its own past performance. "The minute a hospital thinks it's as good as it can be," says one IHI leader, "we tell them to go to Sweden and see how good *they* are."

There are many factors behind this standout performance, but one big factor is Jönköping County's focus on meeting the needs of a patient named Esther. I sat in on a panel discussion where Göran Henriks, the system's chief of learning and innovation, told stories in great detail, and with real emotion, about the worries, stresses, and problems in Esther's life, and how his system had spent years redesigning its services to meet her needs. But why her? I wondered. What's so special about Esther? Eventually it dawned on me that Esther was not a real person—she was a hypothetical character with a compelling story. Jönköping County had used its Esther Project to create a human face for technical debates over strategy, operations, and quality—and to create a sense of urgency for delivering results. "What's best for Esther?" became a rallying cry that drove doctors, nurses, and administrators in their quest for improvement and reform.[4]

Whether it's chilling tales of nuclear terrorism, or uplifting stories of happy patients, the object is to play "mind games" with your colleagues—to influence how they evaluate their environment and charge them up for change. The opposite of urgency, after all, is complacency, and, as Professor Kotter explains, "Almost always, complacent individuals do not view themselves as complacent. They see themselves as behaving quite rationally, given the circumstances."

5. IN A BUSINESS ENVIRONMENT THAT NEVER STOPS CHANGING, CHANGE AGENTS CAN NEVER STOP LEARNING.

Sure, it is the job of leaders to be effective and engaging teachers—to rally their colleagues around a distinctive set of ideas and a well-designed strategy for bringing those ideas to life.

But the best leaders I've met, regardless of their industry, experience, or personal style, have also been insatiable *learners*.

Think about some of the characters we've met thus far and how they've learned to respond to a fast-changing world. Dean Esserman learns from the network of reform-minded chiefs and open-minded criminologists with whom he has been swapping ideas for two decades. Donald Berwick and his colleagues at IHI learned from teachers as diverse as the founders of the quality movement and the leaders of the women's movement. The doctors and administrators at Virginia Mason Medical Center have learned about new ways to run a hospital from the ways in which Toyota builds cars. The marketers at Pedigree learned new ways to position their brand and connect with customers by relearning the brand's history and getting reacquainted with the ideas and values of its founders.

It goes back to those plainspoken words from that unknown Texas genius with which I began the introduction: "If all you ever do is all you've ever done, then all you'll ever get is all you ever got." That's true for organizations, and it's true for people who run organizations. In a business environment that never stops changing, leaders can never stop learning.

Part II

SHAKING UP YOUR INDUSTRY

CHAPTER FOUR

ARE YOU THE MOST OF ANYTHING? WHY BEING DIFFERENT MAKES ALL THE DIFFERENCE

Fun interview I did w/ Serena Williams last year at @Zappos office! (q's came via Twitter) - http://bit.ly/zserena

5:10 PM JUN 25TH FROM WEB

Headshaving day at Zappos! Employees shaving each other's heads. I will be completely bald later!

2:32 PM MAY 20TH FROM TWITPIC

Busy day! Great lunch w/ @tonyrobbins after he toured our offices, @livestrongceo coming now for tour, meeting, then dinner!

6:23 PM MAR 30TH FROM WEB

Wow, Zappos employee just proposed at our Kentucky employee holiday party! Right after DJ played Beyonce's "Put a Ring on It"

9: 14 PM JAN 8TH FROM TXT

—**SELECT "TWEETS" FROM TONY HSIEH, CEO, ZAPPOS.COM, INC.**

A VISIT TO THE HEADQUARTERS OF Zappos.com, the billion-dollar-a-year online retailer based in Henderson, Nevada, is almost as entertaining as a visit to the Las Vegas Strip less than twenty minutes away—and much more rewarding. At one level, the experience feels like business time travel. The seven hundred or so employees in Henderson (another seven hundred or so work at a fulfillment center just south of Louisville, Kentucky) look like a cast of characters from the original Internet boom. The youthful crew is fond of funky clothes, loud tattoos, and the occasional body piercing. There is free food, a nap room, and offbeat cubicle decor. Banners hung around the offices declare the company's core values, from "Create Fun and a Little Weirdness" to "Be Adventurous, Creative, and Open-Minded" and "Be Humble." At the time of my visit there was even a full-time life coach, Dr. David Vik, a retired chiropractor who had delivered more than a million adjustments in his first career, and who was counseling Zapponians on how to be happier and more productive. Dr. Vik, who moved on from Zappos at the end of 2009, produced an annual planner for employees filled with pithy aphorisms ("Change is strange because you have to re-arrange") and hands-on advice ("Set your 30-day goal and downsize it").

But Zappos is not a cultural artifact from the go-go years of the late twentieth century. It is one of the great business success stories of the early twenty-first century. *Inc.* magazine, the bible of entrepreneurship, has called Zappos "arguably the decade's most innovative startup." The company has been hailed on the cover of *Fortune* as one of the country's best places to work, and Tony Hsieh (pronounced *shay*), the thirtysomething CEO, has become an executive role model. The soft-spoken, self-effacing Hsieh has done a star turn on programs from *Nightline* to *Oprah* to Donald Trump's *Celebrity Apprentice*. As of mid-2010, in perhaps the ultimate measure of cultural relevance, Hsieh had passed the 1.7 *million* follower mark on Twitter—putting him in the company of Martha Stewart, Taylor Swift, and 50 Cent.[1]

Hsieh, it should be noted, is a Twitter enthusiast of the first order. He has written a long essay called "How Twitter Can Make You a Better (and Happier) Person." Among the service's virtues, he argues, are its capacity to reframe what's happening ("Twitter encourages me to search for ways to view reality in a funnier and/or more positive way"); to reinforce gratitude ("Twitter helps me notice and appreciate the little things in life"); and to promote positive values ("Twitter constantly reminds me of who I want to be, and what I want Zappos to stand for"). In late 2008, when Zappos made the difficult decision to trim its workforce by 8 percent despite record sales, Hsieh encouraged his colleagues, nearly five hundred of whom also use Twitter, to share their experiences and emotions—a commitment to honest dialogue, observers said, that kept anxiety low and morale high.[2]

On the day of my visit to headquarters, the CEO offers to show me what life at Zappos looks like—a formal walk-through that quickly becomes the workplace equivalent of a Las Vegas revue. He grabs a "tour flag" from the lobby, hoists it high as we set out, and the place, already buzzing with energy, goes a bit nuts. One department we pass makes a ruckus with whistles and handheld clackers; members of the performance-shoe department ring cowbells as they catch sight of the flag; the fashion team turns on music and snaps photos as we walk by; other departments wave pom-poms, burst into applause, and, in general, do their best to cause a rowdy scene. The tour ends with a visit to the Room of Royalty, where Dr. Vik outfits me with a crown, sits me on a throne, and snaps a photograph as a keepsake.

The experience of visiting Zappos is surprising, entertaining, and carefully designed—much like the experience that Hsieh and his colleagues work to create for their customers. The colorful surroundings, boundless energy, and nonstop tweeting are all in the service of serious business, because they are part of such a unique way of doing business. Zappos, which celebrated its tenth anniversary in June 2009, is a high-profile game changer that has grown fast, made money, and redefined the standards of service for Internet retail. As recently as

2004, the company sold less than $200 million worth of merchandise. In 2008, it passed the billion-dollar mark, and continues to post double-digit growth in a severe retail downturn.

Indeed, a month after its tenth birthday, in a powerful validation of how Zappos works, Internet giant Amazon.com agreed to use stock, eventually valued at $1.2 billion, to buy the company—even as it vowed to keep its hands *off* the company, so it could do things its way. It was a huge and hugely unexpected deal that made a surprising amount of sense. Sure, Amazon is highly regarded for the way it serves customers. But its model is driven by muscle: low costs, huge warehouses, smart software. Zappos does much of that too, but what makes it special is the depth of the human connections it has forged with customers. As Amazon founder Jeff Bezos said when he announced the deal, "I get all weak-kneed when I see a customer-obsessed company."

How has Zappos managed to shake up the brutally competitive world of fashion retail? A big part of the answer, as with Amazon, involves economics and logistics. The company offers an absurdly huge selection of shoes, clothes, handbags, and fashion accessories—although shoes remain the sole (pun intended) of the operation. Its fulfillment center in Shepherdsville, Kentucky, south of Louisville, which I visited a few months after my trip to Las Vegas, holds nearly *four million* pairs of shoes and other fashion items. (My recurring thought, as I scanned the aisles of boots, pumps, and footwear of all kinds, was that this was Imelda Marcos's version of paradise.) The company only sells merchandise it has on its shelves (no delays or back orders) and ships the items to customers for free. It also offers full refunds and free shipping for customers who return their purchases—up to a year after they order.

It sounds like a prescription for chaos—tens of thousands of returns coming in, even as tens of thousands of orders go out—but it's crucial to the company's success. Zappos's operating efficiencies and open-ended return policies mean customers who are unsure about sizes and styles can order lots of different options, keep what they like, and ship back the rest. "We take the risk out of buying online," Hsieh explains. "If someone likes to try ten different pairs of shoes with ten outfits, we encourage them to order all ten pairs and return the ones that don't work." It's an easy-to-understand offer with hard-to-beat appeal. In its first decade, Zappos shipped orders to ten million different customers. On any given day, more than 75 percent of the shipments go to repeat customers, whose average order is between $130 and $145, substantially more than the average order for first-time buyers.

So the Zappos value proposition is a winner. But it's the company's performance art that really seals the deal. Everything about how Zappos does business is meant to reassure, amuse, and otherwise engage customers, even as it attends to the basics of price, selection, and shipping. For example, the company's free-delivery policy guarantees that orders will arrive within four or five business days—a perfectly reasonable timetable, other than in a severe fashion emergency. But since the warehouse sits just down the road from the UPS sorting hub, items can sometimes leave as late as 1:00 A.M. and arrive the next morning. So for repeat customers, Zappos almost always provides free *next-day* delivery as a "surprise upgrade"—an unexpected benefit that leaves a lasting impression.

"Some customers order as late as midnight and get free delivery by eight o'clock the next morning," Hsieh explains. "People ask me if it is expensive to do that. It is *very* expensive. But we are willing to invest to create a 'wow' experience that generates customer loyalty. Our whole philosophy is to take most of the money we would spend on marketing, put it into the customer experience, and let word of mouth be our true form of marketing. Repeat customers buy more and become our best advocates."

Moreover, unlike virtually any other Internet retailer on the planet (including Amazon), Zappos encourages its customers to communicate by telephone. It publishes its 800 number at the top of every page of the website, populates its call center with highly trained employees (no outsourcing), imposes no scripts or time limits on its agents, and injects a large dose of personality into the process. (For years, callers could choose to hear a "joke of the day" before getting down to business, or ask to hear the standard menu of options read by celebrities such as Gladys Knight and the Pips.)

According to Hsieh, cutting-edge Zappos handles more than *five thousand* old-fashioned telephone calls per day, and almost all of its Internet-savvy customers call at some point during their history with the company. Why? Because Zappos makes it so easy to pick up the phone, reach a human being, explain what you need, and ask for help—no matter how strange the question or how long it takes to answer. Indeed, according to *The New Yorker*, which published an in-depth account of life "inside the online shoe utopia," the longest call in Zappos history took place on July 5, 2009, and lasted five hours, twenty-five minutes, and thirty-one seconds, easily besting the previous record of just over four hours. The new-record call, which was handled by a twenty-two-year-old Zapponian named Britnee Brown, focused on the merits of an exotic shoe brand called Masai Barefoot Technology—and on the caller's sister. The previous-record call, handled by a Zapponian named Jennifer, dealt with the customer's health problems, which affected the kinds of shoes she wore, and with stories about her childhood. No wonder that the amused and amazed writer, Alexandra Jacobs, concluded that customer service at Zappos "occasionally resembled protracted talk therapy."[3]

One of Tony Hsieh's favorite customer-service stories, which he often shares as a lighthearted case study during serious presentations to business audiences, underscores how differently Zappos behaves from most retailers. It seems that Hsieh was a featured speaker at a sales conference in Santa Monica, California, for Skechers, the popular footwear brand. After the day's business, three Skechers executives and three Zappos executives (including Hsieh) went out for a night of carousing. After, in his words, "hopping one or two bars too many," they all wound up back at the hotel, a little tipsy, a lot hungry, and with room service shut down for the night. "Where on earth can we find a pizza?" wondered one of the Skechers executives. "Hey, Zappos is all about customer service," Hsieh cracked. "Call our 1-800 number." So the executive put his phone on speaker, dialed Zappos, and asked with an air of desperation how he could get a pizza delivered to the hotel. "There was an awkward silence for a moment," Hsieh reports. "'You do know you called Zappos, right?'" the employee said. "'But hold on and I'll see what I can do.'" Sure enough, after a minute or two, the customer-service operator came back on the line with the names and phone numbers of pizza joints in Santa Monica that delivered late into the night. Little did that employee know that he or she had left a huge impression on a major supplier—and provided an amusing case study of precisely the kind of behavior the CEO is trying to instill throughout the organization.

That kind of over-the-top responsiveness from a frontline employee is rare, although not as rare as you might think, at Zappos at least. Since the company does not sell items for which it is out of stock, customers who can't find what they need on the site often call asking for help. One hard-and-fast rule is that if a customer calls looking for a specific item in a specific size, and Zappos is out of stock, the rep will search the websites of at least three of Zappos's competitors, and if he or she finds the item in stock there, actively direct the customer to that site—in other words, make it as easy as possible for a customer to buy from someone else. "Obviously, in that case, we lose the sale," Hsieh says. "But we've served the customer."

Even more rare is a company that chooses where to locate its headquarters based in large part on being able to attract and retain these kinds of high-touch employees. In the early days, Zappos, like so many Internet-based start-ups, was headquartered in San Francisco. But as the young company got bigger, Tony Hsieh and his executive colleagues worried that the Bay Area was just not the kind of place to support a business that required this level of intense, personal, telephone-based service. The city was expensive, many ambitious young people saw customer-service jobs as a stepping-stone to something else, and the business culture valued technological prowess (coding) over people skills (connecting). So Hsieh and his colleagues drew up a list of cities—including Phoenix, Arizona; Portland, Oregon; and Des Moines, Iowa—where the costs were reasonable, the people were friendly, and the infrastructure was advanced. Eventually, they settled on Las Vegas. Rather than just locating customer service there, they relocated the entire company there—because, Hsieh says, service *is* the company.[4]

"We *want* to talk to our customers," the CEO argues, although even he hopes customers don't make a habit of five-hour conversations or inquiries about pizza. "We *encourage* them to call. I speak at branding conferences and there's always lots of debate: Consumers are being bombarded by thousands of marketing messages, how do you get yours to stand out? Well, as unsexy and low tech as it sounds, the telephone is really powerful. Most companies look at the telephone as an expense. We look at it as one of the best branding devices out there. You have your customer's undivided attention. If you get the interaction right, if you focus not on 'closing the sale' but on doing exactly what's best for that customer, it's something they'll remember and tell their friends and family about."

EXTREME THINKING—THE COMPANIES WITH THE STRONGEST OPINIONS WIN

IT ALWAYS FEELS RISKY, AND at times it can feel downright scary, to start from scratch and do something new, whether it's launching an entrepreneurial venture or championing a game-changing venture inside an established organization. There are so many uncertainties, so many variables, so much that can go wrong—especially in an environment with so little room for error. But when it comes to thriving in an age of widespread uncertainty and rapid-fire change, the only thing more worrisome than the prospect of too much experimentation and change may be the reality of *too little* experimentation and change—especially when there are too many competitors chasing too few customers with products and services that look too much alike. If you do things the same way everyone else in your field does things, why would you expect to do any better?

At least that's what occurred to me as I listened in on one of those hush-hush, invitation-only conferences for CEOs and top executives. This conference was for leaders of regional banks across the United States. The setting was beautiful, but the mood was somber. Much of the talk was about how tough the business had become: credit markets were wreaking havoc with profit margins; acquisitions were creating a handful of giants that were putting the squeeze on rivals; customers had become demanding, fickle, impossible to please. (This was, by the way, well before the worldwide financial meltdown, when bankers thought TARP was what groundskeepers used to cover an infield during a rain delay.) There were lots of bankers, with lots of problems, looking for lots of sympathy from one another.

It was enough to make me, as an outsider, feel sympathetic too—until one industry insider explained an overlooked source of the bankers' pain. This market-research guru runs a firm that has conducted thousands of "mystery shops" and interviews with frontline employees at retail banks. He told the executives that during their visits, his firm's researchers always ask bank employees a simple question: "As a customer, why should I choose your bank over the competition?" And two-thirds of the time, he reported, frontline employees have no meaningful answer to that question—they either say nothing (and look to excuse themselves from the conversation as quickly as possible), or, in his words, they "make something up on the fly."

The bank executives seemed unsurprised. I was stunned. How can the leaders of any company expect to outperform the competition when their own people can't explain what makes them different from the competition and better than they've been in the past? That's the real problem with so many organizations today, whether the macroeconomic forecast calls for boom, bust, or something in between. It is also the huge opportunity for executives, entrepreneurs, and innovators of all stripes who are prepared to shake up their industries by doing something truly distinctive.

> When it comes to thriving in an age of rapid-fire change, the only thing more worrisome than too much experimentation may be *too little* experimentation. If you do things the same way everyone else does things, why would you expect to do any better?

Ray Davis, president and CEO of Umpqua Holdings, based in Portland, Oregon, was not one of the bankers feeling sorry for himself at that conference—and *all* of his people understand what makes their organization different from the competition. Davis took charge in 1994, when Umpqua was a pipsqueak of an outfit with six branches in and around the southern Oregon town of Roseburg, assets of $140 million, and, in his words, a "plain vanilla" strategy. Since then Umpqua has been one of the regional-banking industry's rising stars. It has 184 branches stretching from San Francisco to Seattle, assets of $11.5 billion, and a unique strategy that positions Umpqua as a lifestyle brand rather than as just another local bank. Davis and his colleagues like to answer their phones with the greeting, "Welcome to the World's Greatest Bank, how can I help you?" and the training department is called "World's Greatest Bank University."[5]

It's corny, maybe even a little goofy, but it's a declaration of independence from business as usual. "If the only way you compete is on price, offering the highest interest rate, then you might as well close your doors," Davis says. "Is it 'unreasonable' for us to aspire to be the world's greatest bank? Sure. But that's how you succeed, by being unreasonable."

It's not unreasonable to argue that Umpqua's fifteen-year track record of growth has little to do with the products it markets, which are similar (if not virtually identical) to the products offered by other banks. It collects deposits, issues credit cards, writes mortgages, and offers business customers lines of credit and real-estate financing—just like the competition. What's distinctive about Umpqua has to do with how it offers those products—its commitment to reimagining the experience of interacting with a bank. Davis puts is this way: "If you took a person, blindfolded them, sent them to a bank, and took the blindfold off, 99 percent of them would say, 'I'm in some bank somewhere.' We want our customers, when they take off that blindfold, to say, 'I'm in an *Umpqua* bank.' We don't want the experience of banking here to feel like banking anywhere else."

That's why Umpqua designs its branches to appeal to all the senses. What should a bank *look* like? In Umpqua's case, its branches evoke the spirit of a sleek hangout space, more like Starbucks or a well-appointed art gallery than the neighborhood savings and loan. Many of the branches are decorated with works from local artists, a way to keep the environment fresh and visually arresting. What should a bank *sound* like? In Umpqua's case, it's the sound of music. The bank signs up-and-coming bands to its Discover Local Music project (slogan: "Bank to your own beat") and invites customers to listen to songs on in-branch kiosks or download them from the Web. It even sells compilation CDs of the best songs. What should a bank *smell* like? Being the Pacific Northwest, the answer, of course, is coffee. Branch employees are happy to brew customers a cup of the bank's own Umpqua Blend, and they end every transaction with a piece of gold-wrapped chocolate served on a silver platter. (That's what Umpqua *tastes* like.)[6]

Moreover, during and after hours, the beautifully appointed

branches host community activities as well as banking activities. There are book clubs, movie nights, neighborhood meetings, "business therapy" gatherings, and "stitch and bitch" sessions where participants knit and gossip. Umpqua's Innovation Lab, a branch filled with high-tech gadgets in Portland's South Waterfront neighborhood, even hosts bowling leagues—not with balls and pins, but with Wii video bowling on 144-inch high-definition screens.

Why does Umpqua bother? To answer the make-or-break question that confounds so many other banks: Why should I choose you over the competition? To change the conversation with customers and the community, to make itself interesting in a world where most banks are boring, to become a passion brand in an industry sorely devoid of passion. "People come to the South Portland store in the middle of the day with their bowling shirts on," Davis marvels. "Some customers are waiting to see their banker, and others are bowling! It's incredible. It creates an environment where people say, 'That was fun, let's go back.'"

This distinctive personality and market presence, it should be noted, has served Umpqua well during the financial meltdown. Since mid-2007 the Pacific Northwest in general, and Oregon in particular, have been devastated (even more than the rest of the country) by the double whammy of a job-eliminating recession and a wealth-evaporating collapse in real-estate prices. An article in the *New York Times* argued that prosperous and progressive Portland "affords an ideal window onto the spiral of fear and diminished expectations assailing the [national] economy." Not surprisingly, given its prominence in the region, Wall Street hit Umpqua hard in terms of its stock price. But the bank's track record of financial appreciation was still truly impressive. Back in 1994, when Davis took over, Umpqua's market value was a trifling $18 million. By mid-2010, despite all the economic setbacks, and even after investors had turned their backs on banks, Umpqua's market value was $1.5 *billion*.[7]

Indeed, even as Wall Street's nerves frayed with respect to nearly all banks, community confidence in Davis's bank remained high. He took to the road, on a CEO barnstorming tour, reassuring executives, entrepreneurs, and just-plain folks that Umpqua was healthy and that the region would recover. Umpqua stepped in to acquire the deposits of a community bank in Clark County, Washington (just over the border from Oregon), that regulators closed. And the organization as a whole maintained its upbeat, high-energy posture. On June 24, 2009, as the Pacific Northwest economy worsened and spirits sagged, Umpqua held a "Random Acts of Kindness Day." Employees fanned out across their cities, towns, and neighborhoods and offered free ice cream (in Yuba City, California), milk shakes and strawberry short-cake (in Salem, Oregon), and pet treats in animal clinics (in Napa, California). A TV station in Bend, Oregon, captured the surprise of residents who got coffee, crepes, and other treats—and then invited passersby to share stories of something kind they'd done for a stranger. What was the point of this feel-good exercise? "To lift people's spirits and encourage a viral effect within each community," according to Umpqua's explanation of the program.

CEO Davis explains his bank's approach to business, in boom times or dark times, this way: "In an industry like ours, which is so old, where people are used to doing things one way, with blinders on, this model is not just shifting the paradigm. It's crashing and burning and nuking the paradigm! That's how you stay relevant. And if you can't stay relevant, you're done. The banks that are failing have no value proposition—nothing—other than, 'We are a bank and we will offer you a higher rate.' We have a one-of-a-kind value proposition in our industry."

The lesson is as simple as it is subversive: it's not good enough to be "pretty good" at everything anymore. You have to be *the most of something:* the most elegant, the most colorful, the most responsive, the most focused. For decades, organizations and their leaders were comfortable with strategies and practices that kept them in the middle of the road—that's where the customers were, that's what felt safe and secure. In the new world of business, with so much change, so much pressure, so many new ways to do just about everything, the middle of the road has become the road to nowhere. As Jim Hightower, the colorful Texas populist, is fond of saying, "There's nothing in the middle of the road but yellow stripes and dead armadillos." To which we might add companies and their leaders struggling to stand out from the crowd, even as they play by the same old rules in a crowded marketplace.

Harvard Business School professor Youngme Moon has emerged as an eloquent and distinctive voice on strategy, competition, and brands—and especially on the theme of why being different makes all the difference. She teaches one of HBS's most popular courses (on consumer marketing), she has written some of its bestselling case studies, and, a few years ago, she coauthored, to my mind, one of the most provocative articles that *Harvard Business Review* has published in years. (I'll discuss that essay in the next chapter.) So it's no surprise that her latest book, called *Different,* is both refreshing in its honesty and challenging in its implications for established companies (and cautious leaders) in all sorts of industries.

Professor Moon's message is as simple as it is powerful: most companies, in most industries, have a kind of tunnel vision. They chase the same opportunities that every other company is chasing; they miss the same opportunities that everyone else is missing because those opportunities are hiding in plain sight. It's the companies and brands that see a different game that win big—but all too often, the big companies in a field see things exactly the same way.

"In category after category," she writes, "companies have gotten so locked into a particular cadence of competition that they appear to have lost sight of their mandate—which is to create meaningful grooves of separation from one another. Consequently, the harder they compete, the less differentiated they become. . . . Products are no longer competing against each other; they are collapsing into each other in the minds of anyone who consumes them."

The most successful entrepreneurs and organizations aim to create what she calls "idea brands"—products and services whose performance and personality challenge the limits and assumptions of entire categories. Idea brands share three characteristics, according to Professor Moon: they offer something that is hard to come by; they reflect a commitment to a big idea; and they are intensely human. Cirque du Soleil is an idea brand, a circus that reimagined and re-invented what a circus could be. So is Harley-Davidson, which in-vented the concept of the white-collar, weekend "biker outlaw." So is something as prosaic as Dove soap, whose Campaign for Real Beauty rejected preconceived ideas from the worlds of fashion and style about glamour and body type. As Professor Moon argues, it created a beauty brand for women who are tired of trying to be beautiful.

"Idea brands are not perfect brands," she warns. "Far from it. They are polarizing brands. They are lopsided brands. They are brands de-voted to the skew. But because they do such an exquisite job of cap-turing our contradictions, they end up teaching us lessons about the inadequacies of our reductionist tools, lessons that they play back to us in fabulous style. They may not make much sense on paper, but they make perfect sense to us."[8]

> It's not good enough to be "pretty good" at every-thing. You have to be the most of something: the most elegant, the most colorful, the most respon-sive, the most focused. In the new world of busi-ness, the middle of the road has become the road to nowhere.

It makes perfect sense to me. No one would accuse Zappos or Umpqua Bank of playing in the middle of the road—even if no one would confuse one company's strategy with the other's. Umpqua is built around physical retailing, while Zappos operates in the virtual realm. Umpqua is colorful and entertaining, but, as a bank, does not embrace the zanier sides of life that help to define life at Zappos. (You won't find many pierced eyebrows or visible tattoos on its employees.) And that's the point: there's no one right strategy that separates a company from the crowd, no one experience that brings a strategy to life. As different as they are from each other, Umpqua and Zappos are even more different from the other players in their fields. They are "extremists" in the best sense of the word. They have made big bets on ideas that they consider indispensable, and that most of their rivals find unfathomable. They don't just have strategies, they have *opinions*—opinions, it should be said, that don't appeal to everyone, which is what makes them so much more appealing than organizations that think like everyone else.

For an extreme example of the power of extreme opinions, consider Michael O'Leary, the combative, controversial, and endlessly colorful CEO of Ireland's Ryanair. O'Leary has achieved in Europe what only Southwest Airlines has achieved in the United States. He has built a carrier that has grown fast, stayed healthy, and generated billions of dollars of wealth in an industry known for endless supplies of red ink. The company took flight in the mid-1980s with the aim of breaking the stranglehold of British Airways and Aer Lingus on travel between Ireland and England. It started small (it had two routes and carried eighty thousand passengers in 1986) and lost money. Then O'Leary, who became CEO in January 1994, devised a game-changing strategy that produced head-spinning results. In 2009, the company flew more than 850 routes, carried nearly sixty million passengers, and generated revenue of roughly $4 billion. Its share price grew *fivefold* between 1999 and 2009—ridiculously great performance in a ridiculously tough industry—and the CEO has become one of the wealthiest men in Ireland.

All of which has inspired O'Leary to pick countless public spats, from calling European regulators "morons" to dismissing British Airways as "expensive bastards" to suggesting that travel agents be "taken out and shot." He's even taken potshots at people like me. "Business books are bullshit," he told the author of a book about him, "and are usually written by wankers." One profile argued that O'Leary "revels in his persona as national pugilist and provocateur, alternately charming and offending." That's an understatement. As the *Wall Street Journal* noted, when Britain's advertising regulatory authorities questioned Ryanair's claims that it was quicker and cheaper for travelers to take its flights between London and Brussels than to ride the train, not only did the CEO refuse to back down—he sent the panel copies of *Mathematics for Dummies*.[9]

Trash talk notwithstanding, no other airline in Europe has delivered business results that come remotely close to what Ryanair has delivered over the last fifteen years. That's because no other airline has been as extreme as Ryanair in its devotion to a particular way of doing business—a model that is relentless and creative about cutting costs, lowering fares, and charging customers for anything and everything beyond the ticket itself. Here's how one account described the Ryanair formula: "If you want to check a bag, you pay extra. If you want soft drinks or pretzels on the flight, you pay extra. If you want an air-sickness bag, too bad—Ryanair has removed those . . . If there's a cost to be cut, it's been cut." Another account put it this way: "Most airlines fight to trim costs. Ryanair struggles to find the few ounces of fat it hasn't already cut."[10]

Put simply, unlike its middle-of-the-skies rivals, Ryanair knows *exactly* what it's the most of—insanely low costs and a colorfully high profile that doesn't inspire warm feelings among customers, but does inspire them to fly more than ever. As the CEO explained to a slightly appalled American reporter, Ryanair promises cheap fares, on-time schedules, minimal cancellations, and few lost bags: "But if you want anything more—go away! Will we put you in a hotel room if your flight was cancelled? No! Go away. Will we give you a refund on a nonrefundable ticket because your granny died unexpectedly? No!

Go away. We're not interested in your sob stories! What part of 'no refund' do you not understand?"[11]

Seth Godin, the acclaimed marketing guru, wrote a funny line about poultry with serious implications for standout performance in fields with lousy economics and lots of competition. "Tastes like chicken," he cracked, "is not a compliment." Translation: in a world in which so many companies present the same bland, nondescript fare, is it any wonder that so few customers feel energized about what these companies have to offer? That's what makes it so jarring to encounter free-spirited Zappos, experience-minded Umpqua Bank, even foulmouthed Ryanair. They are organizations with strong opinions about where their industry can and should be going, about what really matters to their customers and which customers matter most to their long-term success.

> Most companies, in most industries, have a kind of tunnel vision. They chase the same opportunities that every other company is chasing; they miss the same opportunities that everyone else is missing. It's the companies and brands that see a different game that win big.

Jason Fried and David Heinemeier Hansson are a lot more polite than Michael O'Leary, and they've even written a business book of their own. They are also two of the most opinionated young entrepreneurs I've come across in years. (In fact, they object when people use the word *entrepreneur* to describe them. The term is "outdated and loaded with baggage," they argue, which is why they prefer to be called "starters.") Their fast-growing software company, 37signals, embraces a set of extreme ideas about how to meet the needs of the people who use its products.

That's why the company doesn't just have users, it has raving fans, and its two leaders are certified Internet celebrities. (A *Wired* profile called them the "Brash Boys" of software and described a ballroom packed with programmers awaiting a keynote by Hansson as exuding "the kind of giddy excitement that greets the opening chords of a Hannah Montana concert.") Its signature offerings, such as Basecamp project-management software, Highrise contact-management software, and Ruby on Rails, a popular Web-programming template, are models of simplicity in an industry haunted by complexity. Software created by 37signals is distinguished by its limited features, its unrivaled ease of use, and the company's reluctance to add lots of new functionality.[12]

Indeed, it is this commitment to extreme simplicity that generates such extreme devotion from the more than three million people who rely on the products to manage their projects or build their businesses. How does 37signals avoid the "bloatware" and "feature creep" that have become defining features of life in the software industry? "When you're competing against companies that have so much more, the only answer is to do less," Fried and Hansson told me when I visited their offices in Chicago. "Conventional wisdom says that to beat your competitors, you need to one-up them. If their product has four features, you need five. If they are spending 'x' on development, you have to spend two or three times 'x.' In fact, the right answer is to do less than your competitors to beat them. Instead of one-upping other companies, *one-down* them. Instead of outdoing other products, *underdo* them."

I get it, I responded: less is more, right? The two entrepreneurs shook their heads. "No, less is less—because more is not better! Everyone tries to do too much: solve too many problems, build products with too many features. We say 'no' to almost everything. If you include every decent idea that comes along, you'll just wind up with a half-assed version of your product. What you want to do is build half a product that kicks ass."

Those strong opinions don't just apply to how 37signals develops products, it applies to how its leaders run the company. As strategists, Fried and Hansson focus on customers with smaller budgets, less bureaucracy, and fewer headaches. Most technology companies are obsessed with the "enterprise" market—Fortune 500 giants with big problems and thus big budgets with which to solve them. 37signals builds software for solo entrepreneurs and small companies—a market it calls the Fortune 5,000,000. "We solve the simple problems and leave the hairy, difficult, nasty problems to everyone else," the company likes to say.

As entrepreneurs (sorry, *starters*), they push themselves to spend less money and add fewer colleagues than more conventional executives might. "Don't hire people," they implore in *Getting Real*, their free, Web-based book filled with great advice for Internet-savvy innovators. "Is the work that's burdening you really necessary? What if you just don't do it? Can you solve the problem with a slice of software or a change of practice instead?" As young people running their own lives, they insist on working fewer hours and holding as few meetings as possible. Forget the long days and all-nighters that are such a part of Internet lore. 37signals has adopted a four-day workweek, the better to keep everyone fresh, energized, and free of distractions.

"Forgoing sleep is a bad idea," they warn young, all-nighter enthusiasts in *Rework*, a business bestseller they published in 2010. (The sort of young, all-nighter enthusiasts who use their software and buy their books, and thus need their sage advice.) "Creativity is one of the first things to go when you lose sleep. What distinguishes people who are ten times more effective than the norm is not that they work ten times as hard; it's that they use their creativity to come up with solutions that require one-tenth of the effort. Without sleep, you stop coming up with those one-tenth solutions."[13]

All told, the 37signals philosophy is a challenge to a business culture addicted to more. "Revenue growth in and of itself is not a goal," Fried and Hansson insist. "We are about profits—profits per employee. And growth forever is not sustainable. There is a right size for certain things, at least if you want to do them well." Which is why, as leaders, Fried and Hansson are not content with being pretty good at everything; they are determined to be the most of something. "We are enemies of mediocrity," declares CEO Fried. "If you try to make everyone happy, you end up with mediocrity. Our company has opinions, and we build products and do business based on those opinions. We need more opinionated companies."

> Seth Godin, the marketing guru, wrote a funny line about poultry with serious implications for standout performance in fields with lots of competition. "Tastes like chicken," he cracked, "is not a compliment."

My friend and former *Fast Company* colleague Daniel H. Pink has an especially poignant way of making this very important point. In his bestseller *Drive*, which explores "the surprising truth about what motivates us," Dan identifies with clarity and cleverness the three big drivers of performance and success: autonomy, mastery, and purpose. Most of his analysis speaks to the roots of individual performance, but it's easy to extend his insights to business performance. In particular, he urges individuals to ask a question of themselves that I believe leaders should ask of their companies as well.[14]

In his book, Dan tells a story about Clare Booth Luce, the accomplished playwright, journalist, and Republican member of Congress. In 1962, Luce had a meeting with President Kennedy, who was, at the time, pursuing an ambitious agenda domestically and overseas. She worried about his diffuse priorities. "A great man," she advised him, "is one sentence." President Lincoln's sentence was obvious: "He preserved the union and freed the slaves." So was FDR's: "He lifted us out of a great depression and helped us win a world war." What, Luce challenged the president, was to be his sentence?

What a powerful question—not just for great presidents, but for great companies too. Time and again, as I've gotten to know organizations that are winning big in tough industries, I've been struck by the clarity, simplicity, and originality of the defining ideas that drive them—their version of Luce's sentence. I don't mean that they have a clever slogan or a well-crafted mission statement. I mean that they have a well-defined and widely shared sense of the impact they want to have in their field and the legacy they hope to leave in their wake. As you think about the ideas you stand for and the difference you hope to make, ask yourself, What's your company's sentence?

EXTREME RESULTS—WHAT BUSINESS CAN LEARN FROM THE FOUR-MINUTE MILE

I'VE NEVER BEEN A BIG fan of applying sports metaphors to business. Most executives have sat through enough high-decibel pep talks about teamwork, coaching, and camaraderie to last a lifetime (or at least a career). But as I reflect on the competitive zeal of innovators from Zappos to 37signals, and the depth of their commitment to shaking up their industries, one legendary athletic achievement does shed some light on how to win big when most of your rivals play by the same rules. That achievement took place more than half a century ago, when a twenty-five-year-old medical student became the first person in history to run a mile in less than four minutes—a barrier that, until it was finally broken, was thought to be out of reach.

Like many people, I knew the basic story of Roger Bannister, who, on May 6, 1954, busted through the four-minute barrier with a time of three minutes, fifty-nine and four-tenths of a second. But it was not until I read a remarkable account by the British journalist and runner John Bryant that I understood the story behind the story—

and the lessons it holds for leaders who want to bust through barriers in their fields. In *3:59.4—The Quest to Break the 4 Minute Mile*, Bryant reminds us that runners had been chasing the goal seriously since at least 1886, and that the challenge involved the most brilliant coaches and gifted athletes in North America, Europe, and Australia. "For years milers had been striving against the clock, but the elusive four minutes had always beaten them," he writes. "It had become as much a psychological barrier as a physical one. And like an unconquerable mountain, the closer it was approached, the more daunting it seemed."[15]

This was truly the Holy Grail of athletic achievement. It's fascinating to read about the pressure, the crowds, the media swirl as runners tried in vain to break the mark, which, Bryant says, "had taken on an almost mythical power." He also reminds us that Bannister was an outlier and iconoclast—a full-time student who had little use for coaches and devised his own system for preparing to race. The British press "constantly ran stories criticizing his 'lone wolf' approach," Bryant notes, and urged him to adopt a more conventional regimen of training and coaching.

So the four-minute barrier stood for decades—and when it fell, the circumstances defied the confident predictions of the best minds in the sport. According to Bryant, the experts believed they knew the precise conditions under which the mark would fall. It would have to be in perfect weather—68 degrees and no wind. On a particular kind of track—hard, dry clay. Probably in Scandinavia (to meet the first two conditions) and in front of a huge, boisterous crowd urging the runner on to his best-ever performance. But Bannister did it on a cold day, on a wet track, at a small meet in Oxford, England, before a crowd of just a few thousand people.

When Bannister broke the mark, even his most ardent rivals breathed a sigh of relief. *At last, somebody did it!* And once they saw it could be done, they did it too. Just forty-six days after Bannister's feat, John Landy, an Australian runner, not only broke the barrier but crushed it, with a time of 3 minutes 58 seconds. Then, just a year after Bannister's achievement, three runners broke the four-minute barrier *in a single race*. Within three years, sixteen more runners celebrated. Over the last half century, more than a thousand runners have conquered a barrier that had once been considered hopelessly out of reach.

What goes for runners goes for leaders running organizations. In business, progress does not move in straight lines. It is not slow, steady, incremental. Whether it's an executive, an entrepreneur, or a technologist, an innovator changes the game, and that which was thought to be unreachable becomes a benchmark, something for others to admire and shoot for. Lexus has run the four-minute mile in automobiles: Who could have predicted that a mass-market carmaker from Japan would launch the best-selling luxury auto brand in North America? Umpqua has run the four-minute mile in financial services: Who could have imagined that the experience of visiting a bank branch would involve great art, cool music, good coffee, and video bowling? Henry Ford's West Bloomfield facility has run the four-minute mile in health care: Who could conceive of a hospital that blends high-quality care, high-touch service, and high-powered prevention, all in a way that remains affordable and accessible?

Professor Yoram (Jerry) Wind and Colin Crook of the Wharton School have written eloquently about the lessons for business of the four-minute mile. In their book, *The Power of Impossible Thinking,* they devote an entire chapter to an assessment of Bannister's feat and emphasize the mind-set behind it rather than the physical achievement. How is it, Wind and Crook wonder, that so many runners smashed the four-minute barrier in the three years after Bannister became the first to do it: "Was there a sudden growth spurt in human evolution? Was there a genetic engineering experiment that created a new race of super-runners? No, the basic human equipment was the same. What changed was the mental model. The runners of the past had been held back by a mind-set that said they could not surpass the four-minute mile. When that limit was broken, the others saw that they could do something they had previously thought impossible."[16]

That's the real promise of start-from-scratch innovation. Most thinking about strategy, competition, and innovation emphasizes the intricacies of business models: revenues, costs, niches, leverage. But *mental models* are what separate organizations that are the most of something from those that are pretty good at everything. As Wind and Crook explain, "Our [mental] models are so powerful, invisible, and persistent that when the old model no longer explains what is happening, we keep trying to make our experiences fit into them." Which is why, at first blush, the organizations we've met thus far can seem exotic, eccentric, hard to fathom. They don't just outperform their rivals. *They transform the sense of what's possible in their fields.* They don't accept the limitations, trade-offs, and middle-of-the-road sensibilities that define conventional wisdom in their fields. That's what makes them so unusual—and so important.

Robert MacDonald, one of the most offbeat and opinionated insurance-industry executives I've met (yes, I know, he doesn't have tons of competition), uses different language to describe the same phenomenon. The art of starting something new, he says, is a matter of "reminiscing about the future." That is, conjuring up a set of ideas and practices that are so extreme that established companies can't begin to make sense of them, let alone respond to them—and painting a vivid picture of what your organization can become if it delivers on its change-the-game agenda. That was the spirit behind LifeUSA, MacDonald's memorable contribution to an industry whose record of innovation is pretty forgettable. "If we had listened to the experts," he says, "we would have limited our goals and focused on the states around Minnesota, where we were based. But because we reminisced about the future, we started out as a national company competing against the giants of the field. We painted a picture of the future we wanted to create."

That picture became a compelling reality. LifeUSA took shape at a time when the insurance business was synonymous with poor service, slow decision making, and bureaucratic complacency. (Some things never change.) MacDonald's response? A blank-sheet-of-paper outfit infused as much by the lightning-quick pace of Silicon Valley as by the humdrum pace of life in Hartford and the industry's other outposts. He vowed that the company would make commission payments to agents within twenty-four hours, issue policies to customers within forty-eight hours, and respond to questions within forty-eight minutes—unheard-of promises at the time. He paid independent agents in part with stock options (again, an unheard-of practice) and shared both ownership and detailed information about the business with all rank-and-file employees. "How we did business was as important as what we sold," MacDonald told me. "The big companies simply couldn't treat people the way we did, either because the bureaucracy wouldn't allow it, or because they had no concept of how to do it."

Thanks to its one-of-a-kind ideas and practices, LifeUSA started fast, got big, and went public. In just a decade, the company signed up eighty-five thousand agents and attracted $6 billion worth of assets—off-the-charts performance that got the attention of Allianz, the German insurance giant, which paid a huge price to acquire MacDonald's outfit, and then put him and his unorthodox colleagues in charge of its life-insurance business in North America. "I remember when we started," MacDonald says. "People asked, 'How can you compete with Prudential and New York Life?' My answer was, and I didn't mean to seem arrogant, 'How can they compete with us?' They were responding to yesterday's market. We were reminiscing about the future. If we'd tried to be a little better than Prudential or New York Life, we would have failed. We had to do something completely different."[17]

The improbable rise of Magazine Luiza, one of Brazil's most-admired companies, is an even more dramatic example of what happens when a start-from-scratch competitor embraces, in the language of Wind and Crook, the power of impossible thinking. This family-owned department store, headquartered in the small city of Franca, five hours north of São Paulo, has emerged as the third-largest non-food retailer in the country—and its CEO, a tiny (four-foot nine-inch), irrepressible entrepreneur by the name of Luiza Helena Trajano Rodrigues (the niece of the company's cofounder, who was also named Luiza), has become a closely watched innovator among Brazil's class. She and her organization are featured on the cover of magazines, and there is so much interest among business professors that the company's website has a section to help with their research. "Luiza Helena is a celebrity among business leaders," says Marco Pellegatti, a director of the Amana-Key Group, a Brazilian management-training firm. "But she is also well known in the rural parts of the country. She has folk appeal—simple, straightforward, shrewd."

One obvious reason for the company's visibility is its eye-opening success. As recently as 2003, Magazine Luiza (in Portuguese, a "magazine" is a small store that sells a wide range of merchandise) had about 180 locations and a few thousand employees, with annual sales of 920 million reais ($490 million). In 2009, it had 450 locations with 13,000 employees, and sales of 3.6 billion reais. Moreover, despite the Brazilian economy's history of wild gyrations, the company has made money every year since 1992, shortly after Luiza Helena Rodrigues took charge.

What's more striking than Magazine Luiza's track record of growth, though, is its game plan for achieving that growth. The company has become big, powerful—*rich*—by meeting the needs of Brazil's *poorest* shoppers. Unlike its two major national competitors, Casas Bahia and Ponto Frio, not to mention foreign-owned retailers such as Walmart and Carrefour, the company has not built the bulk of its business around well-to-do customers in big urban areas—the most sought-after market in Brazil, with its famously skewed distribution of wealth. Rather, it has focused on low-income customers in small cities and rural areas and devised a set of business practices to allow these customers to purchase durable goods (washers, dryers, refrigerators, computers) that were beyond their reach until Magazine Luiza came along. Even when it enters big cities (on September 21, 2008, the company took São Paulo by storm when it opened forty-four stores in one day), it focuses on neighborhoods and customers who are overlooked by the retail establishment. To be sure, the other big retailers can't help but do business with the "bottom of the pyramid"—if only because in a country like Brazil, the bottom of the pyramid holds so many people. But no retailer has been as aggressive, as creative, as assertive as Magazine Luiza in looking at the bottom of the pyramid as the foundation of its business.

In other words, Luiza Helena Rodrigues and her colleagues saw a huge market opportunity where their mainstream rivals saw an extremely limited market, and they have built a hugely successful organization as a result. According to Frederico Trajano Rodrigues, executive director of sales and marketing (and the CEO's son), more than 70 percent of Magazine Luiza's customers are low-income shoppers, and the business of the company is about more than just commercial transactions. "For a poor Brazilian family to buy a refrigerator, for a woman who works every day to buy her first washing machine, this is not merely a purchase," he told me. "It changes and improves the quality of life. Our business strategy, our innovations, and our culture make it possible for us to address this segment of the market."

There are all kinds of reasons why Magazine Luiza has been so confident about adopting such a brash and unorthodox game plan for competition. One huge (and admittedly hard to replicate) reason is the fact that the CEO literally grew up in the business, which gives her tremendous confidence to champion ideas that more conventional leaders would consider too risky. Luiza Helena began working in the store as a young child, and she absorbed the unique sense of mission, purpose, and customer involvement around which the enterprise was founded. "When my aunts started the business, the very first thing they did was to promote a public contest through a popular local radio [show] to choose a new name," Luiza Helena told researchers from the Harvard Business School, who prepared a case study on the company. "It was a huge success. After a few days of amazing participation, the [audience] chose 'Magazine Luiza' as the winner. From the very beginning, the company was truly customer centered, and we have tried to maintain this essence."

Marco Pellegatti, the consultant from Amana-Key, has watched closely and worked with the CEO as she has translated a lifetime of experience into an ongoing series of timely innovations. Luiza Helena "started working at the store almost as a child, on the retail floor, and she worked her way up the ranks to CEO," he told me. "She has experience in virtually every area and position in the company. That's why she's light-years ahead of everyone else in terms of entrepreneurial vision and strategic thinking. Yet at the same time, and this is so important, she is not the least bit afraid to or ashamed of admitting doubts and fears in many situations. It is not at all uncommon for her to call upon people, particularly people from the front lines, to ask for their input on issues that she's unsure of. People know this is how she operates, and they are eager to contribute to her thinking."

In particular, Pellegatti points to the company's biannual strategy session, in which literally thousands of employees come together to take part in a group exercise to plan the future. This gathering, known inside Magazine Luiza as the Encontrão ("Big Meeting"), is where the company's most important initiatives get formed, critiqued, and improved upon—by employees at every level of the company. Before they attend the meeting, though, thousands of rank-and-file workers answer two questions that drive much of the discussion: First, What are we not doing that we should start doing right away? Second, What should we immediately stop doing in order to allow for the emergence of the new? The answers are collected, compiled, analyzed, and create the foundation for the Big Meeting. "This kind of grass-roots dialogue allows for the creation of richer strategies," Pellegatti argues, "since it leverages the diversity of the workforce. It also makes for greater engagement and faster and more accurate execution, since everyone feels like they have a stake in the strategy."

In other words, since Magazine Luiza is so clear about the difference it aims to make in the lives of its low-income customers, and so open to inviting employees at all levels to shape how it delivers on that mission, it gives itself the freedom to invent wildly different ways of doing business. A case in point: the company's Liquidação Fantástica (Fantastic Sales) program, which runs for just six hours on the first Saturday each January starting at 5:00 A.M. In these Fantastic Sales, a way to clear out the shelves for the start of a new year, merchandise is marked down by as much as 70 percent. Lines begin forming outside the stores several days in advance and can grow to as many as twenty thousand people before the doors open on Saturday morning. Magazine Luiza turns the lines into carnivals, providing entertainment, organizing sales by local vendors, and otherwise keeping spirits high. Literally millions of Brazilians participate in the Liquidação Fantástica every January.

On a more substantial note, the company has mastered the art and science of financing customer purchases with credit: how to evaluate risks, structure payments, and collect overdue debts. As the *New York Times* explained, in an article that marveled at the company's growth and profitability, "Through the store's strategy of selling in installments and providing affordable credit in a country with some of the world's highest interest rates, [it] has managed to bolster the spending power of the poor in Latin America's biggest consumer market. And by requiring customers to return to the store each month to make payments in person, the strategy has enticed many new purchases with a steady diet of blowout sales—prices can be reduced by as much as 70 percent—on . . . furniture, refrigerators, and other household goods." According to the Harvard Business School case study, 80 percent of the company's sales were on credit, and its 4 percent default rate was one-third of the Brazilian average.[18]

Another huge factor in Magazine Luiza's growth was the creation of "virtual" stores—small outlets specifically designed for rural towns and poor neighborhoods in high-cost urban centers. These locations carry little or no merchandise, and cost about 15 percent of what it costs to build a more traditional store. But they allow customers to learn about appliances, furniture, and consumer electronics, to figure out what they want to buy and what they can afford. The company guarantees home delivery within forty-eight hours of the purchase. In other words, customers get full access to Magazine Luiza's inventory of durable goods, without the company having to maintain expensive physical stocks or absorb big real-estate expenses.

> Since Magazine Luiza is so clear about the difference it aims to make with its customers, and so open to inviting employees at all levels to shape how it executes that mission, it gives itself the freedom to invent wildly different ways of doing business.

Magazine Luiza launched these outlets (there are sixty today) in the early 1990s, long before Internet kiosks became a familiar piece of the retail landscape. Early on, says Frederico Rodrigues, who led the project, the company relied on print catalogs and amateur video. "We'd 'camcorder' the products and show them on a screen." He laughs. "Now we have a sophisticated Web catalog, a very nice system." The stores have also become popular hangout spaces and destinations, through a strategy that Magazine Luiza calls "social insertion." The company partners with nonprofits and other groups to offer cooking lessons, computer training, health tips, English classes, and the like. ATM machines and free Internet access also keeps the number of visitors (and potential customers) high.

Remarkably, adds Rodrigues, despite the well-documented success of the virtual stores, establishment retailers have been slow to offer their twist on Magazine Luiza's innovation. "They looked at it with skepticism," he says, "so much so that for years nobody copied the idea. And thanks to everything we learned from the virtual stores— the images, the database, the supply chain for home delivery—we got a head start on e-commerce. We're now the second-largest online retailer in Brazil. The effort to serve low-income customers helped us to pioneer the use of the Internet for e-commerce in Brazil, which allows us to reach higher-income customers. Innovation takes you to places you never expected to go."

EXTREME MAKEOVER—HOW TO "CRUMPLE IT UP" AND "WORK BACKWARD"

To be sure, the easiest way to create an extreme competitor—an organization capable of running the four-minute mile in its industry—is to start with a set of extreme opinions and build a company around them. That's why so many start-ups have come so far so fast and have had such an enormous impact—even when they go head-to-head with giant rivals that can draw on more money, power, and traditional clout. They are successful precisely because they don't look, talk, behave, or compete like other companies in their fields. They are outliers, extremists, game changers. They don't, in the delicious words of Seth Godin, "taste like chicken."

What's also striking about such start-from-scratch innovators is that their extreme opinions often leave the old guard baffled, confused, and unable to muster an extreme makeover. That's why I devoted the first three chapters of this book to strategies for helping long-established organizations make deep-seated transformation. It's certainly possible for incumbents to devise creative responses to fast-changing markets, fast-moving technologies, and demanding customers. But most big companies fail miserably at making big change, and the biggest obstacle is the pull of old mental models—how comfortable it feels to be pretty good at everything, how unsettling it feels to become the most of something.

For years, Michael O'Leary and his colleagues at Ryanair have expressed their disdain for Europe's airline establishment, yet the establishment has never really gotten off the ground in terms of a response. Or think about the competitive skies on this side of the Atlantic, and how the major airlines greeted the rise of Southwest and JetBlue—fiercely opinionated newcomers (albeit much more civil than Ryanair) that combined low costs and friendly service to challenge the preeminence of Delta, United, and the rest. Did the leaders of the U.S. airline establishment ask searching questions about the customer experience that had gone unasked for decades? Did they challenge habits and practices that kept them stuck in the middle of the road and devise a new sense of purpose to inspire a new era of prosperity? Hardly. Instead, they made a halfhearted effort to mimic their blank-sheet-of-paper competitors—and then quickly gave up when they realized that they didn't have the deeply held beliefs or most-of-something ideas to match what their rivals were doing.

The story line would be depressing were it not so familiar. Delta launched Song, so obviously modeled on JetBlue, on April 15, 2003—and the perpetually out-of-tune division flew its last flight on April 30, 2008. (It was not a great sign of support when Gerald Grinstein, Delta's CEO at the time, began calling his new business unit, "Swan Song.") United launched TED, its unoriginal twist on Southwest, on February 12, 2004—and TED came in for a final landing five years later. The big carriers understood that new rivals were changing the game and challenging their supremacy. But their middle-of-the-road sensibilities limited their response. They could not develop a new set of strategic opinions, so they could not devise an original strategy with which to leapfrog the competition.

But you don't have to be a blank-sheet-of-paper start-up to embrace a blank-sheet-of-paper *mind-set*. Indeed, compare how Delta and

United responded to turbulence in their industry with how Humana, the health-insurance company based in Louisville, Kentucky, has responded to turmoil in its industry. Humana is a huge organization with twenty-eight thousand employees, eleven million covered lives, and annual revenues of $29 billion. It's also right in the middle of the traumatic changes—and fierce political debates—sweeping the health-care system. How does an organization with such a vast reach, under so much pressure, rethink its assumptions and practices? By creating a freethinking team whose job is to generate strong opinions about tough problems and experiment with start-from-scratch answers.

Humana's Innovation Center, which occupies the tenth floor of a high-rise tower in downtown Louisville, is a dull-sounding name for a game-changing approach to strategy. The fifty or so members of the team, most of whom have never before worked in health care, have been charged with helping to shake up the company's culture, challenge its assumptions, and experiment with new technologies, products, and services. It's not just about research and development. It's about questions and answers—new perspectives on what's wrong with health care and how to fix it. There's a reason why, for years, the team's website was called "Crumple It Up." That was the basic idea—to identify established practices, throw them away, and sketch out alternatives.[19]

When I toured the Innovation Center, I asked Greg Matthews, a former HR executive who became a director of consumer innovation, if there was a clear-eyed definition of success for the unit, given that its members have played such an open-ended role at the company as catalysts and provocateurs. Part of the work over the years, he said, has been to create new products and services that represent tangible innovations that help to establish best practice—Humana's "personal nurses" unit, for example, and its easy-to-understand SmartSummary customer statements, both of which have been widely embraced in the marketplace. In the future, he added, the Innovation Center was likely to evolve back toward this product-oriented focus—to devise and define new offerings for the marketplace.

But at the time of my visit, he emphasized, and for the prior several years, the group's focus had been on developing a far-reaching point of view that *redefines* the marketplace—and gets widely embraced by employees. The team members at the Innovation Center relish their status as freethinkers. When I first met Matthews, for example, he handed me a business card that featured a photo of his face on top of a stick figure holding a wrinkled sheet of paper that said "Crumple It Up," along with handwritten scribbles (Twitter account, cell-phone number, etc.) to evoke the sketch-your-ideas sensibility. When I met one of Matthews's colleagues, who'd spent four years as an advocate for innovation inside Humana, he handed me a business card that described his personal change-the-game mission. It read simply, "Health Bad Make Good." Translation: try all sorts of programs and projects on the theory that small experiments can lead to big insights that create huge opportunities for change. "The 'crumple-it-up' approach," he says, "is that you test a bunch of things really quickly, see what works, and shelve the ones that don't work."

That's why, over the last few years, the Innovation Center sponsored such an extensive array of unlikely initiatives (unlikely, that is, for a cautious field such as health insurance). One intentionally silly project, Relatively Hilarious, was a mobile-communications platform to help senior citizens swap jokes with their families. (Laughter, it turns out, really is the best medicine, although this particular service didn't tickle the market's funny bone.) Meanwhile, working with Trek, the hot bicycle manufacturer, and Crispin Porter + Bogusky, the cool ad agency, Humana launched B-cycle, a bike-sharing service and social network to promote commuting on two wheels—and better fitness in the process.

The Humana Games for Health project (HG4H) taps video technology as a platform for encouraging players to break a sweat. In one game, called the Horsepower Challenge, Humana issued pedometers to five Louisville schools and used wireless technology to measure how many steps participating sixth graders walked. Their real-world jaunts powered a virtual school bus—the more kids walked, the farther the bus traveled. As of late 2009, the game was being played by thousands of kids in a total of twenty different cities and was showing real promise in terms of increasing exercise rates. (Physical activity increased by 35 percent among the players in the Challenge.)

These are small steps, but they are meant to be first steps in a journey to redefine what it means to be a health-insurance company and to define a new generation of products and services. "The health-care system today is really about managing sickness," Matthews told me, and in some sense that's as it should be. "But our vision is to help this organization broaden its focus to include life and happiness, which we believe is a much bigger business. We are trying all sorts of experiments, crumpling things up left and right, testing new products and services. But we are really advocating a philosophy. Every time we present a project or a program, it is in the context of our point of view: Can we move this company, and perhaps the whole industry, from the land of sickness and death to the land of life and happiness? There is a social revolution in health, and we have to be a part of it."

You don't have to be a blank-sheet-of-paper start-up to embrace a blank-sheet-of-paper *mind-set*. At Humana, the Innovation Center has developed a website called "Crumple It Up." The mission— identify established practices, throw them away, and sketch out alternatives.

So one way for an incumbent to generate strong opinions is to assemble a small group of smart people and encourage them to think freely. Gamal Aziz, president and COO of MGM Grand Las Vegas, has devised a different way to unleash most-of-something strategies inside a pretty-good-at-everything organization. His technique, called "working backward," fueled years of remarkable growth at the hotel as his industry boomed, and the style of thinking it encouraged made it possible to respond quickly and creatively as the boom turned to bust. We began this chapter with a visit to a blank-sheet-of-paper innovator, headquartered twenty minutes outside of Las Vegas, that shook up the field of Internet retail. It seems fitting to close the chapter with a visit to the Strip itself, and an established organization that unleashed a blank-sheet-of-paper mind-set to shake up its field.

Aziz took charge of the MGM Grand in 2001, when the hotel was successful (annual revenues of roughly $700 million) and profitable (earnings of about $170 million), but nothing spectacular. It was the sort of so-so setting that could have sustained years of business as usual. Instead, Aziz and his colleagues unleashed a torrent of innovations that reshaped the hotel, remade the business, and generated rave reviews. Annual revenues jumped to $1.2 billion, profits rose to nearly $400 million, the MGM Grand became one of the world's largest hotels (with 6,763 rooms and 10,000 employees), and the experience began to live up to the promise of delivering "Maximum Vegas."

Aziz's growth strategy worked because he taught his colleagues the value of "working backward" from the future. They engaged in an exercise to look at every aspect of the hotel's performance—rooms, restaurants, shops, shows—and evaluate it with a start-from-scratch mind-set. The challenge was no longer: How do we make marginal improvements over current results? It was: What is the highest and best use for this venue or shop, if we could sketch ideas on a blank sheet of paper and build it today? How does present performance compare with ideal potential performance? And how do we work backward from where we know we could be to achieve this performance? "It's easy to make small improvements in what you are doing already," Aziz explained to me over lunch at the Mansion at MGM Grand, a collection of exquisite villas reserved for special guests. "It's harder to capture what you're missing. But that's the real challenge for innovators. And that's what we did with working backward."

It's a mind game of sorts that led to a whole new mind-set—and a staggering array of opinions about how the property could reinvent itself. Early on in his tenure, for example, Aziz looked at Gatsby's restaurant, which was generating sales of $2 million and decent profits. A traditional improvement plan might have aimed to raise sales by 10 percent a year. But Aziz posed a different challenge: If the space were empty, and we could open any type of restaurant, what might the results be? He figured that if he could recruit a big-name chef and create a dynamic experience, the space could generate $5 million in sales and much bigger profits. So the organization no longer measured Gatsby's as generating $2 million in positive sales. It was *losing* $3 million in potential sales. Soon thereafter, MGM Grand closed Gatsby's and opened Nobhill Tavern by Chef Michael Mina. A few years after the new restaurant opened, it was generating sales of $6.5 million—far ahead of Aziz's ideal projections.[20]

Aziz used the same approach to the hotel's much-loved Brown Derby restaurant, its version of the storied Hollywood eatery that was famous for hosting the movie establishment and for inventing the Cobb salad. Back in 2005, the Brown Derby was a perfectly solid performer for the MGM Grand, generating $8 million in revenue and $1.5 million in profit. (The restaurant was also entrenched because it was a personal favorite of many of the executives of both MGM Grand and its parent company, a comfortable place to have a working lunch or dinner.) But Aziz knew that this respectable space could be downright dazzling if he created a truly unique venue, as opposed to a Las Vegas spin on an old Hollywood institution. Enter celebrity chef Tom Colicchio and Craftsteak, which now generates $18 million in revenue and $4.6 million in profit annually. The demise of their unofficial company cafeteria may have disappointed some of Aziz's executive colleagues, but the performance of its replacement certainly satisfied their appetite for business results.

No commitment to incremental improvement could have justi-
fied these changes. And they were just two of many tangible innovations Aziz and his colleagues unleashed. It was a frontline executive,
for example, who, during a fairly routine (albeit pretty lavish) upgrade
of the top two floors of the MGM Grand, suggested to Aziz that he
think more ambitiously about the space as a separate "hotel within
a hotel," with its own style, amenities, target audience, and brand. A
by-the-book renovation quickly became a game-changing innovation,
and thus was born the hugely successful Skylofts offering, with room
prices that run into the thousands of dollars per night. Talk about a
twist: Skylofts is a member of the prestigious Leading Small Hotels
in the World, even though it occupies the top two floors of one of the
biggest hotels in the world!

Overall, Aziz and his team pledged, using the working-backward
methodology, to unveil a major initiative (a new shop, show, or restaurant) every three months for forty-eight months—a breathtaking
commitment by any standard. Not only did they meet this commitment, but they nearly doubled it, launching thirty major innovations
in Aziz's first four years that transformed a middlebrow brand into one
of the darlings of the Strip.

My first conversation with Gamal Aziz was in 2007, boom times
for Las Vegas. My final conversation was more than two years later,
after the boom had turned to bust, leaving many bright-and-shiny Las
Vegas properties with a decidedly cloudy future. Yet the MGM Grand
was weathering the downturn better than most of its competitors, and
far better than its parent company, debt-plagued MGM Mirage. (Remarkably, even during the worst moments of the meltdown in Las
Vegas and the economy more generally, occupancy rates at the MGM
Grand remained, on average, above 90 percent.) Aziz, meanwhile,
as he continued to run one of the world's largest hotels, was also ex-
porting the brand around the world, in his additional role as CEO
of MGM Mirage Hospitality, which was opening a variety of properties (under the brand names MGM Grand, Bellagio, and Skylofts) in

Egypt, the United Arab Emirates, Vietnam, China, Morocco, India, and elsewhere. Even as he expanded the brand's footprint around the world, though, Aziz understood that what happened at the MGM Grand itself was a demonstration project to developers, partners, and customers around the world about the quality of the experience and the power of the culture. When it came to creativity and innovation, what happened in Vegas couldn't stay in Vegas.

Indeed, Aziz tells the story of a powerful Arab sheikh who asked to visit the MGM Grand in Las Vegas and see what the fuss was about. This sheikh was in discussions with MGM Mirage Hospitality about opening a huge property in his country, so Aziz was happy to host him and show off the cutting-edge restaurants, clubs, and shows. But what this Arab ruler really wanted to see, and what he spent most of his visit studying, was MGM Grand University—the training arm that maintains and develops the culture, teaches frontline employees the innovation techniques that have come to define the hotel, and otherwise cultivates the property's human connections. "He really appreciated that you can't understand the brand without understanding the people," Aziz told me. "And you can't understand the innovations we've introduced unless you understand the 'culture of ideas' that brought them to life. Our culture really is our flagship."

So how did the flagship property hold its own during what Aziz calls "the incredibly messy crisis" that brought Las Vegas to its knees—and brought his parent company, MGM Mirage, to the verge of bankruptcy before it began a financial turnaround? By remaining consistent in its commitment to new ideas and strong opinions. Years of innovation at the MGM Grand had created a culture of engagement that made the huge hotel more agile than it had ever been. In flush times, executives might debate the merits of opening a new club or an exclusive pool, chefs and bartenders might compete to develop the most unusual dishes or the most exotic cocktails. In the downturn, the debates were about cutting costs without reducing service and doing more with less.

During the boom times, for example, the hotel's fifteen-minute preshift meeting, a daily ritual in which thousands of frontline employees gather in small groups for updates and discussions, might focus on which celebrities were at the hotel or which club had the hottest DJ. During the dark times, the preshift might focus on saving energy, eliminating waste, or helping employees hang on to their homes despite the wave of foreclosures that was sweeping Las Vegas. "There is a daily conversation among all the people in the company," Aziz says, "no matter what's happening in the economy."

CHAPTER FIVE

DIFFERENT ON PURPOSE— MOTIVATION, INSPIRATION, AND THE HEART OF INNOVATION

Hear ye, hear ye, on behalf of this company that is new and is ours and could be special, we do proclaim the following: Whereas, this Academy was created based on the premise that we, the citizens of DaVita Village, never forget that we have accepted responsibility for the essential care of fellow human beings.

Whereas, as individuals and as a company, we will make mistakes, but we will admit them, learn from them, and grow from them.

Whereas, as to the meaning of life . . . we hold the conviction that one does not search for and find it, but rather one works for and builds it.

We hereby proclaim you leaders of our community in its quest to build the Greatest Dialysis Company the World Has Ever Seen!

—EXCERPTS, DAVITA ACADEMY GRADUATION
PROCLAMATION

IF YOU WANT TO EXPERIENCE the joys and heartaches of organizational life—not to mention the
joys and heartaches of life itself—spend time at one of the fifteen hundred kidney-dialysis centers operated by DaVita Inc., a fast-growing
company that treats nearly one-third of all the dialysis patients in
the United States. A visit to Zappos headquarters leaves you infused
with a sense of youthful vigor. A visit to Umpqua Bank leaves you
entertained and caffeinated. A visit to DaVita leaves you touched and
humbled about what it means to do something exceptional under exceptionally difficult conditions. Lots of leaders tell themselves that
their work feels tough because they work in such tough fields, with
aggressive competitors, hard-to-please customers, and little room for
error. But few fields come close to dialysis in terms of the pressures on
the companies that provide the treatment, the demands on the employees who interact with patients, and the life-or-death stakes of the
service itself. This is one of the most daunting environments imaginable in which to build a high-performance organization and create
long-lasting economic value—a field in which you must be the most
of something, because being pretty good at everything is a surefire
prescription for failure.

Consider the time I spent in Reidsville, North Carolina, a rural
town of fewer than fifteen thousand people in the north-central part
of the state. Reidsville is a lovely place, dotted with more churches
than a visitor can count and well-maintained fields of corn, soybeans,
and tobacco. The high school football team is a powerhouse, with
seventeen state titles, more than any other city or town in North Carolina. But for years, Reidsville has been feeling the effects of global
economic restructuring. Tobacco, needless to say, is not the cash crop
it used to be, and the American Tobacco Company closed its huge
facility here back in 1994. Meanwhile, sitting as it does close to the
rusting textile mills of Burlington, Reidsville also has suffered the
nonstop flight of jobs to Latin America and Asia. It's been a while
since this picturesque community was the picture of health.

Much the same can be said for the people inside the DaVita center. Being a dialysis patient means that you suffer from end-stage renal disease (ESRD), that is, a lack of function in both kidneys, often due to diabetes or high blood pressure. Dialysis does what damaged kidneys cannot—clean the blood of water, minerals, and built-up toxins that would be fatal without the process. A single treatment lasts up to four hours, and treatments must take place three times a week, fifty-two weeks a year, every year for the rest of your life (or until you are fortunate enough to get a kidney transplant).

In other words, as explained in an absorbing front-page article in the *Wall Street Journal*, dialysis "is one of the great life-extending treatments of all time." Small wonder, then, that the number of Americans on dialysis has doubled over the last two decades, or that this single center, in this tiny town, can handle twenty patients at a time, and stays open Monday through Saturday. It is a busy place whose work is never done, a place to which patients may drive fifty or sixty miles, and arrive at the crack of dawn, to spend hours hooked up to a dialyzer to stay alive.[1]

But dialysis, for all its lifesaving marvels, puts enormous physical and emotional strains on patients and their families, so much so that a fair portion of ESRD patients eventually stop treatment—knowing full well what awaits them. The *Journal* piece offers an almost unreadably sad account of the decision by a forty-one-year-old carpenter named Joe Mole who, after twenty-two years with diabetes, nearly four years of dialysis, and several unsuccessful efforts to secure a donor kidney, skipped three treatments and suffered the inevitable outcome. "Some patients can reverse course after missing a dialysis treatment or two," the *Journal* noted, "but at a certain point there's no turning back." Joe Mole chose not to turn back, a life-ending decision that was about both chronic pain and psychological exhaustion.

This sobering context is what made my visit to Reidsville so memorable, and so unexpectedly uplifting. The place is bright and cheery, filled with smiles and positive energy in plentiful supply. Enter the lobby and you encounter the Wall of Fame, a fixture at virtually every DaVita facility. The theme here is "Compassionate Hands Bridging Hearts and Lives." Nurses, patient-care technicians, dietitians, social workers, and other members of the DaVita team have left their handprints on the wall, along with photos of themselves. Each patient gets a photo too, attached by a Band-Aid to a heart. Inside the heart, patients write messages to people in their lives—friends, family, and more often than not, DaVita employees—who keep their spirits high and make their treatments easier to handle. It's a lovely tribute to the bond between the staff and its patients, who spend literally hundreds of hours together every year.

Eddie, a fiftysomething diabetic who also suffers from high blood pressure, is winding down the day's session when I stop by. Because of his illness, Eddie had to give up his job at an auto dealership, but he still has the energy to umpire amateur baseball, a game he loves and played into his forties. Somehow, despite a long drive to Reidsville and four hours of dialysis, he also has the energy to give Linda, a DaVita staffer working a few feet away, an endless (and endlessly entertaining) supply of guff.

"How do you feel?" Eddie is asked. "I feel great! I'm in a great mood. Of course, Linda is in a terrible mood. She's *always* in a terrible mood," he says. "Do you really drive yourself here?" a visitor wonders. "Yes I do," he says with satisfaction. "It's easier for Linda, though. She rides her broomstick." And so it goes until Linda is out of earshot, at which point Eddie, who has been on dialysis for more than two years, and remains hopeful about qualifying for a kidney, looks serious, lowers his voice, and says: "I'm going to tell you something. Linda and these ladies have saved my life. I've taken dialysis at other places, including some big hospitals, but there's no comparison with here. These people are extraordinary."

Seventy miles down the road in Durham, in a DaVita center on the west side of town, the client base reflects a different slice of North Carolina life. Durham is part of the Research Triangle region, with its big-time universities, cutting-edge medical research, and high-tech entrepreneurs. There are twenty-eight treatment stations here, and they run two shifts a day, six days a week. There are also beds for "nocturnal" dialysis, an attractive option for patients with demanding jobs. They arrive in the evening, stay hooked up for eight hours, sleep through the night, and head to work in the morning.

Lynn Guerrant is the facility administrator (FA) for DaVita Durham West. Each of DaVita's 1,450 centers has an FA (basically, the CEO of the facility), and they have a huge day-to-day impact on quality, turnover, and morale. Guerrant has loads of professional credentials (she's an intensive-care nurse with master's degrees in both education and administration) and she exudes the air of a natural leader. As we walk the floor, she gently ribs one sixty-year-old patient, who swears that, "I've been behaving myself." (A few weeks earlier, he was discovered with a pack of cigarettes hidden in his socks.) Guerrant isn't so sure. "I'll send a tech to talk to him," she says. "Patients tell people like me what they think we want to hear."

This facility (one of two in Durham) serves more than a hundred patients, twenty of whom are on waiting lists for kidneys. They include college professors, high-powered executives, gospel musicians, and a bunch of younger people (ages nineteen to thirty-six) about whom Guerrant worries—a lot. "It's tough to adjust your lifestyle when you're young," she says. "This condition affects what you can eat, how much you can drink, even intimacy. But if you want the best results, and if you want to stay in compliance for a kidney, you can't misbehave." That's why she's organized a program that pairs the most challenging patients with DaVita staffers who stay on them about diet, exercise, and overall lifestyle. "It can be disheartening" when people don't take care of themselves, Guerrant admits. "But this is like a family. Our patients spend so much time with us. We never give up."

As tough as dialysis is on the heartstrings, it's just as tough on the purse strings. DaVita and other treatment providers must navigate the treacherous crosscurrents of medical advances, government mandates, insurance-industry practices, and never-ending demands to lower expenses and improve outcomes. Roughly 80 percent of DaVita's patients are covered by Medicare, which, most analysts agree, does not reimburse providers for the full costs of the basic treatment. (The *New York Times* has called dialysis "the closest thing the United States has to nationalized health care.") So companies have to keep a tight rein on expenses, generate extra revenue by administering medication and providing add-on services, and stay in the good graces of (better-paying) private insurers, which cover a minority of patients for a limited time.[2]

Still, through it all, DaVita has thrived. Kent J. Thiry, its hard-charging CEO, took command in October 1999, when the company was on the verge of bankruptcy, literally running out of cash, and under investigation by the SEC. Since then DaVita basically started from scratch and started something big. In 1999, it had revenues of $1.4 billion, losses of $56.4 million, and a share price of about $2. Less than ten years later, it had revenues of $5.7 billion, net income of $374 million, and a share price of more than $60. Here's how a Stanford Business School case summarized DaVita's performance six years after Thiry arrived: "The company's market capitalization had grown from $200 million to more than $5 billion, the clinical outcomes had become the best in the industry, the company's organic growth was the highest in the industry, and employee retention had improved dramatically with a 50 percent reduction in turnover."[3]

All of which, from the perspective of achieving exceptional results under exceptionally difficult conditions, raises two questions: If the dialysis process is so demanding, how do DaVita centers manage to feel so spirited and full of life? And if the economics are so punishing, how has DaVita been such a success in terms of growth, profitability, and shareholder value? The answers speak to the power of designing a one-of-a-kind business around a unique (and extreme) set of ideas—and to the virtues of building an organization around a sense of personal engagement and emotional attachment that goes beyond the dollars-and-cents logic of business itself.

Bill Shannon, who spent several years as DaVita's chief wisdom officer (his actual title), offered some unconventional wisdom about what makes the organization tick. "We are different on purpose," he explains. "We are a community first and a company second. We want people to feel and behave like citizens of a village, the DaVita Village, and to embrace the rights and responsibilities that come with citizenship. The goal isn't financial performance. The goal is for people to be part of something they are proud of, a sustainable community that becomes an example to others. That means giving people a voice, giving them a vote, giving them skills, not just to be better managers and business leaders, but better people and citizen leaders."

Life at DaVita is filled with symbols, rituals, and traditions that bear little resemblance to life inside conventional organizations. When Thiry took over in 1999, the company was called Total Renal Care, not exactly the warmest identity. After generating a bunch of alternative names, the company put the final choices up to a vote of eight hundred members of the workforce, chosen to express the will of their colleagues in a form of representative democracy. (Two-thirds of the eight-hundred-person electoral college were nurses.) The name DaVita (inspired, it is said, by an Italian phrase that means "gives life") won in a landslide. (The winning name was unveiled at a rally that felt like an election-night victory celebration.) There's an official company song ("On DaVita," to the tune of "On Wisconsin"), and an unofficial company movie (*The Man in the Iron Mask*, in which the Three Musketeers come out of retirement to save France from King Louis XIV). Thiry looks for any and every opportunity to don his Musketeer uniform, brandish his sword, and rally colleagues to conquer a goal or slay a problem.

At the DaVita offices in El Segundo, California, there's a wooden footbridge across which thousands of employees have walked to signify their passage into a new way of working. Many of the company's training programs, organized by DaVita University, include the sort of pomp and circumstance that goes with college life. The wildly spirited Nationwide Meeting, in which thousands of employees celebrate awards, mourn the death of patients, and connect with the emotional side of their work, is something to behold. At the 2008 meeting, Congressman John Lewis, the celebrated veteran of the civil rights movement, seemed genuinely stunned by the intensity of the DaVita faithful. "I have not seen such an enthused and moving audience in Washington, D.C.," he said, "since I came here almost forty-five years ago, when Martin Luther King Jr. stood on the steps of the Lincoln Memorial." The crowd took its enthusiasm to a whole new level.

So the way to deliver outsized business results in a field with huge problems is to promote a strong culture, right? That's not the whole story, argues Thiry: "There's a Buddhist phrase I use a lot, 'One cannot pour from an empty cup.' Dialysis is a grueling job. You can't make a mistake, or the patient dies. About 17 percent of our patients die each year anyway, despite all we do. So we have to make the experience of working here a little easier, a little more fulfilling. If we didn't create an environment where people feel free to sing songs, to laugh, to come to work in funny outfits, all the business strategies and HR practices in the world wouldn't make a difference.

"But we don't work this way because of the business we're in or the people we care for," he continues. "When I explain our ideas, I never play the patient card. I believe this is how *every* organization should work. And I stay away from 'linkage' between how we treat each other and how the business performs. We don't do return-on-investment calculations for this stuff; that's like calculating ROI for having a nicer family. We have flipped the means and the ends. Having an adequately profitable business is the means. Building a real community of human beings is the end."

"ONE FOR ALL AND ALL FOR ONE!"—THE COMPANIES WITH THE STRONGEST *EMOTIONS* WIN

I SUSPECT THAT SOME READERS, as impressed as they may be by the spirit of the DaVita workforce, are dubious about how the company works—its full-throated appeals to community, even democracy, over tough-minded calls for efficiency and profitability. You skeptics are not alone. By virtue of his track record over the past decade, CEO Kent Thiry has been asked to address business schools and executive conferences about how DaVita has performed so well in such a grueling environment. How do traditional leaders react to his company's untraditional priorities and practices?

"My gut tells me that half the audience thinks it's bullshit," he says candidly. "A quarter thinks we're naive. The rest think we're on to something. Those are the people I try to reach. I ask them: How much time did you spend this month checking on your values and creating a greater sense of empathy among your leaders? CEOs are happy to carve out time to check on productivity, R&D, sales. But unless you bring the same rigor to checking on how people treat each other, to refreshing and sustaining the behaviors you claim to value, you never get anywhere."

Truth be told, I was skeptical at first—or at least puzzled by the outsized emotions and larger-than-life rituals at the company. This is an organization whose affinity for call-and-response interaction rivals the level of audience participation at a Bruce Springsteen concert. When the CEO cries, "One for all!" his colleagues cry, "All for one!" When he shouts, "We said!" they shout, "We did!" The graduation proclamation from the DaVita Academy, an intense, two-day program that has trained tens of thousands of frontline employees, will never be confused with HR boilerplate: "By the powers vested in me by generations of dialysis patients, past, present, and future, with serious respect, sincere gratitude, and warm affection, we hereby proclaim you graduates of the DaVita Academy . . ." (CEO Thiry wrote the language himself, a sign of the importance he places on the program.) As I reviewed videos and webcasts of various company events, it dawned on me that I had never seen so many businesspeople shed so many tears in public. This is a company that is not afraid to wear its heart on its sleeve or shout its enthusiasm to the rafters.

It's also a company that's not afraid to insist that its high-ranking executives invest themselves with the same degree of emotional commitment as the nurses and technicians on the front lines. Early on in the turnaround process, Thiry designed a program called "Adopt a Center" in which senior executives (including the CEO himself) would be required to develop a personal connection to a specific dialysis treatment facility—to spend time there, get to know the staff and patients, even do some basic work. When Thiry first told me about the plan, I assumed the idea was for executives to teach rank-and-file employees the basics of the business. This was a company, after all, that was fighting for its life. But that wasn't the idea at all. The goal was for caregivers to teach the executives why the business mattered. This was a company, after all, whose "customers" were literally fighting for their lives.

Later, as DaVita's financial condition stabilized, Thiry raised his expectations for senior executives in a formal program called Reality 101. Every official with the title of vice president or above spends a week on the front lines of a dialysis center, helping to set up and tear down equipment, assisting in basic procedures such as blood-pressure monitoring, and simply experiencing in human terms the highs and lows, the laughter and tears, that everyone experiences in a typical week at one of these remarkable places. One of the great threats to the health of big organizations, he argues, is when executives allow themselves to lose touch with what happens in the trenches, and when people in the trenches come to believe that the people in headquarters don't understand their day-to-day struggles and problems. Reality 101 is one of many DaVita initiatives to maintain and strengthen a sense of empathy, not just between the company's people and its patients, but between the company's high-ranking executives and its frontline staff.

"This whole thing could not have happened if we relied simply on working through the executives," Thiry told me. "The key to the transformation was that the frontline people, who got energized about the notion of a different kind of place to work and be a part of, swept along the executives. Two-thirds of the executives who got 'converted' in this process weren't converted by me, they were converted by the energy and enthusiasm they saw in the centers. They experienced personally and emotionally how hard it is to take care of patients, how responsible you feel when you're operating that equipment and delivering treatment. We had Harvard Business School grads who were scared pantless when they had to actually spend time in the centers. This experience creates a reservoir of empathy that would not otherwise exist. A lot of executives allow their empathy muscles to atrophy. Reality 101 reawakens the empathy muscle."

DaVita CEO Kent Thiry asks: "How much time did you spend this month checking on your values? CEOs are happy to check on productivity, R&D, sales. But unless you bring the same rigor to checking on how people treat each other, you never get anywhere."

In Chapter 4, we highlighted the distinction between business models and mental models and argued that new mental models are what allow blank-sheet-of-paper innovators to transform the sense of what's possible in their industries. But sustaining performance—building an organization that can "run the four-minute mile" and stay the course over the long haul—is as much about cultivating a spirit of grassroots energy, enthusiasm, and engagement as unleashing a set of game-changing ideas. I saw it time and again, from Umpqua Bank in the Pacific Northwest to Magazine Luiza in southern Brazil: companies built around strong opinions are at their best when rank-and-file colleagues share and express strong *emotions.*

In his inspiring and instructive book *Rules of Thumb,* my friend and *Fast Company* cofounder Alan Webber identifies two questions that demand the attention of leaders. The first is familiar: What keeps you up at night? What are the problems that nag at you? The second is less familiar, but even more important: What gets you up in the morning? What keeps you and your people more committed than ever, more engaged than ever, more excited than ever, particularly as the environment around you gets tougher and more demanding than ever?[4]

That's a question every organization needs to ask and answer if it hopes to prosper in an era of hypercompetition and nonstop dislocation. Even the most disruptive and creative leaders recognize that long-term success is not just about thinking differently from other companies. It is also, and perhaps more important, about *caring more* than other companies—about customers, about colleagues, about how the organization conducts itself in a world with endless temptations to cut corners and compromise on values. For leaders, the pressing question isn't just what separates you from the competition in the marketplace. It's also what holds you together in the workplace.

Of course, the best leaders have known this all along. There's a wonderful biography of Vince Lombardi by David Maraniss, the Pulitzer Prize–winning reporter at the *Washington Post.* After the Green Bay Packers captured their first-ever Super Bowl, Maraniss writes, Coach Lombardi, as tough an SOB as there was on the American sporting scene, found himself in high demand as a speaker to executive audiences, who wanted him to translate his principles for victory on the gridiron to success in work and life. (His first business talk, Maraniss notes, was to a big American Management Association conference in New York City, and Lombardi "considered it a seminal moment in his emergence as a public figure known for more than winning football games.") In what became a recurring message to corporate America, he set out seven principles of competition and leadership, most of which you'd expect from the greatest football coach of all time. But his most important principle was also the most surprising: Love is more powerful than hate.

"The love I'm speaking of is loyalty, which is the greatest of loves," Lombardi told his audiences. "Teamwork, the love that one man has for another and that he respects the dignity of another. . . . I am not speaking of detraction. You show me a man who belittles another and I will show you a man who is not a leader. . . . Heart power is the strength of your company. Heart power is the strength of the Green Bay Packers. Heart power is the strength of America and hate power is the weakness of the world."[5]

That spirit of tough love explains why DaVita works the way it does. The demands on the company's workforce are intense and relentless. Its 35,500 employees care for more than 116,000 patients, which means they provide more than 16 *million* treatments per year. That's millions of opportunities to overlook a symptom, misdiagnose a problem, or otherwise make a small mistake that could have deadly consequences. The Stanford case study identified the four "critical factors for success" in the dialysis industry, the first of which was "painstaking attention to operational details." That kind of pressure can bring out the worst in an organization and its people—or, with a strong enough sense of identity and emotional attachment, it can bring out the best in an organization and its people.

> Forget the question, What keeps you up at night? The bigger question is, What gets you up in the morning? What keeps your people more committed than ever, even as the environment gets more demanding than ever?

In *Drive*, Dan Pink tells a story about one of his former bosses, Robert B. Reich, who was secretary of labor under President Clinton. As Reich traveled the country visiting workplaces and searching for high-performance organizations, he administered an informal diagnostic he called "the pronoun test." He'd walk the floors and hallways of factories and offices and pose some simple questions about the company and its culture. "If the answers I get back describe the company in terms like 'they' or 'them,' I know it's one kind of company," Reich explained. "If the answers are put in terms like 'we' or 'us' I know it's a different kind of company." The answers themselves didn't much matter, he concluded. What mattered was whether the organization was a "we" company or a "they" company. At the heart of "we" companies, Reich argued, was a sense of shared ownership and a commitment to shared information. What's also required, I'd argue, is a spirit of shared emotions—an explicit commitment, not just to the well-being of the organization, but to the well-being of one another.[6]

The people at DaVita understand this better than just about any organization I've met. One of the core themes of the company's culture is that "Everything Speaks." That is, even the most trivial issues—what the facilities look like, how colleagues communicate with one another, small gestures of individual kindness or selfishness—send huge signals about the health of the entire organization. Another theme is "No Brag, Just Fact." Thiry and his colleagues are well aware that plenty of companies with toxic workplaces talk a good game about the level of commitment among their people. But the only thing that matters at DaVita are the day-to-day realities of the quality of care it is delivering and the quality of the culture that delivers the care.

"As a leader, you have to be as creative, rigorous, and disciplined about the human side of enterprise as you are about technology or finance," the CEO argues. "This is hard. Unless you figure out, together, how people should behave at work, and create the kind of language and rituals and systems you need to reinforce that behavior, you never get there. At DaVita, we do a lot to remind people that despite the crushing realities of their day-to-day professional lives, we want to treat each other differently. We want to care about each other with the same intensity that we care for our patients."

In his heartfelt book *Love Is the Killer App* (published a few years ago, cleverly enough, on Valentine's Day), Tim Sanders, then chief solutions officer at Yahoo!, made the case that as economic conditions get more turbulent, and corporate rivalries get more fierce, positive emotions get to be a defining element of success. "As the world becomes more competitive," he writes, "we also compete for people's emotions. . . . It's not completely important what people think about you—it is, however, totally important how they feel about you. People are hungry for compassion. And the tougher the times are, the more important it becomes."[7]

Here's one small example of that larger point, a touching story that made me sit up and take notice when I read it in my local newspaper. Boston's legendary Dana-Farber Cancer Institute, where sick kids get some of the best care in the world, was building a new facility on its busy campus. Every morning, in bitter temperatures and biting wind, ironworkers showed up for work and moved the building a little closer to completion. No news there. The news was what was happening before the shift began. "It has become a beloved ritual at Dana-Farber," the *Boston Globe* reported. "Every day, children who come to the clinic write their names on sheets of paper and tape them to the windows of the walkway for ironworkers to see. And, every day, the ironworkers paint the names onto I-beams and hoist them into place as they add floors to the new 14-story Yawkey Center for Cancer Care.

"The building's steel skeleton is now a brightly colored, seven-story monument to scores of children receiving treatment at the clinic—Lia, Alex, and Sam; Taylor, Izzy, and Danny. For the young cancer patients, who press their noses to the glass to watch new names added every day, the steel and spray-paint tribute has given them a few moments of joy and a towering symbol of hope. 'It's fabulous,' said [eighteen-month-old] Kristen [Hoenshell]'s mother, Elizabeth, as she held her daughter and marveled at the rainbow of names. 'It's just a simple little act that means so much.'"

The *Globe* account, understandably, focused on the impact of this daily ritual on the kids and their parents. "They don't have to do this, the guys," Kristen's mother told the newspaper. "They could just do their job . . . and give us a building that we can get treatment at, but they go the extra step and that's huge." But think about the impact on the job. Is there any doubt that these union members worked harder and smarter, that they paid even more attention to quality, because their "simple little act" gave their work a greater sense of meaning? "Everybody saw the kids smiling," foreman Mike Walsh, from Iron-workers Local 7, told the reporter. "And that's what you want to do, keep them smiling."[8]

For these tough-as-nails ironworkers, work had become personal, which meant they devoted themselves to their work with a renewed sense of personal responsibility. That's the difference between new ventures built on a hot product or a cool piece of technology—a foun-dation for success that can evaporate as quickly as it materializes—and those built on both most-of-something ideas and an all-for-one sense of shared commitment. If you want to start from scratch and shake things up, whether as an independent venture or a team or busi-ness unit inside an established organization, how you work will be as decisive as what you think.

Even the most creative leaders recognize that suc-cess is not just about thinking differently. It is also about *caring more*. The question isn't just what separates you from the competition in the mar-ketplace. It's what holds you together in the work-place.

Roy Spence, one of the toughest-minded business thinkers I know, is a cofounder of GSD&M, the legendary advertising agency based in Austin, Texas. In a provocative and saucy book, *It's Not What You Sell, It's What You Stand For*, Spence explains the extreme ideas behind many of the one-of-a-kind organizations he has studied or worked with over the years, from BMW to Whole Foods Market to the U.S. Air Force. Sure, these and other organizations are built around strong opinions, stellar products and services, and (of course) clever advertising. But Spence is adamant that behind every great brand is an authentic sense of purpose—"a definitive statement about the difference you are trying to make in the world"—and a workplace with the "energy and vitality" to bring that purpose to life.[9]

His own firm walks the purpose-driven talk. His coauthor, Haley Rushing, serves as GSD&M's "chief purposologist" and cofounder of its Purpose Institute. Spence and Rushing argue that the virtue of being clear about purpose and identity—what makes your organization different, what difference it is trying to make in its field and in the lives of its employees—is that it creates the strength to resist mimicking the stale ideas and outmoded practices of the competition. "You can look at an opportunity or a challenge," they explain, "and ask yourself, 'Is this the right thing to do given our purpose? Does this further our cause?' If it does, you do it. If it doesn't, you don't. If it's proof to your purpose, embrace it. If it violates your purpose, kick it out on its ass." (I told you the book was saucy.)

In a chapter on the mission and culture at Texas A&M, the huge (forty-eight thousand students), rabidly conservative, steeped-in-tradition university that traces its history to 1871, Spence and Rushing highlight a saying about the school that students have been reciting for decades: "From the outside looking in, you can't understand it. From the inside looking out, you can't explain it." That's a neat way to capture how it feels to change the sense of what's possible in your field—and a reminder of why so few leaders muster the commitment to build an organization with a unique sense of itself. The rituals at Texas A&M include Silver Taps, Muster, Midnight Yell, Fish Camp, and the Aggie Ring—memorable events that define life at the school. "The unique culture you encounter when you step foot in 'Aggieland,'" argue Spence and Rushing, "is like nothing you'll experience on any other college campus."

It sounds a lot like life among the warmhearted, patient-obsessed nurses and social workers at DaVita—and among the gadget-crazed propeller-heads at Geek Squad, the young, largely male, tech-support specialists who travel to your home or office, or help you in a Best Buy store, with a troublesome computer, mobile phone, home-theater system, or other device. There's no denying that the Geek Squad has a distinctive style of working. The company's field agents wear a bizarre and recognizable uniform: white short-sleeve dress shirts, black clip-on ties, black pants, white socks, and black shoes (with the Geek Squad logo in the sole). They drive to client locations in identical cars: black-and-white VW Beetles with the Geek Squad logo on the door. And their job titles speak for themselves. Robert Stephens, the company's outspoken founder, is called the chief inspector. His rank-and-file colleagues are "special agents." Geeks who work inside the stores are "counterintelligence agents."

There's also no denying the Geek Squad's growth. Stephens started the company in 1994, when he was a college student. Best Buy acquired it back in 2002, when it had sixty employees and annual revenues of $3 million. Today, still under the founder's leadership, the Geek Squad employs more than fifteen thousand agents, generates more than $1 billion in annual revenue, and is a crucial part of Best Buy's strategy to provide high-touch service as well as high-tech gadgets.

Still, when I sat down with Robert Stephens at Best Buy headquarters, outside of Minneapolis, I was not prepared for how savvy and tough-minded he is about the right way for colleagues to work together and for frontline employees to deliver unforgettable service. I wanted to talk about how a young entrepreneur could shake things up inside a giant company like Best Buy. He wanted to talk about the discipline it takes for young Geeks to deliver great results inside the homes of confused and frustrated customers.

Just like at DaVita or Texas A&M, Stephens is a big believer in ritual, tradition, and cultural indoctrination. There is, for example, the matter of the uniform. "It's a litmus test for some people," Stephens told me. "They say, 'I'm not wearing that!' In which case we know they're not ready to sign on." The uniform is also a symbol of well, uniformity. It reinforces the message that there are consistent ways in which the fifteen-thousand-plus Geeks are expected to behave with customers and among themselves. "Wearing a tie used to be a sign of conformity," says Stephens. "Now it's like an act of rebellion—nobody dresses up anymore. The uniforms are visible and distinct. Plus, he jokes, "those ties let me apply a little pressure around the neck!"

To emphasize his point, the chief inspector hands me a copy of *The Little Orange Book*, a truly remarkable guide to great service (produced by the squad's so-called Ministry of Propaganda) that Stephens intends as a bible of sorts for how Geeks do their work. Here's the six-point pledge that every Geek is expected to sign: "I will: 1. Never violate the trust of my clients or disrespect their property. 2. Never say, 'I don't know.' Instead, say, 'I'll find out.' 3. Always understand that my clients' time is more valuable than my own. 4. Assume every problem is my fault, unless proven otherwise. 5. Consider my job done only when my client is completely overwhelmed with joy. And instead of assuming they're happy, I'll ask them. 6. Keep every promise I make. Including this one."

Lofty goals, which Geeks are expected to fulfill with great attention to detail. It is official policy that employees drive their Geek-mobiles at five miles per hour below the speed limit. They are also expected to arrive for appointments five minutes before the designated time and offer to take off their shoes before entering the client's home. And don't even think about pocket protectors! Geeks are forbidden to put anything—pens, eyeglasses, screwdrivers—in the pocket of their white shirt. If it all seems a touch fanatical, well, maybe that's what it takes to do something remarkable. And that's the ultimate goal for Robert Stephens, who also likes to say that "marketing is a tax you pay for being unremarkable."

Tony Hsieh of Zappos makes much the same argument about his business, which may be why he spends so little time or money on traditional marketing. His company initially championed its over-the-top performance for customers as a matter of strategy, a way to avoid being pigeonholed as an online shoe retailer. Sure, Zappos started out selling footwear. But if it developed a reputation for killer service and a fun-loving personality, the CEO reasoned, it would be easier to expand into new categories, from fashion to cosmetics to housewares (all of which it has done). "Then a funny thing happened that we didn't expect," Hsieh goes on. "When people saw they were working on something beyond profits, or being the biggest retailer in a certain category, when they were working on something that meant something to them, they became much more engaged. There's a difference between motivation and inspiration. You can accomplish stuff by motivating employees. But you can accomplish much more by inspiring people around a vision with meaning to them and that you're passionate about."

If you want evidence of the rank-and-file sense of mission at Hsieh's organization, thumb through an eight-hundred-page tome called the *Zappos Culture Book*. Every year, the CEO invites his employees to contribute a riff, rant, or serious essay that captures what it feels like to work at the company. He promises that Zappos will publish the responses verbatim, other than corrections for spelling and typos, and share them with job candidates, suppliers, business partners, and customers. He also gathers lots of candid workplace photos and groups them under headings such as, "What would Zappos look like if we were all 10 feet tall?" and "How does Zappos freak its freak?" and "How much do Zapponians care about hair?"

The book, filled with heartfelt tributes, earnest poetry, and bizarre entries of all sorts, is a strange and wonderful window into what makes the company and its people tick, and their deep sense of engagement with both their work and their colleagues. In the 2008 edition, Abbie M., from the customer-loyalty department, writes about the death of her sister, and how her Zappos colleagues "never stopped calling, never stopped emailing, sent flowers and cards, gave hugs and just plain listened to me." Michelle S., from human resources, praises "real friends and intimate friendships. Gossip. Conversations using random slang and swearing. Casual dress taken to the extreme. Changing change with more change." (I know what you're thinking: Where do *we* find HR people like that?) Jimmy A. from finance says simply, "Zappos culture is the confluence of genius and insanity."

One reason Zapponians work with such a sense of camaraderie and shared identity is that the company makes it easy for new recruits to leave if the Zappos way of working is not for them. It's a demanding job, answering phones and solving customer problems for hours at a time, and doing it with a sense of humor and style. And it doesn't pay all that well (about $11 an hour for newcomers). So when Zappos hires employees, it provides a four-week training period that immerses them in the company's strategy, values, and obsession with customers. During those four weeks, it is impossible not to understand what a career at Zappos will feel like: the expectations, the intensity, the commitment.

A week into the crash course, it's time for "The Offer." This hard-charging company, which works diligently to recruit highly qualified people, says to its new hires: "If you quit today, we will pay you for the amount of time you've worked, plus we will pay a $2,000 bonus." *Zappos actually bribes new employees to leave!* Why? Because if you're willing to take The Offer, you obviously don't have the sense of commitment the organization needs. There is a hard-to-fake energy, a kind of zealotry, about the Zappos culture, which means, by definition, it's not for everybody. So Zappos wants to learn if there's a bad fit between what makes the organization tick and what makes individual employees tick, and it's willing to pay to learn sooner rather than later. (The Offer stands for the duration of the training period.)

> **Why does Zappos pay recruits $2,000 to quit? Because there is a kind of zealotry about the Zappos culture, which means it's not for everybody. Zappos wants to learn if there's a bad fit between what makes the organization tick and what makes employees tick.**

Indeed, Tony Hsieh and his colleagues keep raising the size of the quit-now bonus, to encourage more recruits to opt out. (Fewer than 3 percent of new employees choose to leave.) It started at $100, went to $500, then $1,000, and may go higher than $2,000 as the company gets bigger. But the ultimate value of this unusual practice, Hsieh argues, is the message it sends to people who stay. "The biggest benefit," he says, "is not that it sorts out people who don't believe in the long-term vision of what Zappos stands for, although that is important. The biggest benefit comes from all the people who decide not to take the offer. Those people had to go home, think about whether this was a company they were prepared to commit to, talk about it with their family and friends. They wind up more engaged than they would have been if we had not offered the chance to leave."

"COMPANIES AND THE CUSTOMERS WHO HATE THEM"— FROM ENRAGEMENT TO ENGAGEMENT

A FEW YEARS BACK, THE *Harvard Business Review* published one of the most quietly subversive management essays I've read in a long time. One of its big-name authors was Gail McGovern, who had served as executive vice president of AT&T (where she ran the $26-billion residential long-distance unit) and president of Fidelity Personal Investments, which had four million customers and managed $500 billion worth of assets. At the time the essay appeared, she was a professor at the Harvard Business School, and she has since gone on to become president and CEO of the American Red Cross. The second author was Harvard Business School professor Youngme Moon, whose work I discussed in Chapter 4.

Those are some serious establishment credentials, which is what made the essay's antiestablishment argument so arresting: two bright lights of Big Business were shining a spotlight on the dark side of how so many businesses operate. "One of the most influential propositions in marketing," McGovern and Moon wrote, "is that customer satisfaction begets loyalty, and loyalty begets profits. Why, then, do so many companies infuriate their customers by binding them with contracts, bleeding them with fees, confounding them with fine print, and otherwise penalizing them for their business? Because, unfortunately, it pays. Companies have found that confused and ill-informed customers, who often end up making poor purchasing decisions, can be highly profitable indeed." That's some pretty tough stuff from a pretty important executive.[10]

Thus far, our take on the link between emotion and innovation has focused on the positive, from the culture of caring and community at DaVita to the spirit of fun and games at Zappos. Yet much of business—*most* of business, I suppose—is infused by the negative. "Heart power" may be what fuels championship teams, as Vince Lombardi set forth more than forty years ago, and love may be the "killer app," as Tim Sanders argued more recently, but there's a reason the essay by Gail McGovern and Youngme Moon was titled, "Companies and the Customers Who Hate Them." It's one emotion, sad to say, that's always in plentiful supply. Think of it as terms of enragement. Companies continue to behave in ways that drive their customers crazy: outlandish baggage fees from airlines, rigged overdraft charges from banks, impossible-to-understand contracts from rental-car companies, countless other indignities both large and small, substantial and trivial.

Indeed, *HBR's* unsparing review of financial results in a range of industries (retail banking, cell-phone service, credit cards) demonstrated how so many companies depend on their most dissatisfied customers for so much of their profits. That is, they make their best money from customers whose decisions *are the least good for them.* The essay challenged executives to answer four questions that define worst (albeit common) practices, and to reckon with the implications of their answers: "Are our most profitable customers those who have the most reason to be dissatisfied with us? Do we have rules we want customers to break because doing so generates profits? Do we make it difficult for customers to understand or abide by our rules, and do we actually help customers break them? Do we depend on contracts to prevent customers from defecting?" A remarkably large number of organizations, McGovern and Moon fretted, if they told the truth, would respond yes to some or all of those questions.

As provocative as it was, the *HBR* essay wasn't meant to be an attack on big companies. It was an earnest appeal by a big-company executive to save her colleagues from themselves. Gaming the system, McGovern and Moon warned, was an open invitation for blank-sheet-of-paper newcomers to right wrongs and change the game. "Businesses that prey on customers are perpetually vulnerable to their pent-up hostility," they wrote. "Sometimes all it takes to drive mass defection is the appearance of a customer-friendly competitor."

Well, that's not *all* it takes. The warning by McGovern and Moon certainly helps to explain the luxurious rise of Lexus, the pop-star popularity of 37signals, and the transformation of DaVita from basket case to best-of-breed case study. But the success of these and other game changers isn't just about providing better terms and conditions to customers. It is also, and primarily, about crafting stronger terms of engagement *with* customers. That's the real promise of start-from-scratch innovation, whether by a hungry start-up or a longtime in-cumbent. The most enduring source of advantage, the most effective way to become the most of something, is for emotionally charged em-ployees to capture the imagination of emotionally drained customers. Even in fields desperate for reform—simpler prices, fewer gimmicks—the opportunity to shake things up is as much about how you behave as what you offer. The late Arnold Glasow, an old-school business humorist who devoted himself to helping companies connect more deeply with their customers, put it eloquently years ago. "Nothing splendid was ever created in cold blood," he wrote. "Every great ac-complishment is the story of a flaming heart."[11]

The emergence of Life Time Fitness, a fast-growing company in a perpetually troubled industry, is a perfect illustration of the tough-minded message from Gail McGovern and Youngme Moon to the establishment—and of Arnold Glasow's big-hearted invitation to in-novators. In a field notorious for bait-and-switch pricing, punitive contracts, shoddy service, and occasional trips to bankruptcy court by some of its biggest players, Life Time Fitness unveiled an agenda to shake up (and shape up) the competition. Its founder, industry veteran Bahram Akradi, who got his start as a nineteen-year-old en-try-level employee doing menial tasks in an old-school health club, promised to eliminate the worst business practices—those that en-raged customers—and to design facilities that would dazzle with their vast size, wide offerings, elegant style, and member-centric policies. Indeed, McGovern's essay cites his company as a newcomer prepared "to challenge the industry's bad behavior."

Under the Life Time Fitness model, customers pay modest up-front fees (with a full money-back guarantee) and don't sign long-term contracts. Instead, memberships run on a month-to-month basis ($50–$100 per month for an individual, $100–$150 for a family) and can be canceled for any reason at any time—no penalties, forfeited de-posits, or hidden charges. In return, the company builds huge (more than 100,000 square feet) all-in-one clubs that are to exercise what Disneyland is to entertainment or The Home Depot is to renovation—an endless source of options, choices, and stimulation. The clubs feature indoor and outdoor pools, basketball courts, yoga studios, racquetball and squash courts, rock-climbing walls, hundreds of pieces of cardio and resistance-training equipment, cafés, spas—resortlike facilities that are open seven days a week, twenty-four hours a day, 364 and a half days per year. (Only Scrooge exercises on Christmas morning, it seems.)

> The most enduring source of competitive advantage is for emotionally charged employees to capture the imagination of emotionally drained customers. The opportunity to shake things up is as much about how you behave as what you offer.

It's a newfangled strategy for a workout company—and a strategy that has worked out big in the market. As of mid-2010, Life Time Fitness had seventeen thousand employees, roughly a million adult members, annual revenues of $770 million, and a stock-market value of more than $1.5 billion. The typical club (there are more than eighty in eighteen states) has 25 trainers and dietitians, 250 total employees, and gets nearly 70,000 visits per month. The no-contract, cancel-at-any-time strategy has its perils. In 2008, as the economy melted down, consumers got more interested in shaping up their wallets than their waistlines, so Life Time Fitness throttled back its hypercharged expansion plans. Still, the company as a whole got fifty million member visits that year, up from forty-two million in 2007. Meanwhile, Bally Total Fitness, one of the well-known, mass-market giants in the field, filed for bankruptcy protection in both 2007 and 2008, and Crunch, a high-end brand with clubs in Manhattan, Los Angeles, Miami, and other urban centers, filed for bankruptcy in 2009.

"The 'standard' business model was to charge a huge up-front fee, lock people in with long-term contracts, and sell as many memberships as you could as quickly as you could," explains founder and CEO Akradi, whom I visited at company headquarters in Chanhassen, Minnesota, west of Minneapolis. (Akradi himself is a fitness fanatic and leads famously intense spinning classes for members.) "Almost everything we looked at in terms of how this industry did business was designed from the club's point of view: What's good for me, not what's good for you. We were treating customers the wrong way, selling memberships the wrong way, serving members the wrong way—and yet people kept coming back!

"So we asked, 'What would this industry be like if we did things the right way?'" he continues. "What would a club look like if members designed it? What would the membership offer look like if the customer wrote it? What would the hours of operation be if customers set them? *What if we let customers dictate how we did things?* That's why we did away with contracts. A contract makes you fat and lazy. We have to win over every one of our customers every month. It forces us to keep getting better."

Importantly, though, Akradi's long-term goal is not just to rewrite terms and conditions in his business. It is to write new terms of engagement with his customers. "If we think of ourselves as a health-club company, the opportunities are limited," he says. "If we think of ourselves as a *healthy-way-of-life* company, the opportunities are endless. We don't build 'gyms'—dreary places where people try to escape from their ailments or postpone old age. We build destinations that make exercise and nutrition fun, positive, and bright. There's a rational side: Am I losing weight, am I feeling better? But there's an emotional side too: Am I surrounded by people who are trying to help me, is this a place I *want* to be, not just where I *should* be?"

That's why the company emphasizes the creation of "clubs within a club"—highly tailored training opportunities, workout routines, discussion groups, public events, and social networking for customers with all-consuming interests in activities such as distance running, triathlons, or cycling. Overall, Life Time Fitness is pretty fanatical about the power of combining "virtual" communities of interest outside the walls of its clubs with the physical activities and exercises that take place within the clubs. Tens of thousands of customers routinely interact with trainers and their fellow members even when they're not at the facilities.

"The old way to run this business was to sign up as many members as possible, get them on long-term contracts, and then hope that a lot of them didn't show up very much," says Jeffrey Zwiefel, executive vice president of operations. "Because if they did show up, you wouldn't have room for them. Our logic is the complete opposite of that. If we see that one of our members hasn't been by in a month or two, that doesn't make us happy: 'They're paying us but not using the facility.' It makes us nervous, so we'll reach out to that member and ask them to come in. We *want* high rates of utilization. We have to win over our customers every month, which means we want them engaged, certainly when they're here, but even when they're not here."

One ultrapopular case in point is Life Time Ultimate Hoops (slogan: Oncourt. Online. 24/7). The company organizes after-work basketball leagues as if they were the run-up to the NBA playoffs or "March Madness" for the NCAA. The company has a polished, colorful website that posts schedules, standings, box scores, individual player rankings, action shots, even Twitter-fueled trash talk. Sure, the pick-and-rolls happen on the hardwood. But there seems to be as much action off the court as on the court.

Meanwhile, rank-and-file employees write "personal mission statements" to be sure that what pumps them up is in sync with how the organization is trying to pump up customers. "Our people must understand why we do what we do, and what we are trying to do in the world," says Jess Elmquist, who runs Life Time University, which plays a big role in selecting, educating, and certifying the fast-growing staff. "We are a 'missional' company, and our people have to be wrapped around that mission. It shapes who we hire, how we train, whom we promote. We have a zero-tolerance policy when it comes to casting the wrong people."

The ultimate goal is to achieve what company executives like to call "operating to artistry"—a blend of well-chosen offerings, high-energy spaces, and thoroughly engaged staffers meant to transform long-standing terms of enragement into deeply felt terms of engagement. Indeed, the open-to-the-public Life Time Fitness club next door to headquarters is called the Artistry Center. It's where the company experiments with new equipment, programs, colors, foods, music—all the strands of the multifaceted experience it is trying to create and the attachments it is trying to strengthen.

Why call this large and busy facility the Artistry Center as opposed to, say, the R&D Center? "We are 'scientific' about what we do," replies the founder and CEO. "But when you are dealing every day with tens of thousands of employees and hundreds of thousands of members, you really are dealing with human emotions. We are trying to bring lots of different elements into a kind of harmonious execution, like a symphony or a sculpture, and that's as much about art as it is about science."

"THE PATH TO SAMENESS IS THE PATH TO DEATH"— COMPANIES AND THE CUSTOMERS WHO CAN'T LIVE WITHOUT THEM

THE SOCIAL SCIENTISTS AT GALLUP Inc., the world-renowned polling and research firm, spend most of their time crunching numbers as opposed to dwelling on symphony or sculpture. But they would no doubt endorse Bahram Akradi's enthusiasm for "operating to artistry" inside his business, because they understand where value comes from in a turbulent business environment. A Gallup team spent years analyzing data from nearly two thousand business units at ten different companies, in fields such as financial services, professional services, and retail. Their goal was to identify what factors explained loyalty, repeat purchases, willingness to select premium services—the positive, value-creating behaviors that companies hope to see in their customers. The critical variable, researchers found, was neither the lowest price nor the highest quality, but the depth and consistency of the human interactions between a company and its customers. "It's important not to think like an economist or an engineer when you're assessing the employee-customer interaction," the study noted. "Emotions, it turns out, inform both sides' judgments and behavior even more powerfully than rationality does."

Intriguingly, the analysis found only small differences in behavior between customers who were "rationally satisfied" with their experience on the one hand and those who were "rationally dissatisfied" on the other. The big differences were between customers who were "rationally satisfied" and those who were "emotionally engaged" with the company and its people. The researchers actually created a hierarchy of engagement to describe the strength of these emotional and psychological ties. The first level is *confidence*: "Does this company always deliver on its promises?" The second level is *integrity*: "Does this company treat me the way I deserve to be treated?" The third level is *pride*: "Do I have a sense of positive identification with the company?" The fourth and highest level is *passion*: "Is the company irreplaceable in my life and a perfect fit for me?"[12]

Indeed, when Gallup staffers conduct research on behalf of a client (let's call it Company X), they make it a point to ask customers this make-or-break question: "Could you imagine a world without Company X?" Talk about a high-stakes test! It's a lofty goal to imagine that customers would say no, that a company is irreplaceable in their lives, but organizations that aim to change the game in their field aim to achieve that level of engagement in the market. After all, in every industry you can name, there are so many brands, so many choices, so many claims, *so much clutter*, that the central challenge for any company is to rise above the fray. Put simply, if your customers *can* live without you, eventually they *will* live without you. "Truly passionate customers are relatively rare," the study concludes. "They are customers for life, and they are worth their weight in gold."

How many companies can you name that would pass the Gallup test? Apple leaps to mind, what with tens of millions of gadget enthusiasts hooked on its people-friendly technology and convention-tweaking attitude. Lexus makes the grade as well. Its commitment to designing not just impressive cars, but an immersive ownership experience (borrowing, in part, from Apple's genius), has produced a highly engaged and fiercely loyal customer base, luxury enthusiasts who could not imagine sitting behind the wheel of another brand, even with all its high-profile problems and headlines. Those are the obvious answers. For a less obvious (but no less instructive) answer, I traveled to western Canada to spend time with a company that is virtually invisible outside the markets in which it does business, yet utterly indispensable inside those markets. It is, quite simply, one of the most unusual retailers I've ever encountered—a start-from-scratch innovator that depends for its growth and success on a level of engagement in the lives of its customers that is without peer.

> In every industry, there are so many brands, so many choices, so much clutter, that the challenge is to rise above the fray. Put simply, if your customers can live without you, eventually they will.

The moment I stepped foot in London Drugs in Richmond, British Columbia, a fast-growing city south of Vancouver, I understood that this was not some middle-of-the-road retail outfit. Sure, there was an ultramodern pharmacy, with handsomely appointed private areas for one-on-one consultations, and the typical small-ticket items you find in Walgreens or CVS: snacks, batteries, greeting cards, tchotchkes of all kinds. At the same time, the store offered a dazzling array of computers, consumer electronics, and home-entertainment equipment—products that were selling for thousands (even tens of thousands) of dollars and whose quality and sophistication were plain to see. The photography department stocked high-end cameras that even the most talented professionals would be happy to use, as well as fine art paper that cost $110 for twenty sheets. There were plush leather chairs, private-label tables, and bedroom sets, loads of small appliances. The store also featured a gorgeous and extensive collection of high-end cosmetics, including perfumes that sold for hundreds of dollars an ounce, and a beautifully designed day spa, where women were enjoying facials, massage, and other break-from-the-routine indulgences.

But that was just the start of my long walk through many aisles. Need to mail a letter or ship a package? The store includes a branch of the Canadian postal system. Worried about the health of your dog or a risk to your family vacation? You can buy pet or travel insurance. In a hurry to pay a speeding ticket? You can do that here. Planning a walk *down* the aisle? You can get a marriage license at London Drugs! Put simply, this store, one of two in Richmond, and one of seventy-two (and counting) the company operates in Canada's four western provinces, offers a collection of goods and services, products and price points, big-ticket items and little necessities, that defy easy description or neat categorization. London Drugs is a company that has become the most of something in its field by figuring out how to offer something for everyone in its market, a company that attracts customers for life because it has worked its way so deeply into the lives of its customers.

"You mean not every 'drugstore' sells marriage licenses?" cracks the tireless and infectiously upbeat G. W. (Wynne) Powell, the CEO of London Drugs. "We're one of the most popular places in Vancouver to get a marriage license! First of all, we're convenient—govern-

ment offices aren't open at 9:30 at night. Second of all, this is the
ultimate feel-good moment, deciding to get married, so why stand in
front of a bureaucrat to get the application? Plus, maybe you need a
new camera to celebrate the decision—try getting that at City Hall!
It's really not that crazy when you think about it."

It may not sound crazy to Wynne Powell, but when's the last time
you went to the same store for prescription antibiotics, a fifty-two-inch
high-definition TV, insurance for your cat, and a marriage license?
"The collection of products and services we offer may not make sense
to outsiders who see us for the first time, but it makes perfect sense
to our customers," he replies. "People say we have a 'cult-like status'
in our markets. I prefer to think of it as the 'magic' of London Drugs.
We do millions of pharmacy transactions a year. Under the Canadian drug-price-control system, profitability comes from professional
dispensing fees rather than markups on the drugs. But the pharmacy
is where everything starts, it's the heart of our business. We are more
concerned with being part of people's lives than with maximizing
each transaction. Our brand is about a lifetime commitment to customers. If they trust us with their health, they'll trust us with their
computer, home entertainment, and other parts of their lives."

Even, it turns out, with where they live. In recent years, as the
economy in western Canada boomed and real-estate costs soared,
London Drugs had to get more creative about how and where it
opens stores in urban neighborhoods. One solution has been to develop condominium complexes around their new outlets. A London
Drugs store in Kerrisdale Village, a section of downtown Vancouver
north of the airport, was part of a $45-million complex with sixty large
condos. An even bigger store at Broadway and Vine, due north from
Kerrisdale, was part of a $55-million development that featured 133
condos—nearly all of which were sold before the place opened.

"We build these condos as though we'd live in them ourselves,
and our customers trust us on that," Powell says. "We do all the wireless networks and home electronics, so the systems are impeccable.

And the fact that there's a London Drugs as part of the complex is also a big selling point. I've had customers tell me, 'I bought this condo because the store is right underneath me.' It's quite a revelation when you think about it."

Actually, it's downright bizarre—sophisticated city dwellers eager to buy condos because a *drugstore* is building them! That kind of drawing power speaks to the power of the company's brand, and to the depth of its engagement with customers. London Drugs started in 1945, as a game-changing newcomer that offered discount prices, extended hours, and a colorful way of doing business thanks to its founder, Sam Bass. (The company is now a unit of the HY Louie Group, a highly regarded, family-owned operation that is more than 105 years old.) Over the years, as it opened locations in and around British Columbia, the organization (with eighty-four hundred employees and estimated sales well above C$1 billion) has faced calls to get much bigger much faster—to extend its footprint across the whole of Canada. Instead, it has chosen to go deeper into familiar geographies and markets, to offer its already-fanatical customers an ever-greater array of products and services, thus playing an ever-larger role in their lives.[13]

Kenneth B. Wong is a high-profile professor of marketing at Queen's University and a longtime student of the company. "If you look at the business textbooks," he argues matter-of-factly, "London Drugs should not exist. They violate the cardinal rule that you must be a luxury brand or a bargain-basement brand. Within the stores, they run each department exactly the way it is supposed to be run. Where they are selling superexpensive cameras, they operate the department like an upscale boutique with a smart and knowledgeable staff. Where they are selling liquidation goods, a dollar-store environment, you won't find an employee in sight.

"The way it holds together," he continues, "the reason it coheres, is that customers believe no matter what they are buying, whether it costs thousands of dollars or ninety-nine cents, they are getting tremendous value from an organization they trust. You can't think of London Drugs as just a physical entity. It's a state of mind, a unique approach to doing business."

That state of mind, that unique approach to doing business with customers, translates into uniquely rewarding behavior *from* customers. Analysts estimate that 80 percent of the population of British Columbia shops at London Drugs on a regular basis—*80 percent!*—and that the lifetime value of these shoppers, in terms of total sales, is something like C$400,000 each. That's what it means to be irreplaceable, and that's why this independent, homegrown organization, which should be wilting under competitive pressure from global juggernauts such as Walmart and Best Buy, has been downright unbeatable. Indeed, unlike many independent retailers, London Drugs does not shy away from locating its stores in the shadow of the global giants. "We love to be close to our competition," says CEO Powell. "Everybody sees how different we are." (By the way, analysts also estimate that sales-per-square-foot at London Drugs, a common gauge of retail productivity, are *four times* the comparable figure at Walmart.)

"There's no hubris there," argues Wong. "They don't fool themselves into thinking they are any better than they are. They understand that London Drugs is a legendary brand in British Columbia. They also understand that when they move into a new region, the brand means nothing. So they move in with one store, establish a reputation, and go from there. That's a lot different from, say, Starbucks, which presumed that a model that worked in Seattle was going to work everywhere else. At London Drugs, there is no one uniform model they're going to use everywhere."

The company has expanded eastward, into Alberta, Saskatchewan, and Manitoba, but slowly, methodically, and only after the clamor in a neighboring province is too loud to ignore. When the company opened its first location in Winnipeg, its debut presence in Manitoba, more than a thousand shoppers lined up to welcome the new store—a *drugstore*, remember. Before venturing into Winnipeg,

London Drugs considered bypassing Saskatchewan, the province between Alberta and Manitoba. Saskatchewan is small, poor, rural, with
a history of left-wing politics—not exactly a prescription for retail success. But that sort of strategic move, the right move, perhaps from the
perspective of short-term economics, was the wrong move for long-
term engagement.

"It would have been very rude to 'skip over' a province as we moved
to the east," Powell says. "It would have sent the wrong message about
who we are and how we feel about our customers. As it turns out, our
locations in Saskatchewan have the highest per-store sales growth of
any of our stores anywhere, double-digit growth in difficult times. We
did what we believed was the right thing to do, rather than what pure
economics might have told us to do—and that was the proper call. We
don't think the same as a lot of other retailers. The path to sameness
is the path to death."

CHAPTER SIX

RADICALLY PRACTICAL (II)— FIVE NEW RULES FOR STARTING SOMETHING NEW

WHAT'S THE DIFFERENCE BETWEEN innovators who dare to start something new and managers who are content to improve what already exists? This simple question is at the heart of every strategy, technique, and case study presented in the last two chapters. Whether, as with classic start-ups such as Zappos or Life Time Fitness, the opportunity was to establish a new company around blank-sheet-of-paper ideas, or, as with the reinvention of MGM Grand and DaVita, the challenge was to unleash blank-sheet-of-paper innovation inside an established company, I've tried to describe and make sense of what it takes to change the game in fields defined by too many competitors chasing too few customers with products and service that look too much alike. Which, by the way, defines pretty much *every* field.

A similar question is at the heart of some truly original research by Professor Saras D. Sarasvathy, who teaches entrepreneurship at the Darden Graduate School of Business at the University of Virginia. It's been a long time since I've encountered academic work as fresh, relevant, and compelling as what Sarasvathy has produced, in a meticulously argued book and a collection of essays and white papers, one of which features the pithy title, "What Makes Entrepreneurs Entrepreneurial?" Her research explores whether there is such a thing as "entrepreneurial thinking"—and whether it differs in important ways from how MBAs and traditional executives size up problems and identify opportunities.[1]

The answer, Sarasvathy concludes, is an emphatic yes, and the differences boil down to the "causal" reasoning used by traditional managers versus the "effectual" reasoning used by entrepreneurs. Causal reasoning "begins with a predetermined goal and a given set of means, and seeks to identify the optimal—fastest, cheapest, most efficient, etc.—alternative to achieve that goal." This is the world of exhaustive (and exhausting) business plans, finely tuned ROI calculations, and portfolio diversification. Effectual reasoning, on the other hand, "does not begin with a specific goal. Instead, it begins with a given set of means and allows goals to emerge contingently over time from the varied imagination and diverse aspirations of the founders and the people they interact with." This is the world of nonstop experimentation, rapid prototyping, guerrilla marketing, and leaps of faith.

But the real difference between traditional executives and game-changing entrepreneurs, Sarasvathy argues, boils down to a different take on the future. "Causal reasoning is based on the logic, To the extent that we can predict the future, we can control it," she writes. That's why big companies spend so much time on focus groups, market research, and statistical models—the endless analysis that encourages decision-making paralysis. Effectual reasoning, on the other hand, "is based on the logic, To the extent that we can control the future, we do not need to predict it."

How do you control the future? *By inventing it yourself.* That is, by doing more with less, by reacting quickly to setbacks and surprises rather than agonizing over how to avoid them, and by never losing sight of why you got started in the first place—the impact you aim to have in your field and in the world. So whether you aspire to shake up your industry with an independent start-up or shake up your company with an internal venture, here are five new rules for starting something new.

I. IT'S NOT GOOD ENOUGH TO BE "PRETTY GOOD" AT EVERYTHING. BLANK-SHEET-OF-PAPER INNOVATORS FIGURE OUT HOW TO BECOME THE MOST OF SOMETHING.

MOST TRADITIONAL THINKING ABOUT STRATEGY and competition emphasizes the intricacies of money, power, and business models. But the start-from-scratch innovators featured in the last two chapters have prospered based on the audacity of their *mental* models. Robert MacDonald, the one-of-a-kind insurance entrepreneur, says that starting something new is a matter of "reminiscing about the future." Ray Davis, the customer-obsessed CEO of Umpqua Bank, argues that the real work of leadership is to "find the revolution before it finds you"—that is, to be the driving force for transformation in your field, rather than a lagging indicator.

In *Rework*, a concise book that describes their expansive worldview with respect to competition and innovation, the founders of 37signals, the self-declared "enemies of mediocrity," urge their fellow entrepreneurs to "ignore the real world" as the first step to success. "The real world sounds like an awfully depressing place to live," they argue. "It's a place where new ideas, unfamiliar approaches, and foreign concepts *always* lose. The only things that win are what people already know and do, even if those things are flawed and inefficient." Their company, the founders go on, has prospered because it "fails the real-world test" in so many ways—from devising ultrasimple products in a market ruled by complexity, to attracting millions of customers without salespeople or advertising. "The real world isn't a place, it's an excuse," they conclude. "It's a justification for not trying."[2]

Michael O'Leary and his colleagues at Ryanair are more than willing to try new ideas, unfamiliar approaches, and foreign concepts—in an industry where the "real world" truly is a depressing place. A few years ago, when the company ordered new planes, it insisted that they come without window shades, seat pockets, or reclining seats—the easier to clean them and reduce turnaround times. In 2009, it announced plans to eliminate airport check-in counters, mandating that all customers use its website. That same year, in an interview that literally made readers squirm, CEO O'Leary disclosed that he has contemplated installing coin slots in bathroom doors and charging customers to use the facilities. The reasoning: if fewer passengers used the toilet, he could order planes with fewer bathrooms and more seats—thus increasing headcount and per-flight revenues. In the same spirit, O'Leary has talked with regulators and aircraft makers about planes that would allow passengers to sit on "bar stools" with seat belts, another way to sell more tickets on each flight.

It sounds crazy, and compared with standard operating procedure it is. But it's been crazy enough to work. The company's fares keep going down (a one-way average of $56 in 2009) and demand for its services keeps going up. For a decade, passenger traffic has grown at an average annual rate of more than 15 percent, and Ryanair now carries more passengers than any other airline in Europe. The challenger has become the champion. "O'Leary's airline has broadened the horizons of millions of people," London's *Guardian* newspaper concluded. "It is Ryanair which ferries Poland's carpenters and plumbers to seek work in London. It is Ryanair which made Essex accents commonplace on the promenade at St. Tropez. It is Ryanair's cheap flights which made it affordable for Britain's' chattering classes to snap up second homes in the Loire valley, Burgundy and Provence."[3]

It's hard to overcome the pull of conventional wisdom—established ways of doing things, familiar ways to size up markets. That's why it's hard to overstate the impact of blank-sheet-of-paper innovation, and why longtime incumbents find it so hard to muster a strategic alternative. The real promise of starting something new is not merely to improve on what exists. It is to transform what's possible.

2. JUST BECAUSE YOU'RE "THE MOST OF SOMETHING" DOESN'T MEAN YOU CAN'T DO LOTS OF DIFFERENT THINGS. BEING UNIQUE IS NOT ABOUT BEING NARROW.

TONY HSIEH, THE HIGH-PROFILE CEO of Zappos .com, understands that his fast-growing company is revered among shoe lovers for the vast array of footwear it offers, and that its owes much of its success to its mastery of this one product category. But he is adamant that as a brand and as a culture, Zappos is not primarily about selling good shoes—it is about delivering great service, a most-of-something commitment that can take the organization into all sorts of related (and unrelated) categories without diluting what makes it distinctive. Already, Zappos offers clothing, bags, and other fashion accessories, plus housewares and skin care, and Hsieh is reluctant to rule out expanding into all sorts of new fields.

"Most people know us for footwear," he explains. "But internally we think of our company pretty differently. We want the Zappos brand to be about the very best customer service and customer experience. Our hope is that ten years from now, people won't even realize that we started out selling shoes online, they'll just think of us as standing for the best possible service. We've had customers e-mail us and ask, 'Will you please take over the IRS or start an airline?' We won't do that this year or next, but thirty years from now? I wouldn't rule out a Zappos airline."

Hsieh is joking about starting an airline, but at service-crazed London Drugs, that idea is no laughing matter. In Chapter 5, I made the case that London Drugs is so clear about its most-of-something commitment to customers that it has resisted the temptation to expand as quickly as possible across as much of Canada as possible. But this is not to suggest that London Drugs is cautious or conservative. In fact, it is one of the most strategically nimble companies I've seen. Back in 1999, as the number of store locations was increasing, company executives, who travel nonstop to walk the aisles and interact with employees and customers, found it harder and harder to get reliable flights to the cities and towns they had to visit. So the company purchased a Lear Jet. But rather than treat the plane as a cost center, ever-entrepreneurial London Drugs created a for-profit business. Thus was born London Air Services, with Wynne Powell as its president and CEO.

Today, the service has ten aircraft (eight jets plus two helicopters), a spanking-new hangar and operations center in Vancouver, and a position as the go-to private carrier for Hollywood celebrities making movies in western Canada, Canadian executives traveling from mines and oil fields to visit customers in Asia, and the parade of movers and shakers visiting British Columbia before, during, and after the 2010 Winter Olympics. In barely a decade, London Air Services has built a sterling reputation for high-end service and technical excellence. (Its helicopter division even trains pilots for the U.S. government.) Early in the venture's history, Canada's *Marketing* magazine put this question on its cover: "What's a pharmacy chain doing running a charter airline?" No one asks that question now. As one 2009 media report put it, "At a time when Air Canada is struggling to stay afloat, London Air Services continues to soar."[4]

Professor Kenneth Wong likes to say that London Drugs is less a physical entity and more a "state of mind." That's not a bad way to describe, in general, what it means to be the most of something in your field. Sure, a strong set of strategic opinions allows an organization and its people to remain focused and disciplined—to stay on their unique course and avoid the middle of the road. But it can also be a road map to think bigger and aim higher, to apply its one-of-a-kind ideas in as many directions as possible.

3. LONG-TERM SUCCESS IS ABOUT MORE THAN THINKING HARDER THAN THE COMPETITION. IT'S ALSO ABOUT CARING MORE THAN THE COMPETITION.

KENT THIRY AND HIS COLLEAGUES at DaVita make no apologies for an outsized corporate culture that wears its heart on its sleeve—it's how they avoid being worn down by the demands of their business. "So much of what we do, with the rituals and the costumes, are little ways, cute ways, cheesy ways, of reminding us of what we hope to create and how we want to behave," the CEO explains. "Why do people say a prayer every day? To remind themselves of how they aspire to live and behave every day. Why do you go to church every week? To be reminded of the values that are important to you."

The leaders at Magazine Luiza, the Brazilian retailer whose growth has confounded its mainstream rivals, also make a direct connection between what they think and how they work. Among business professors and management consultants, Magazine Luiza's unorthodox business strategy is the stuff of admiration and curiosity. But among rank-and-file Brazilians, the company's larger-than-life workplace rituals and open-book culture generate as much attention and acclaim as its focus on low-income customers. Every Monday morning, for example, employees around the country (there are stores in seven of Brazil's twenty-seven states) assemble to sing songs, say a prayer, do exercises, and celebrate birthdays and the arrival of new colleagues. Every Thursday, staffers watch an entertaining forty-five-minute broadcast (TV Luiza) in which executives discuss the latest wrinkles in tactics, high-performing employees share their best practices, and everyone reviews the latest ads and promotions. Meanwhile, the company shares detailed information on revenues, costs, margins, and profits across the organization. "We are very open in terms of strategy and results," says Frederico Rodrigues, "very transparent, with very granular numbers, from the CEO right down to the cleaning staff."

This is not, Rodrigues insists, just a better way for any company to operate. It is a *necessary* way for his company to operate, since the margin for error in its model is so small. Magazine Luiza has figured out how to enable low-income customers to make big-ticket purchases in part through sound financial analysis and conservative risk management. (The company has a 50-50 joint venture with one of Brazil's largest banks to underwrite the credit program.) But its long-term success has more to do with savvy employees and good on-the-spot judgment. Frontline staffers have wide autonomy to approve credit for customers who need it—and individual responsibility to work out payment plans for customers who fall behind. Unlike the subprime mortgage fiasco in the United States, which collapsed in an orgy of portfolio securitization and computer-driven abstraction, the credit process at Magazine Luiza remains local, personal, and highly accountable. There is nothing "synthetic" about how the company offers loans and interacts with customers.

"You cannot run a company in the markets we serve without this culture," he says. "You cannot provide this level of service without people deeply committed to the organization. Our sales associates have about the same purchasing power as our customers; they understand their needs, which products are best for them, what they can afford. That's why they have so much power in the credit-approval process. They also have responsibilities when problems arise. The collection process in Brazil can be tough, harsh, and we don't want that. If the associates who approve the loans also have to help customers who run into trouble, they are not going to strain the relationship. They are going to remain committed to those customers. I cannot imagine running our business without this culture."

4. IN A WORLD OF ENDLESS CHOICE, COMPANIES MUST ENGAGE CUSTOMERS EMOTIONALLY, NOT JUST SATISFY THEM RATIONALLY. REMEMBER, IF YOUR CUSTOMERS CAN LIVE WITHOUT YOU, EVENTUALLY THEY WILL.

THAT'S THE SIMPLE (AND POWERFUL) lesson behind Gallup's research on the relationship between companies and their customers. The differences in behavior between customers who were "rationally satisfied" with products and services versus those who were "emotionally engaged" were striking—and had a striking impact on business performance. Overall, Gallup found, "fully engaged" customers "deliver a 23% premium over the average customer in terms of share of wallet, profitability, revenue, and relationship growth." And these terms of engagement, the research adds, are driven as much by psychological connections as by business considerations: "Every interaction an employee has with a customer represents an opportunity to build that customer's emotional connection—or to diminish it."[5]

That's why, like Ray Davis at Umpqua Bank, Bahram Akradi obsesses over the "sensory experience" of interacting with Life Time Fitness and its staff. He pays careful attention to what the clubs look like, what the fabrics and finishes in the locker rooms feel like, what the health-conscious meals taste like—the five senses. Unlike Umpqua, Life Time Fitness does not have its own music label. But it does have a national director of music, a well-known, Brazilian-born DJ who selects just the right beats for the wide range of exercises and activities at the clubs, beats designed to maximize what Akradi calls the "sixth sense" of energy.

The Zappos blend of unconventional strategy, high-touch service, and one-of-a-kind culture has created a deeply felt connection with customers who are eager to share their sense of enthusiasm. One case in point among many: a much-buzzed-about testimonial called "I Heart Zappos" from a blogger named Zaz Lamarr. A few weeks after her mother died, Lamarr posted an entry about an unexpected encounter with Zappos. Her mother had lost lots of weight during a long illness, and her old shoes were all too big. So Lamarr, in an effort to lift her mom's spirits, ordered seven pairs of shoes online. Only two pairs fit, but Lamarr, who was busy attending to her sick mother, never got around to returning the others.

After her mother died, Lamarr received an e-mail from Zappos about the unreturned shoes. She explained her situation, and a Zappos employee offered to send a UPS driver to her house so she wouldn't have to bother with boxes, labels, and the rest. It was a thoughtful gesture, and then that same employee made an even more thoughtful gesture. Here's how Lamarr described it: "When I came home from town, a florist delivery man was just leaving. It was a beautiful arrangement in a basket with white lilies and roses and carnations. Big and lush and fragrant. I opened the card, and it was from Zappos. I burst into tears. I'm a sucker for kindness, and if that isn't one of the nicest things I've ever had happen to me, I don't know what is. So . . . IF YOU BUY SHOES ONLINE, GET THEM FROM ZAPPOS. With hearts like theirs, you know they're good to do business with."[6]

No org chart or policy manual could have inspired this authentic bit of human interaction. It was a frontline employee, moved by a customer's loss, and guided by the company's relentless focus on service, who chose to do something special without asking permission. That small gesture sent a big signal about the kind of organization Zappos aspires to be. Lamarr's post rocketed around the Web, led to countless links from other bloggers, and became the subject of approving accounts in online news sites. Months after the post, a Google search for "Zappos" turned up Lamarr's tribute among the top-ranked links—a word-of-mouth message of untold value, another piece of folklore that separates the company from the competition.

"We don't have a process or procedure for this," Tony Hsieh explains. "How can we? You can't predict all the situations that are going to come up. But if you get the culture right, these things happen on their own. You create thousands of stories, and those stories spread the word about Zappos. We're not trying to maximize every transaction. We're trying to build a lifelong relationship with each of our customers, one call at a time."

5. STARTING SOMETHING NEW DOESN'T ALWAYS MEAN STARTING A NEW COMPANY. YOU DON'T NEED TO BE A BLANK-SHEET-OF-PAPER ENTREPRENEUR TO EMBRACE A BLANK-SHEET-OF-PAPER MIND-SET.

THESE LAST TWO CHAPTERS, UNLIKE the first three, have emphasized the transformative potential of entrepreneurial start-ups. From Umpqua Bank to Zappos, from LifeUSA to Life Time Fitness, the most direct way to shake up an industry is to launch a company that aims to "run the four-minute mile" in its industry. But starting something new doesn't have to mean starting from scratch. Some big, established organizations can become the "most of something" in their field—if they can find ways to challenge middle-of-the-road thinking and develop strongly felt opinions that respond to fast-changing markets, fast-moving technologies, and fickle customers.

That's the appeal of Gamal Aziz's "working backward" methodology at MGM Grand, which we explored in Chapter 4. It turned blank-sheet-of-paper thinking into a routine part of thinking about the business. For decades, the Las Vegas model of innovation has been to literally "blow things up." Companies would dynamite a hotel or casino that had lost its luster, and, from the ashes, build something more glamorous. At the MGM Grand, Aziz demonstrated that organizations can embrace deeply disruptive ideas without deep-sixing what came before, as long as leaders give everyone the tools to work backward from the future. "We have kept morale high even in this environment," he says. "Our people are coming up with extraordinary ideas. There is an ongoing conversation, a commitment to fresh thinking, that is as powerful in tough times as in good times."

PART III

CHALLENGING YOURSELF

LEADERSHIP WITHOUT ALL THE ANSWERS—AMBITION, HUMBITION, AND THE POWER OF HIDDEN GENIUS

This orchestra has been performing for more than 35 years, which shows that a wonderfully original idea, even a radical idea, can have great longevity as long as you continue to adapt and refine it. There is such a depth of engagement among the players, a willingness to hold each other accountable, a sense of individual responsibility for the whole performance, that it creates a special energy on stage. We hear it all the time: There's something more "palpable" about an Orpheus concert, because everyone plays with so much commitment. There's a different kind of connection between the audience and the orchestra.

—GRAHAM PARKER, EXECUTIVE DIRECTOR,
ORPHEUS CHAMBER ORCHESTRA

HOW DO YOU GET TO Carnegie Hall? Practice, practice, practice. It's an old joke, but for the violinists, cellists, clarinetists, percussionists, and other accomplished musicians working in a fourth-floor rehearsal space at the Riverside Church on Manhattan's Upper West Side, this particular practice is no laughing matter. In just eight days, the renowned Orpheus Chamber Orchestra will play to a sold-out audience at Carnegie Hall and premiere a twenty-eight-minute piece by Ravi Shankar, the legendary teacher, composer, and sitar player. In his incomparable seven-decade career, Shankar has collaborated with everyone from French flutist Jean-Pierre Rampal to George Harrison of the Beatles and performed everywhere from Woodstock and the Concert for Bangladesh (which he organized with Harrison) to Europe's grandest concert halls. He has written music for ballets and films (including *Gandhi*), won three Grammys, and single-handedly introduced the world to the beauty and power of Indian classical music.

This latest piece, it turns out, is the third concerto for sitar and orchestra that Ravi Shankar has composed. In the first (written in 1971 for the London Symphony) and the second (written in 1981 for the New York Philharmonic), Shankar himself performed as the sitar soloist. For Concerto No. 3, written specifically for Orpheus, his daughter, Anoushka Shankar, a rising world-music star in her own right (and the half sister of nine-time Grammy winner Norah Jones), will perform as the sitar soloist. This transition between generations (at the time of the rehearsals, Ravi Shankar was eighty-nine while Anoushka was twenty-seven) gives the piece added poignancy—and creates added pressure for the orchestra, which aims to do justice to the musical vision of the composer and to shine a light on the talents of his daughter.

Maybe that's why so many of the musicians in the room have such strong opinions about how the piece is sounding. "Let's start with the overture and go from there," suggests violinist Renée Jolles, a member of Orpheus since 2004 and a highly regarded solo artist in her own right. The group begins rehearsing and the feedback begins flying. Many of the musicians are literally on the edge of their chairs, listening for the subtleties of how their colleagues are playing. There are suggestions for the brass: "Every one of the eighth notes is quite long," a voice says. "The brass needs to be very colorful." There are suggestions for the violins and cellos: "What you want there is a Western string sound, very rich."

As the rehearsal proceeds, cellist Melissa Meell, an Orpheus member since 2001, who has performed in virtually every major concert hall in the world, wonders about the overall pacing of the overture: "Is it my imagination, or have we slowed down a bit?" Julia Lichten, another accomplished cellist, has different concerns: "It's the relationship between the winds and the strings that's disturbing to me." As the harpist worries over the intricacies of her part, one smart aleck quips: "Get in touch with your inner sitar!" Frank Morelli, a celebrated bassoon player who has been part of Orpheus since 1978, has plenty to say about the music—and even more to say about the rehearsal itself, from how long the group is spending on each discussion to when it's time to return from a break.

Meanwhile, Anoushka Shankar sits barefoot on an oversized cushion, tunes her sitar, and pays close attention as orchestra members debate and critique their performance thus far. She provides a note of reassurance ("everything you're working on sounds great"), plays a few of her parts, and then offers to share the untold saga behind the concerto—a fable of sorts that Ravi Shankar conjured up as he composed the piece. As she speaks, members of the orchestra listen as closely to her telling of this tale as they do her playing of the sitar.

"When my dad wrote this, he had a balletic story in mind," she explains to the rapt group. "It's the story of a princess. In the first movement, which is really about innocence, she's a clumsy young girl who befriends a servant boy. The king sends him away, which is why the second movement is full of pathos and heartbreak. The princess grows up, she lives a good life, but she misses her friend. In the third movement, she is an adult, and she has many suitors. But the servant boy, who has made his fortune in the world, comes back in disguise and is reunited with the princess. My father wrote my sister a letter and asked her, when she comes to the show, if she can tell that it's a story about a princess and a servant boy. Knowing that makes it easier for me to express myself through the course of the piece."

The same goes for the orchestra—which, after Anoushka's soft-spoken discourse, attacks the music with a renewed sense of vigor and confidence. "When she shared her father's story with us, we just loved that," explained Julia Lichten after the rehearsal. "To hear her describe so specifically what he had in mind. When you play it, you can try to enter that world." Melissa Meell echoed her fellow cellist's enthusiasm about the story and the score: "There's a misconception about classical musicians, that we're 'proper' and that we play in this 'proper' style. When people think of classical music they think of stiff upper lip and starched collar. Orpheus doesn't play that way. We don't play Mozart that way, and we certainly won't play Shankar that way."[1]

The main reason Orpheus plays so differently from most orchestras is that it operates so differently from most orchestras. The rehearsal I watched had most of the elements you'd associate with the creation of a great performance: a compelling score, world-class musicians, strong opinions, and, in the spirit of the old joke, lots of practice. But conspicuously absent was the most familiar ingredient in classical-music success—the big-name, huge-ego, all-knowing conductor. That's because Orpheus plays without any conductor whatsoever. Ever since its creation in 1972, and through its rise as one of the most celebrated chamber orchestras in the world, Orpheus has distinguished itself as much by its unusual approach to leadership as by its unsurpassed artistic achievements. It has managed to survive, even thrive, in a field defined by exacting standards, demanding audiences, and tough-minded critics without the most iconic symbol of power and authority, the larger-than-life maestro.

"People say they feel a more visceral connection with us because there is no conductor with his back to the audience," explains Graham Parker who spent nearly eight years as the group's highest-ranking nonmusician and professional staff member. "There's no one blocking the energy, it comes right at you. But Orpheus is not just an orchestra. It's an idea. It's a way of thinking, a way of interacting, a way of listening. What began as an act of artistic rebellion, even revolution, is now about innovation, connection, and transformation." (In June 2010, to promote even more ways of listening, Parker announced that he was leaving Orpheus to run WQXR, the classical-music station in New York City.)

With Orpheus, no one person is expected to have all the answers about the best way to interpret a score, polish a performance, or even deliver a solo, because everyone is invited to contribute ideas and inspiration—on the theory that the musical whole will be more than the sum of the parts. This is an organization that rejects top-down control in favor of peer-to-peer decision making, a group in which frontline players call the big-picture musical shots. It is a diverse collection of strong-willed individuals, each with different talents, experiences, and opinions, that somehow produces the sweet sound of success— recording after recording, performance after performance, year after year.

In the field of classical music, Orpheus is the subject of widespread attention and acclaim. It has released more than seventy recordings in its long history, first with Deutsche Grammophon, more recently with EMI Classics, and has collaborated with many of the world's leading composers and soloists. It presents an annual concert series at Carnegie Hall (the Shankar premiere was part of the 2008–2009 series) and regularly tours the United States, South America, Europe, and Asia. (In 1998, it became the first American orchestra to play in Vietnam since the end of the Vietnam War.) The group has won countless awards, including a Grammy for *Shadow Dances*, a much-praised collection of Stravinsky miniatures. Through the Orpheus Institute, the orchestra teaches its philosophy and methodology to up-and-coming players—a way to spread its ideas as well as its music.

Back in 2002, on the occasion of the group's thirtieth anniversary, the *New York Times* published an unblinking look at the "mystique and myths" surrounding Orpheus. Music critic Barbara Jepson took issue with some of the more extravagant claims made by and for the group (including the proposition that shared musical leadership *always* produces superior results), but she could not deny its power and force. By virtue of its legacy of recordings, awards, and "glowing reviews," she wrote, the group "has proved itself in the cultural marketplace." Orpheus "is without question a breathtakingly precise chamber orchestra," she continued. "Its players characteristically exhibit a sensitive ear for balances and an appealing 'edge of their seat' alertness." At its best, she added, "Orpheus may match the brilliance and vitality of the most venerable and esteemed orchestras, surely achievement enough."[2]

Yet for all its visibility and influence in musical circles, the orchestra has, in many respects, been just as visible and influential in business circles. For years, leadership gurus have tried to understand how it manages to incorporate such a wide range of opinions, master the intricacies of individual pieces, and deliver precise results onstage, without the baton-wielding hand of an ironfisted leader. The group has been the subject of loads of academic research, several video documentaries, and a collection of case studies. In 2007, WorldBlu, a research-and-advisory organization dedicated to promoting grassroots participation in business, named Orpheus to its first-annual list of the world's "most democratic workplaces." The group has held a position in every subsequent list, whose other members in 2009 included a product-design firm, a huge health-care provider, a bakery franchise, a consumer-products outfit, and a manufacturer of aircraft parts.

The most recent academic case study, by the Haas School at the University of California Berkeley, typifies the fascination of business observers with how Orpheus works and the alternative it provides to traditional ways of doing things. In conventional orchestras, the case noted, "Conductors are celebrated geniuses, whereas musicians are, quite literally, relegated to the back of the room. A conductor rarely plays one note during the performance, yet he or she routinely receives all the accolades. The result of this hierarchy in terms of job satisfaction is fascinating. Indeed, conductors are regularly among the most satisfied category of workers—in the same realm as heart surgeons—whereas orchestra musicians' morale ranks just below that of prison guards. The Orpheus Chamber Orchestra turns this conductor-musician relationship on its head."[3]

During the 1990s, when the first Internet boom got all kinds of organizations riled up about new ideas on leadership and executive power, the orchestra turned this interest among business thinkers into a reasonably lucrative business. It held so-called Orpheus Process Demonstrations for corporate giants such as Morgan Stanley, Goldman Sachs, Kraft Foods, and Novartis. These companies would pay the group to rehearse in front of their executives and then ask its members to explain how they were able to make sound bottom-up decisions that normally were made by an all-knowing maestro (not a bad metaphor for a know-it-all CEO). "The trick that Orpheus has pulled off," writer James Traub argued in an essay that described the business world's efforts to learn from the orchestra, "is to establish authority without establishing an authority figure."[4]

Over the years, Orpheus has in fact developed a deep bag of organizational tricks, a system of long-term artistic governance and day-to-day rehearsing, to make sure that its signature "trick"—performing complex pieces of music with great virtuosity—remains as compelling and vibrant as ever. In the beginning, under the guidance of founder Julian Fifer, Orpheus was essentially a direct democracy, in which any member could raise any concern about any piece of music at any time. Today, it is more of a representative democracy—members choose specific colleagues to play designated leadership roles for individual pieces, and those roles can change during the course of both a rehearsal and a concert. It is a system of "rotational leadership" that shares both the excitement and burdens of taking charge.

At Carnegie Hall, for example, the Shankar concerto was the

second of four pieces on the bill. After each piece the orchestra took a bow, left the stage, and then came back, with several players sitting in different places to reflect their new roles in the next piece. It's like a high-stakes game of musical chairs; where you sit is a reflection of what you do at a specific point in the show. Before the concert, designated orchestra members sat in the concert hall itself, listening to their colleagues perform and evaluating the sound for balance, blend, and clarity of expression. This is one group that works hard to evaluate its performance through the eyes and ears of its customers.

It's also hard work—the much-cited rule of thumb is that Orpheus rehearses three times as long as a traditional orchestra to play the same piece—but the payoff is evident in the energy and quality of the live performance. The music stands out because the group that produces it stands together in the spirit (and a system) of shared creation. "Most orchestras leave a lot of talent on the table," Harvard psychology professor J. Richard Hackman, who has studied Orpheus more closely than any other academic, told James Traub. "You wonder how transcendental a particular performance could have been if the musicians had been as engaged as the Orpheus musicians are."

This morning, though, no one is reveling in decades of musical accolades or years of attention from business-school gurus. Instead, everyone is focused on mastering a new piece of music that blends two cultures, joins two generations of sitar stars, and challenges the orchestra to be at its best on one of the world's highest-profile stages. After all, you're only as good as your last performance. "I'd love to hear that, when the horns come in, shocking a little bit," says violinist Renée Jolles. As members of the wind section chat among themselves, someone compliments one of his colleagues. "I know, I do sound great," the musician jokes, brushing aside the kind words. "But that having been said, there's always room for improvement."

Through it all, Anoushka Shankar marvels at the teamwork and creative give-and-take she is witnessing. "The fact that they would play without a conductor is so novel," she says later. "As I was hearing the piece, I was thinking to myself, 'How are they going to keep those rhythms together, how do they start at the same time?' But they do, and they're amazing. It was a beautiful thing to see how that happens."

GROUP GENIUS—"FREEDOM IS A BIGGER GAME THAN POWER"

IT'S LONELY AT THE TOP. If there is a defining conceit at the heart of how so many of us think about leadership—whether the leader in question is the CEO of a global empire or the founder of a start-up itching to take on the Big Boys—it is that of the no-nonsense, hard-charging, often-wrong-but-never-in-doubt boss who enjoys the glories (and bears the burdens) of success on his or her own. We still like to transplant the rugged individualism of the Marlboro Man from the open range to the corner office—the self-possessed corporate cowboy or don't-take-no-for-an-answer entrepreneur who solves thorny problems as they arise and identifies lucrative opportunities before they go mainstream. That's what makes executive life (in theory) so glamorous: Who isn't eager to match wits with brilliant rivals and stay one step ahead of a complex world? Of course, that's also what makes executive life (in reality) so exhausting: What happens when rivals come at you from more directions than ever, when markets change faster than ever, when problems loom larger than ever?

As a business culture, we've made the lure of executive leadership hard to resist—and the job of leadership virtually impossible to do. A harrowing essay in *The Atlantic* (titled, appropriately enough, "It's Lonely at the Top") captures how excruciating it is for many CEOs just to make it through the day. It begins with an account from Rachel Bellow, an executive coach in Manhattan, who describes the calendar of one of her clients. "There was no white space seven days a week, not even Saturdays and Sundays," Bellow marveled. "He was all over the place on his private jet. . . . He would go to nine cities in a single twenty-four-hour period. It was obscene! There is no possible way that this person ever has the capacity to process what he's doing."[5]

The essay, which does a better job of chronicling the crisis of executive life than empathizing with it, sums up the dilemma of the contemporary business leader this way: "The more CEOs work and the more responsibilities they take on, the more isolated they become. Their entourages shield them from workaday headaches. Their spot at the top cuts them off from the people lower down on the corporate totem pole, and thus from reliable, 'un-spun' information. Everyone reporting to them has his own ambitions; everyone wants to look good; everyone wants a promotion. So what's a CEO to do?"

The simple answer (and the not-so-simple subject of the next few chapters) is to rewrite an awful job description that has been obsolete and counterproductive for an awfully long time. Thus far, I've explored a collection of strategies and practices to renew and revive long-established organizations. I've also presented a set of ideas, and a roster of role models, about the best ways to start from scratch, whether it's launching a stand-alone venture or championing a blank-sheet-of-paper initiative inside a big company. I'd like to think that these strategies, practices, and ideas challenge much of the prevailing wisdom about how business works and why organizations succeed. But I'm confident that they require executives to challenge themselves about how *they* work and why *they* expect to succeed. In an era of nonstop pressure and deep-seated change, the way to succeed as a leader without losing your mind is to change the prevailing and long-standing mind-set about what it means to lead.

To be sure, it is a tough mind-set to change. Even a source of business ideas as intelligent as *The Economist* can't seem to get beyond the idea of the leader as lone (and lonely) genius. In late 2009, the magazine looked at the turmoil of the global economy, as well as the ever-changing face of CEOs around the world, and concluded that what business needs are more "raging egomaniacs" and "tightly wound empire-builders" rather than the "faceless" and "anonymous" bosses running so many companies—"bland and boring men and women who can hardly get themselves noticed at cocktail parties, let alone stop the traffic in Moscow or Beijing." You could almost feel the frustration leaping from the pages of the magazine. "Watch the parade of chief executives who appear on CNBC every day," it complained, "or drop in to a high-powered conference, and you begin to wonder whether cloning is more advanced than scientists are letting on to."

As if on cue, just as *The Economist* was bemoaning the lack of charisma and ego in the modern executive suite, *Fortune* named Apple's Steve Jobs the most charismatic executive of his generation, as its CEO of the Decade (which it thoughtfully renamed the Decade of Steve). On the level of substance, it's impossible to quarrel with the choice. How many innovators can make the legitimate claim to have reshaped not just one industry but four: computing (the Mac), music (the iPod), mobile communications (the iPhone), and movies (Pixar)? And how many CEOs can make the legitimate claim that they achieved their wealth and power by making hundreds of millions of people so unbelievably happy that they worship the company and its products with near-religious devotion? On the level of style, though, Jobs clings to a model of leadership that is outmoded, unsustainable, and, for most of us mere mortals, dangerously unrealistic. "It's often noted that he's a showman, a born salesman, a magician who creates a famed reality-distortion field, a tyrannical perfectionist," the magazine's cover story noted approvingly. "It's totally accurate, of course, and the descriptions contribute to his legend."[6]

Sure, it's lonely at the top. But only if you keep your organization's problems to yourself. Today, the way to succeed as a leader without losing your mind is to change the prevailing and long-standing mind-set about what it means to lead.

It's tempting (and it certainly makes for fun reading) to divide executives into stark either-or categories: risk takers or bureaucrats, those with true ambition or those prepared to plod along, brash personalities or drab corporate drones. But for most executives, this fascination with the know-it-all style of leadership has become a prescription for disaster, personally as well as organizationally. The problem with trumpeting the virtues of one-of-a-kind geniuses like Steve Jobs is that—duh—there are so darn few of them. Memo to my friends at both *The Economist* and *Fortune*: it's not a good idea to urge leaders in general to act like a handful of larger-than-life leaders whose success is, almost by definition, impossible to copy.

That's why, in the very first issue of *Fast Company*, we profiled a hotshot executive who was struggling to develop an alternative to a know-it-all leadership style that was working neither for him nor his company. Dave Marsing was a rising star at Intel, the Silicon Valley behemoth, and had run several of the biggest, most expensive, most complex chip-manufacturing facilities—one of the most stressful assignments at a company known for its "only-the-paranoid-survive" culture. Marsing was at his best when the chips were down—until, at age thirty-six, while working to pull a huge, troubled facility out of a major crisis, he suffered a near-fatal heart attack. For years after his heart attack, Marsing told the writer, he would visit cardiac-care units every six months "just to look at the gray faces and remember." As a result, he confronted "the big lie" of command-and-control leadership, reinvented how he defined his job, and went on to run what was, at the time, the most expensive semiconductor facility on earth.[7]

Marsing's challenge, as the title of the article suggested, was to deliver "Killer Results Without Killing Yourself." That's a challenge with which so many executives in so many fields continue to struggle, and which *The Atlantic* essay documented so well. The answer to that challenge is to recognize that the best way to deliver on an ambitious agenda for your organization is to embrace a sense of "humbition" in your personal style and as part of your leadership repertoire.

What's humbition? It's a term I first heard from a savvy change agent (and self-described "possibilitarian") named Jane Harper, a thirty-year veteran of IBM who devoted her career to transforming how this once-famously top-down organization, founded by the larger-than-life Thomas Watson, approaches innovation, collaboration, and leadership. (Harper was part of a worldwide coalition of IBMers who, working closely with Irving Wladawsky-Berger, the senior executive we heard in Chapter 1 discuss the company's "near-death experience," helped Big Blue respond to the big changes of the Internet era.)

Humbition, Harper explains, is the blend of humility and ambition that drives the most successful businesspeople—an antidote to the hubris that infects (and undoes) so many executives and entrepreneurs. (She says the term was coined by researchers at Bell Labs, who were looking to describe the personal attributes of the most effective scientists and engineers.) The smartest business leaders, she argues, are smart enough to admit that they cannot take all the credit for their success. More likely than not, what they've achieved is some combination of good fortune, great colleagueship, and the random collision of smart people and bright ideas.

In a manifesto of sorts that urged up-and-coming IBMers to embrace a new leadership mind-set, Harper and a group of her colleagues offered a compelling description of what it takes to succeed in a complex, fast-moving, hard-to-figure-out world. Their strongly worded advice to aspiring leaders inside IBM should be read as words of wisdom for leaders at every level of all kinds of organizations.

"Humbition is one part humility and one part ambition," they wrote. "We notice that by far the lion's share of world-changing luminaries are humble people. They focus on the work, not themselves. They seek success—they are ambitious—but they are humbled when it arrives. They know that much of that success was luck, timing, and a thousand factors out of their personal control. They feel lucky, not all-powerful. Oddly, the ones operating under a delusion that they are all-powerful are the ones who have yet to reach their potential. . . . [So] be ambitious. Be a leader. But do not belittle others in your pursuit of your ambitions. Raise them up instead. The biggest leader is the one washing the feet of the others."[8]

There are plenty of smart thinkers who echo Jane Harper's case against the know-it-all style of leadership. Keith Sawyer, a professor and creativity guru at Washington University in St. Louis, has literally written the book on where good ideas come from. In *Group Genius*, he emphasizes the relationship between innovation and improvisation—and explains how few leaders are prepared to recognize the messy and hard-to-manage truth about the real logic of business success. That's why Sawyer became intrigued with jazz ensembles, improvisation groups, and, sure enough, the Orpheus Chamber Orchestra. Their styles of communication, interaction, and collaboration, he argues, are more in sync with the surprising ways in which progress gets made in the real world.

Many (perhaps most) executives subscribe to what Sawyer calls *script-think*—"the tendency to think that events are more predictable than they really are." In fact, he says, "Innovation emerges from the bottom up, unpredictably and improvisationally, and it's often only after the innovation has occurred that everyone realizes what's happened. The paradox is that innovation can't be planned, it can't be predicted; it has to be allowed to emerge."[9]

> **Humbition is the blend of humility and ambition that drives the most successful businesspeople—an antidote to the hubris that infects so many executives. The smartest leaders are smart enough to admit they cannot take all the credit for their success.**

Harriet Rubin, one of the great innovators in business-book publishing, and an accomplished author in her own right, uses different language to make a similar point about the relationship between leadership and change. "Freedom is actually a bigger game than power," she reminds executives who are understandably eager to make their mark in the world. "Power is about what you can control. Freedom is about what you can unleash."[10]

Translation: The most effective leaders no longer want the job of solving their organization's biggest problems or identifying its best opportunities. Instead, they recognize that the most powerful ideas can come from the most unexpected places: the quiet genius buried deep inside the organization; the collective genius that surrounds the organization; the hidden genius of customers, suppliers, and other constituencies who would be eager to share what they know if only they were asked. That's the difference between success and failure today, and the distinction between unchecked ambition and sustainable humbition. In their manifesto for hard-charging IBMers, Jane Harper and her colleagues put it this way: "We've all seen managers and executives that rely on authority to motivate people. We don't want any more of those. Don't become one. . . . Motivate people by your passion, by your insights, and most importantly, by your willingness to listen to them."

This new philosophy of leadership doesn't just help to produce killer results—it helps you to avoid killing yourself, as you struggle to solve problems that are tougher than ever, capitalize on opportunities that are bigger than ever, and navigate a business landscape that is more treacherous than ever. Keith Sawyer offers a bracing corrective to executives and entrepreneurs who insist on holding on to unhealthy and unproductive ideas about what it means to be in charge. "We're drawn to the image of the lone genius whose mystical moment of insight changes the world," he argues. "But the lone genius is a myth; instead it's group genius that generates breakthrough innovation. When we collaborate, creativity unfolds across people; the sparks fly faster, and the whole is greater than the sum of the parts."

HIDDEN GENIUS—"THE MORE I KNOW, THE MORE I KNOW THERE IS TO KNOW"

THIS IS NOT, IT SHOULD be said, some starry-eyed paean to the wisdom of crowds or the brilliance of brainstorming. Indeed, as Keith Sawyer demonstrates in one especially persuasive chapter of his book, the process of brainstorming, at least as it's been practiced since its creation in the 1950s by advertising icon Alex Osborn, the "O" in the Madison Avenue firm of BBDO, has been a better marketing success than business tool. "Brainstorming is the most popular creativity technique of all time," Sawyer argues. "There's just one problem: It doesn't work as advertised. . . . Decades of research have consistently shown that brainstorming groups think of far fewer ideas than the same number of people who work alone and later pool their ideas." In fact, Sawyer warns, "In many organizations, the group ends up being dumber than the individual members."

So what does it take to unlock the quiet genius of colleagues, the collective genius of customers, and the hidden genius of potential collaborators of all sorts? The answer is certainly not less leadership. Nor is it more of the same leadership, but with a little less ego and a little smarter approach to brainstorming. What it takes is an entirely new leadership mind-set—a clear-eyed recognition that in a high-pressure, fast-changing world, where the only way to outperform the competition is to outthink the competition, the most successful leaders are the ones who make it their business to get the best ideas from the most people, whatever their background, job title, or position in the hierarchy.

> The most powerful ideas come from the most unexpected places: the quiet genius inside the organization; the collective genius around the organization; the hidden genius of customers and suppliers who'd share what they know if only they were asked.

That's why, in the spirit of humbition, IBM has launched all sorts of initiatives to shake up its culture, challenge its legacy of top-down control, and surface insights from engineers and executives all over the world—including its Innovation Jams, a remarkable experiment to rethink how IBMers think. Talk about group genius: with Innovation Jams, tens of thousands of employees answer questions, share ideas, and influence the company's point of view on new markets, promising technologies, and emerging problems.

Back in 2006, in what has become a much-heralded case study among academic experts on innovation and collaboration, the company posted detailed information on key technologies that had been developed in its labs, and invited rank-and-file participants to suggest ways to turn these nascent technologies into real businesses. Much of the impetus for the 2006 Jam came directly from CEO Samuel J. Palmisano, who has built on the legacy of his predecessor, turnaround guru Lou Gerstner, in changing the game at IBM. As the story goes, during his annual review of the cutting-edge work being done by the company's research division, Palmisano was struck by the enormous potential impact of so many of the technologies in IBM's labs. But he was worried about how he and a small group of senior executives could work through the enormous challenges of figuring out which technologies to commercialize when.

They just weren't smart enough to make those calls, because *nobody* could have been smart enough to make those calls. "One technology promised to forecast the weather so precisely that school districts could tell whether their town would get an inch or two of snow more than their neighbors and therefore have to close school," noted an in-depth account in MIT's *Sloan Management Review*. "Another project would enable the building of an Internet where shoppers could visit 3-D stores and see realistic 3-D demonstrations of products. Yet another new software program would perform real-time translation of speech so that words on China Central Television or the Middle East's Al Jazeera news network could appear in English underneath the speakers without human intervention."[11]

Palmisano's answer was to make it possible for 150,000 participants in 104 countries to spend seventy-two hours debating which were the most promising technologies and what were the most effective ways to bring them to market. After that first round of grassroots interaction, a team of fifty executives spent a week making sense of the conversation, looking for trends, and identifying thirty-one "big ideas" that stood out from among the cacophony. Participants around the world then got *another* seventy-two hours to refine and develop those ideas. Ultimately, IBM wound up investing a total of $100 million in the ten most compelling ideas, from a smart health-care-payment system to intelligent utility networks to integrated mass-transit information systems to branchless banking for remote markets.

In fact, the process worked so well that IBM turned the Jam itself into a business—selling its expertise in virtual collaboration to other big companies eager to discover what their people already knew. What did CEO Sam Palmisano and the senior leadership of IBM get right? "First, [they] had enabled people with big ideas to articulate them to a wider audience, including skeptics, to hear other's complementary ideas and to win funding," the *Sloan Management Review* analysis concluded. "Second, and probably more important, it had allowed people whose ideas weren't quite so big and who hadn't been able to find the place for their ideas within IBM to present them in ways that senior people could understand."

I participated in the company's 2008 Innovation Jam, which was dedicated to describing the "Enterprise of the Future" rather than identifying new business opportunities. I got to lead a discussion about the impact of the financial meltdown on strategy, growth, and innovation. It was a remarkable experience—IBMers (as well as outsiders) from the United States, Brazil, China, India, Finland, and many other countries sharing stories, worries, and perspectives on what the financial meltdown meant for them and their business units.

All told, in the course of seventy-two hours, the Jam attracted nearly 94,000 log-ins and generated nearly 30,000 posts. It included nearly 4,500 posts from India, more than 3,200 posts from China, nearly 1,500 posts from Brazil, and more than a thousand posts from Australia and New Zealand. It was a real-time window into the best thinking at IBM (and at more than a thousand other organizations that participated) on some of the world's toughest problems and some of the biggest issues facing companies everywhere.

Sitting in a control room on the leafy IBM Learning Center campus in Armonk, New York, watching as scientists, engineers, and marketers from every corner of the globe shared their ideas in hundreds of simultaneous conversations, I was struck by the scale and scope of the brainpower at work—and by the limits of the lone genius. How could even the most inspired thinking of one CEO (thinking alongside his or her closest confidants) rival the collective insights of ninety-four thousand Jammers with an endlessly diverse array of backgrounds, experiences, and locations? As IBM's collaboration-minded Jane Harper says, "The more I know, the more I know there is to know."

The Orpheus Chamber Orchestra certainly knows plenty about the power of group genius, in a field where the supremely powerful lone genius (in the persona of the big-name conductor) remains the archetype. But its evolution since the early 1970s (sometimes smoothly, sometimes not so smoothly) is an eye-opening reminder that while freedom, in Harriet Rubin's words, is a "bigger game" than power, the process of unleashing group genius requires an even more rigorous set of ideas about how leadership actually works, and a more intense commitment to working in concert, than the old, familiar (and largely ineffective) command-and-control model. "Freedom is hard," writes James Traub in his *New Yorker* essay about the group and its influence. "Freedom is inefficient. Orpheus routinely spends thirty hours preparing for a two-hour concert—three times as much as a typical orchestra. And yet it's precisely this pain-staking process of arriving, almost unconsciously, at a shared vision that accounts for Orpheus's distinctive sound. . . . It is as if the process that Orpheus uses to achieve a common sense of purpose reproduces itself in the harmony of the music."

Indeed, Orpheus has struggled with devising the best way to unleash maximum rank-and-file participation without making unreasonable demands on its members in terms of their energy, time, and capacity to contribute. Which is why, over the years, it has evolved into a finely tuned model of "rotational leadership" that keeps the creative sparks flying without sparking a backlash or burning out the participants. For example, each piece in a performance gets assigned a "core group" of musicians—a small number of players who discuss, debate, and hold initial rehearsals before the full orchestra convenes. Each piece also gets an individual "concertmaster" who moderates disagreements, steers colleagues in consensus-oriented directions, and guides the substance of rehearsals. (For the Shankar concerto, it was violinist Renée Jolles.) Each piece also gets a "rehearsal coordinator" who injects discipline into the give-and-take and brings order to the freewheeling, creative chaos. (For the Shankar concerto, it was bassoonist Frank Morelli.)

All told, what struck me about the rehearsal I attended was that despite a wide range of opinions from a wide variety of players, the process as a whole was crisp, sharp, and, dare I say, well orchestrated. (Anoushka Shankar was mortified to arrive five minutes late, aware of the group's keen sense of timing not just onstage but when it comes to practice. "I'm so sorry," she told the group. "I've never known a taxi driver to get lost in this part of town.")

Meanwhile, to help guide its long-term trajectory, the orchestra elects three members to serve three-year terms as "artistic directors." These musicians (violist Christof Huebner, clarinetist Alan Kay, and cellist Jonathan Spitz) work with the professional staff on high-stakes issues such as commissioning new music, devising tour schedules, and recording—an effort to migrate the spirit of "rotational leadership" from the musical side of the enterprise to the strategic side. Indeed, one of the great ironies of Orpheus as an organization, as opposed to as an orchestra, is that for much of its history, it relied upon larger-than-life leaders to make big decisions about the business. Founder Julian Fifer was a one-man band when it came to running the show. Harvey Seifter, Fifer's successor, was a hard-charging entrepreneur who drove the group to worldwide fame—and also nearly drove it into the ground through a combination of risky strategies and outsized ego.

Graham Parker, the longtime executive director, made it his mission to apply the principles that have served the group so well in terms of live performance to how it performs as a business. "More and more," he said, "we are asking ourselves, 'How do we translate the idea of rotational leadership from the orchestra to the staff? In every rehearsal, the musicians find ways to communicate, innovate, and hold themselves accountable. We want to do that with the staff and with the trustees as well.'"

In other words, just because Orpheus plays without a conductor doesn't mean it lacks leaders. Quite the opposite. Harvard's Richard Hackman argues that who gets to lead Orpheus is a function of what they have to contribute rather than who they are or where they trained. "Because orchestra members have played together regularly over the years," he notes, "they know one another's special strengths and weaknesses extremely well, and they are not reticent about using that knowledge in an open, matter-of-fact way. Members listen especially intently to what certain of their colleagues have to say when a Mozart piano concerto is being prepared, but to others when the piece is a Rossini overture, and to still others when it is new music by a contemporary composer. . . . [This is] an ensemble that wastes very little of its members' knowledge, skill, and experience."[12]

That's the promise for organizations that are smart enough to ask less of their senior leaders. They manage to unleash *more* from rank-and-file contributors whose talents, passions, and ideas provide a kind of group genius that not even the most brilliant individual could provide on his or her own. "Although the orchestra has no leader on the podium," argues Hackman, "it has much more *leadership* than do orchestras known for their famous conductors."

QUIET GENIUS—"THE ONE THING WE KNOW IS WE DON'T KNOW EVERYTHING"

IT MAY BE LONELY AT the top, but it's comforting to encounter new models of leadership that are humble enough to ask less of a small number of senior executives and ambitious enough to invite bright people throughout the organization to share insights, talents, and ideas. Still, thus far, our case studies of group genius have been as metaphorical as they have been managerial. What rigidly structured organization wouldn't want to operate with the bottom-up artistry of a conductorless orchestra? What open-minded executive wouldn't want to "jam" with brilliant technologists across the planet? But that's not the real world, at least not for most of us. So how do mainstream companies challenge their assumptions about leadership and innovation? How do everyday leaders, worried about their capacity to solve tough problems and identify big opportunities, redefine their job descriptions to make their work (and lives) more sustainable?

The best way to answer those questions is to leave the concert halls and walk the halls of a company whose operations are easier to relate to—and whose style of leadership is hard to resist. Two of the most humbitious (not to mention homespun and entertaining) executives I've ever met are Jim Lavoie and Joe Marino, founders of a fast-growing software company called Rite-Solutions, headquartered near Newport, Rhode Island. Lavoie and Marino are in a deadly serious business. Their company develops command-and-control systems for submarines, combat-system performance-prediction tools for navy warfighters, simulation and training systems for first responders and Homeland Security personnel, and all kinds of other advanced (and highly classified) technologies. Its customers include the Naval Undersea Warfare Command (located just minutes from company headquarters), the U.S. Pacific Fleet, the Naval Space and Warfare Command in San Diego (where Rite-Solutions also has an office), and defense-contracting giants such as Raytheon and General Dynamics. On the commercial side, it builds complex back-office and player-management systems for casinos—mission-critical technologies for a transactions-intensive industry that have to operate, without fail, twenty-four hours a day, seven days a week, 365 days a year. Put simply, this is a company with smart people, building expensive products, for important customers with big problems.

Given that Rite-Solutions plays for such high stakes, and that its products come with big (often multimillion-dollar) price tags, you'd expect Lavoie and Marino to run the proverbial tight ship—to lead according to rigidly top-down principles. In fact, they launched the company in January 2000 as an explicit alternative to the command-and-control environments they'd suffered through their entire careers. They spent twenty years together as senior executives with a company called Analysis & Technology, a highly regarded engineering and IT-services provider. Analysis & Technology did well, went public, and sold itself to a bigger company called Anteon (which, in turn, sold itself to General Dynamics). Lavoie and Marino walked away with a bundle of cash—and a burning desire to demonstrate that it was possible to do cutting-edge work in a no-margin-for-error field with a new set of principles about what leaders do and where good ideas come from.

"We may have started the company, but we knew that we would not be the smartest people here," explains cofounder and CEO Lavoie. "I had spent thirty years in highly structured organizations where good ideas could only flow from the top down and someone's value was defined by the 'box' they sat in rather than the insights they had. Sure, we had real-world experience and a vision of where we wanted the company to be. But how to get there from here, which technologies to choose, which products to develop, we didn't have those answers."

That's a refreshing dose of humility from a sixtysomething leader with an enviable track record of business success. Rite-Solutions president Joe Marino, also a sixtysomething technologist, echoes this self-effacing outlook on leadership. "There's nothing wrong with experience," he says. "The problem is when experience gets in the way of innovation. In technology-driven industries, maybe in most industries, the higher you rise, the more removed you get from what's actually going on. As founders, the one thing we know is that we don't know everything. Our job is to create an environment where people can express their ideas, no matter where they are in the organization, and then to make sense of all the ideas that emerge."

In part this means creating a looser, more flexible, more humane culture than what exists at most defense-oriented companies. Rite-Solutions is filled with whip-smart software programmers, advanced-degree scientists and engineers, and naval-warfare experts who had long stints in the military or civilian government agencies before they signed on with the company—not always the most gregarious, outspoken, freewheeling cast of characters. So Lavoie and Marino have used tremendous creativity to infuse the environment with a sense of informality, personality, even frivolity. For example, a "welcome wagon" delivers flowers, a fruit basket, and a greeting card to the family of new employees, as a way to signal that life at Rite-Solutions will be different from what they've experienced elsewhere. New employees complete a "birth certificate" before they report for duty, which describes their career, hobbies, pets, interests, nicknames, and other personal stuff. A nifty piece of company-developed technology displays the birth certificate whenever an employee interacts by phone or Web with another employee—a quick way to find common ground and start a conversation. At 9:00 A.M. on the first day of work, each new employee gets a welcome-to-the-company bash, complete with pats on the back, all sorts of wrapped gifts, and a general feeling of good cheer and camaraderie.

> "There's nothing wrong with experience," says Rite-Solutions cofounder Joe Marino. "The problem is when experience gets in the way of innovation. As founders, the one thing we know is that we don't know everything."

"Why do so many places throw parties when people *leave* the company?" wonders Marino. "Doesn't it make more sense to celebrate when they arrive? Every important person in that new employee's life knows they've started a new job. It says something to them if their new company celebrates their arrival. We want to make people feel important, because they are important."

This colorful and seemingly inexhaustible set of workplace practices (trust me, there are loads more) creates an infectious sense of energy and sets a playful tone for the organization—with an emphasis on playful. One of the first times I heard Lavoie and Marino explain their ideas about leadership, before I visited Rite-Solutions and saw for myself how things worked, I was at a business conference where the speakers included world-famous explorer Robert Ballard (the man who discovered the *Titanic* and the *Bismarck*), prolific inventor Dean Kamen (who created the Segway personal transporter), and other big-name, high-minded innovators. When it was time for the Rite-Solutions founders to share their ideas, the session began with a pretty offbeat PowerPoint presentation (including a hilarious illustration of Jim Lavoie in women's clothing). Then the talk morphed into a song-and-dance routine. To the tune of "Daisy Bell" (better known as "A Bicycle Built for Two"), Lavoie and Marino sang an original composition ("In a Box, There's No Room for Two") about the limits to creativity inside traditional organizations. "If you want to tap your feet, tap your feet," Lavoie told the amused (and slightly befuddled) audience. "If you want to clap your hands, clap your hands. If you're white, pick one and focus!"

That's pretty good evidence that there's something a little different about this high-powered software developer and military contractor. The evidence that there's something *profoundly* different is when new employees (also on their first day) get issued $10,000 worth of "opinion money" and are invited to become part of the company's internal stock market for ideas—technology that Lavoie and Marino devised to unearth creativity from anywhere and everywhere inside Rite-Solutions. The stock market, Lavoie explains, "is a mechanism to take the employee relationship beyond the transaction level—I pay you, you do a job—to an emotional level where people are entrusted with the future direction of the company, asked for their opinions, listened to, and rewarded for successful ideas. Most companies say, 'This is what we do.' We ask, 'What can we do with what we know?' The stock market helps provide the answers."

Here's how it works: Any member of the company can propose that Rite-Solutions acquire or develop a new technology, enter a new line of business, or make an efficiency improvement that reduces costs. These proposals become stocks, complete with their own ticker symbols, discussion lists, and e-mail alerts. Each stock comes with a detailed description (called an expect-us, as opposed to a prospectus) and begins trading at a price of $10. (The user interface is reminiscent of a Bloomberg terminal, with charts, updates, portfolio valuations, and so on.) Employees signal their enthusiasm for an idea by investing in the stock and, better yet, volunteering to work on the project, to contribute to its so-called Budge-It Items (small steps that move an idea forward). Volunteers share in the proceeds, in the form of real money, if the stock delivers real-world revenue. The market regularly updates a Top 20 list of the most highly thought-of ideas, which get special attention as a result of their grassroots support.[13]

The ideas in Mutual Fun are divided into three categories. "Blue chip" stocks are low-risk proposals that fall into the company's sweet spot. "Futures" are high-risk, high-reward ideas that require Rite-Solutions to stretch as a business or enter an unfamiliar market. "Savings bonds" are ideas to cut costs rather than increase revenue, to help the bottom line without necessarily growing the top line. Over time, as employees buy and sell stocks, an algorithm adjusts prices to reflect the sentiments of the company's highly credentialed engineers and computer scientists, its veteran project managers—as well as its marketers, accountants, even the receptionist. The market also includes "penny stocks," blue-sky ideas where employees are invited to "give their two cents" without having to invest opinion money.

"Mutual Fun allows half-baked ideas to get into the community," CEO Lavoie told a business-school researcher who studied the stock market. "It lets people start chatting about them, making them better, polishing. Informal 'interest networks' form without management, without supervision. When an informal network forms, [we] let it form. . . . What we found when we were at a big company was that we were very innovative at stopping innovation."

The stock market is, without question, a slick application of technology—just the sort of thing Rite-Solutions is respected for in military and commercial circles. But it's also a compelling metaphor for leadership, for what can happen when senior executives combine big ambitions for their company with genuine humility about how to realize those ambitions. For example, one of the earliest stocks on Mutual Fun (ticker symbol: VIEW) was a proposal to apply three-dimensional visualization technology, akin to video games, to help sailors and Homeland Security personnel practice making decisions in emergency situations. Initially, Joe Marino was unenthusiastic about the idea—"I'm not a joystick jockey," he quips—but support among employees was overwhelming. Today, that product line, called

Rite-View, is a huge hit. "Would this have happened if it were just up to the guys at the top?" Marino asks. "Absolutely not. But we could not ignore the fact that so many people were rallying around the idea. This system removes the terrible burden of us always having to be right."

Or consider a more recent product that also had its roots in the stock market. Rite-Solutions has long furnished "asset-tracking" systems for the military—technology that monitors where equipment is and how it's moving around, say, a naval base. Chuck Angell, a veteran employee, thought the company could apply this expertise to civilian use—specifically, to monitor the comings and goings of school buses and whether or not kids are on the proper bus. His expect-us generated tremendous rank-and-file support on the stock market and a product called Rite-Track was born. Sure enough, orders for the innovation have begun to materialize from school administrators eager to reassure parents (and themselves) about student safety. Rite-Track affixes buses with global-positioning systems and outfits kids with a small tag that gets read by a device on the bus. The tags (which contain no personal information about the students) match the right riders to the right bus, and the system issues alerts when things don't match or when riders are missing. (It's also capable of streaming high-quality video onto the bus as part of an edutainment system.)

All told, the CEO reports, the internal stock market, which took shape in January 2005, has paid huge dividends for the company. As of mid-2009, it had generated more than fifty workable ideas for new products, services, and processes. More than fifteen of these ideas had been launched into the marketplace, representing roughly 20 percent of total revenue for Rite-Solutions. The company had also filed patents on twelve innovations that had their origins in the stock market, a crucial addition to its arsenal of intellectual property.

One reason Mutual Fun works, Jim Lavoie argues, is that it distinguishes being creative from being an extrovert. Early on at Rite-Solutions, before the launch of the stock market, the founders tried all kinds of more familiar techniques to surface ideas from rank-and-file colleagues. They convened innovation summits, installed whiteboards throughout the offices, and built an Innovation Room to foster the creative process. There were lots of problems with these techniques, but one big problem is that they required people with good ideas to advocate for their ideas as well—and to do so in public, in front of their colleagues and bosses. "Offsites are for extroverts," the CEO says, "but most of your genius is in introverts. With the stock market, we have a 24-7 forum that introverts see as a safe haven for sharing. They can compose an expect-us at their pace, ask for help from colleagues, see people rallying around their ideas. We're getting an awful lot of fuel for this engine from the quiet people. Don't confuse extroverts with geniuses."

There's another big virtue to the system—it's good at surfacing creative ideas from the most unlikely places. For example, among the core technologies at Rite-Solutions are pattern-recognition algorithms that get used in military applications and at casinos. Rebecca Hosch, a member of the administrative staff, saw a tiny piece of this technology used during a high-tech game of bingo developed for the company Christmas party. (Hey, I told you these folks were geeky.) After some discussions with her daughter, who was frustrated about a project at school, it occurred to Hosch that the technology might also be used in educational settings, to create an entertaining way for students to learn about history or math, or, in her daughter's case, to learn about soil for an agricultural-science class.

So Hosch floated a stock called Win/Play/Learn (ticker symbol: WPL), which attracted a rush of investment from engineers eager to turn her idea into a product. Their enthusiasm led to meetings with Hasbro, the toy giant up the road in Pawtucket. Hosch's idea didn't become a product right away, but Rite-Solutions won a contract to help Hasbro build its VuGo multimedia system, which was introduced the following Christmas. It is a multimillion-dollar relationship that would not have surfaced without the internal stock market.

"We would have never connected those dots," Joe Marino says. "But one employee floated an idea, lots of people got passionate about it, and it led to important new customers and a new line of business." He calls the story an example of the "quiet genius" that goes untapped inside most organizations, because leaders have no capacity to search for ideas in unexpected places.

"We've always said that our most important job is to surface the quiet genius of individual employees and to harvest the collective genius of the whole company," Jim Lavoie concludes. "Creativity at most organizations is a blip when it needs to be a heartbeat. Innovation can't rely on a few specialists in product development. You need dreamers and doers, brainiacs and maniacs, thinkers and tinkerers. It has to be pervasive. The stock market has become a way of life here."

CHAPTER EIGHT

HIDDEN GENIUS AT WORK— FROM SHARED MINDS TO HELPING HANDS

We couldn't have made this discovery without the knowledge, passion, and persistence of volunteers from around the world—a diverse set of minds with expertise in areas from submarines to military history to genealogy. It represented a new model of collaboration that fits the world we live in, and it would not have been possible without the Internet. But the most important tool for this "flock-of-birds" phenomenon is leadership, not technology. Leaders have to understand the motivations of every member of the group, and create an environment where different kinds of people want to think and work together.

—JOHN ABELE, COFOUNDER, BOSTON
SCIENTIFIC, AND AN ORGANIZER OF THE
SEARCH FOR THE USS *GRUNION*

JOHN ABELE'S LIFE AS AN innovator, entrepreneur, and leader has been a long, exciting, rewarding journey. He is a pioneer in the field of less-invasive medicine—a collection of leading-edge technologies that transformed a whole set of surgeries and treatments (for diseases of the heart, lung, brain, and vascular system) into less-traumatic, less-expensive procedures from which patients recover more quickly. Based on those technologies, he built one of the great success stories in the medical-device industry, a company called Boston Scientific. Abele and his cofounder, Peter Nicholas, launched Boston Scientific in 1979, took it public in 1992, and grew it into a global giant. Today, it has twenty-five thousand employees, revenues of more than $8 billion, and a stock-market value of some $12 billion. Like any high-flying company in a fast-moving field, Boston Scientific has had its share of setbacks and controversies over the years, including run-ins with regulators and a huge acquisition that got a big thumbs-down from Wall Street analysts. Still, it stands as an iconic and influential company that helped to define a whole new industry and turned its founders into billionaires.

For all this success in the corporate world, though, one of the most exciting, rewarding (and certainly the longest) journeys of John Abele's life had nothing to do with medical devices, business plans, or Wall Street. It had to do with solving a heartbreaking mystery that had tugged at him, his family, and sixty-nine other families for more than six decades. On Sunday, May 24, 1942, at the U.S. Navy's submarine base in New London, Connecticut, John and his two older brothers, Bruce and Brad, along with their mother, Kay, had dinner with Mannert Lincoln Abele (who preferred the nickname Jim). At age thirty-eight, Lieutenant Commander Jim Abele was in charge of the USS *Grunion*, a diesel-powered submarine that would set sail the next morning for Pearl Harbor and shortly thereafter to the waters off Alaska's Aleutian Islands, to patrol for Japanese ships threatening U.S. territory. Commander Abele told his wife and three sons nothing of his top-secret mission and sent them home after an uneventful evening. It was the last time John (who was then five years old) would see his father. Jim Abele and his crew of five officers and sixty-four enlisted men disappeared without a trace. For more than sixty years, the navy listed the *Grunion*'s status simply as "overdue, presumed lost."

Hundreds of thousands of American families lost husbands, sons, and fathers in World War II, of course. But there was something about not knowing anything of Jim's fate—where his vessel had gone down, why it had gone down, how it had gone down—that gnawed at the Abeles. Kay refused to accept a death-benefit check from the U.S. government (her husband was missing, she insisted, not dead), and she never remarried. Neither did many other widows of the *Grunion* sailors. As the wife of the missing commander, Kay wrote heartfelt letters to the next of kin of all the missing crewmembers, and many of these family members wrote back—producing a flow of moving and anguished correspondence that went on in some cases for years, and that the Abele family preserved.

As the years went by, John and his brothers never lost interest in their father's unexplained disappearance. They made inquiries with the navy, reached out to historians and other experts in World War II submarine warfare, and struggled to find clues that would help solve the mystery. Brad Abele began assembling what he and his brothers called the "Jim Book," an account of what little information they had gleaned about the final mission of the *Grunion*. Still, despite all their professional success, vast financial resources, and knack for creating things and solving problems (John's brother Bruce is the coinventor of the legendary Polaroid Big Shot camera, which was a favorite of Andy Warhol), the Abele boys could not answer a decades-old question about the fate of their father.

It was the ultimate unsolved mystery—and the ultimate unmet challenge. Until, that is, a lucky break set in motion a journey of discovery that would eventually bring the mystery to a close—and would provide John Abele, a brilliant entrepreneur and business leader, with a lesson in the power of hidden genius to address all sorts of unmet challenges. The Boston Scientific cofounder tells the story with a sense of passion and wonder that is hard to capture on the page. ("It took so many extraordinary personalities to accomplish our mission," he marvels.) Still, let me offer a synopsis of this amazing tale—a story that warms your heart, fires your imagination, and opens your eyes to the new logic of leadership in challenging circumstances.[1]

One day, an Air Force officer and military-history buff named Robert M. Lane walked into an antiques shop in Denver, Colorado, and found a wiring diagram for a Japanese freighter called the *Kano Maru*. Lane collected such artifacts, so he bought the diagram, put it aside for a while, and then decided to learn more about it. He went to a website devoted to Japanese military history, posted the diagram, and asked for help. Within days, a military historian from Japan named Yutaka Iwasaki responded. He told Lane that the *Kano Maru* was a (heavily armed) Japanese supply ship that had operated off the Aleutian Islands during World War II. Iwasaki also translated his notes on an article that was published in 1963 by the captain of the Japanese ship, which told the story of a battle in which the *Kano Maru* sunk an American submarine named *Grunion*.

Thanks to another World War II enthusiast, Bruce Abele got wind of the online exchange, and he and his brothers began a desperate (virtual) search for Iwasaki. Eventually they found an e-mail address for someone named Yutaka Iwasaki—but was it the right one? John Abele sent a message explaining that he was the son of the commander of the *Grunion*, and asking if this Yutaka Iwasaki was the same person who had answered Robert Lane's questions. Within hours, Abele received a reply: "I am he. I pray for the repose of your father's soul."

Iwasaki translated the entire article and sent it to the Abele brothers—a communication that arrived like an answered prayer. The captain's account included a stark, almost minute-by-minute review of the fierce battle, off the Japanese-occupied island of Kiska, which ended on this chilling note: "*Kano Maru*'s forecastle gun fired; fourth shot hit the conning tower of the sub. It is thought the last of *Grunion*." So much for that famous oxymoron "military intelligence." A simple question that the navy had been unable to answer for decades—What happened to the USS *Grunion*?—was answered by two World War II enthusiasts who lived half a world apart and knew nothing of the pain of the Abele family or the families of the other crewmembers.[2]

For John Abele, though, this long-sought news was the beginning of the story, not the end. Fueled by Iwasaki's revelations, he and his brothers set out on a remarkable two-part project. First, they vowed to search for and find the wreckage of the *Grunion*, thousands of feet below the frigid waters of the Bering Sea, and see for themselves their father's final resting place. Second, they vowed to search for and find living relatives of all sixty-nine members of the crew, inform them of the sub's fate, and bring to them the same sense of relief that their family hoped to experience. After more than sixty years, closure was at hand.

It was a truly ambitious project, with hugely long odds, and John Abele pursued it with a sense of humility and a commitment to wide-open, worldwide, grassroots participation. Sure, he was wealthy, well connected, and technologically savvy—a leader with the wherewithal to try to spend his way to success. Instead, inspired by the vital contributions of total strangers like Robert Lane and Yutaka Iwasaki, Abele recognized that there were all sorts of people, from all walks of life, with all kinds of expertise, who would help the search for the sub and the family members of the crew. So he and his brothers issued an invitation to hobbyists, amateur historians, and World War II buffs of all backgrounds to participate in a mission to find the *Grunion*.

Abele was overwhelmed by the brainpower the project unleashed. "We had experts on World War II submarines that participated," he told me. "We had experts on how the navy works, because we needed some connections there. We had experts in explosives, who worked on the 'attack analysis' for the battle. It was amazing! People did the equivalent of PhD theses—not to get attention for themselves, but because they were passionate about the project. There was a purity to the motivation that was quite powerful."

In August 2006, thanks to this outpouring of expertise, along with more incredible detective work from Yutaka Iwasaki ("This could not have happened without him," Abele emphasizes), who tracked down the *Kano Maru*'s log book, and thus shrunk the target area for the search even more, the Abele brothers determined that they had collected enough information to hire the *Aquila*, a rugged, 165-foot commercial-fishing boat, equip it with sonar, and conduct a 250-square-mile search of the ocean floor. Eventually, that search produced images of a long, narrow tube resting three thousand feet below the surface. It was impossible to say what exactly the sonar had turned up, but it was impossible to deny that it might be the *Grunion*. Abele and his brothers vowed to resume the search the next summer, with technology that could get closer to the target and send back images of much higher resolution.

The intriguing results of the search in the Bering Sea inspired a different (and equally remarkable) group of volunteers to search for the descendants of the missing crew. Three amateur genealogists, each of whom were relatives of sailors from the *Grunion*, none of whom had ever met each other, made it their collective mission to track down members of sixty-nine different families, and to persuade the newspaper in each family member's city or town to write an article about their local hero. These so-called sub ladies—Mary Bentz of Bethesda, Maryland; Vickie Rodgers of Mayfield, Kentucky; and Rhonda Raye of Cartersville, Georgia—were so clever and dogged that they became a story of their own, the subject of a feature article in *USA Today* along with other accolades and attention. "She's my best friend, and we've never met," Rodgers told *USA Today* about her relationship with Raye. "I bet we'd email 200 times a day. And I feel like I know a lot of these men. I'm the mother of five, so I feel like a mother to them." (The letters from and to Kay Abele were an important starting point for much of the genealogical research.)[3]

John Abele, who has worked with some of the world's most gifted scientists and engineers, was struck by the quiet genius and collective firepower of the soft-spoken sub ladies. "They knew how to scour obituaries, examine probate records, they did really good historical research," he told me. "It took a year to find some of these relatives. They showed real persistence of the old kind. They also learned how to 'sell' the story to journalists, as a way to get the profiles written. This was an important part of the project for them, a way to celebrate the lives of these lost sailors."

In August 2007, the volunteers from around the world who had become part of the search had reasons of their own to celebrate. With John Abele on board, the *Aquila* returned to the waters off Kiska, this time with a remote-operated vehicle (ROV), a submarine drone equipped with state-of-the-art video cameras. The cameras confirmed what Abele, his brothers, and their many colleagues had so fervently hoped. Here in the North Pacific, a thousand miles off the coast of mainland Alaska, they found what they had been looking for. On that very same day, Mary Bentz found a family member from the sixth-ninth and final sailor on the *Grunion* crew. As one truly wonderful account of the saga put it, "At last, the list was complete: On the same day the *Grunion* was found, the sub ladies had met their goal."[4]

John Abele collected seventy vials of seawater from the area of the wreckage, one for the family of each member of the *Grunion* crew, as well as flowers from Kiska Island, which he sent to the families of Japanese sailors whose ships the *Grunion* had sunk, and came home with the definitive answers that had eluded his family for sixty-five years. On October 2, 2008, the U.S. Navy made official what everyone already knew—their discovery was, in fact the *Grunion*. On October 11, 2008, more than two hundred relatives, including widows (both in their nineties) of two of the sailors, gathered for a memorial service at the site of the *Grunion*'s sister sub, the USS *Cod*, in Cleveland, Ohio. Mary Bentz recited the names of all seventy members of the crew, while the *Grunion*'s original bell, which had been removed before the sub set sail, and was discovered in Greenville, Mississippi (another remarkable tale), tolled in their memory. There were prayers, speeches, and a general sense of a shared experience. "It was like finding a family that has been there all the time, you just never knew you had it," the cofounder of Boston Scientific told me, still moved by the gathering.

For John Abele—inventor, entrepreneur, and business leader— the search for the *Grunion* was first and foremost a lifelong personal challenge. But he also sees it as a challenge to long-held ideas about how projects work and problems get solved. "This story is a collection of improbables," he says, "but improbables that were made possible because a diverse group of people with the right expertise came to- gether and stayed together. This isn't just collective intelligence, it's collective *capability*. We had volunteers from Australia to Israel, and there was a real self-organizing quality to how they worked. But that doesn't mean groups like this don't need leadership. I think of it as the 'collaboration paradox.' Leaders can't be so self-effacing that they become invisible. They have to create a reason to collaborate and a platform to make it possible. If you create the right conditions, it's amazing what can happen."

(MANY) EYES ON THE PRIZE—NETFLIX'S MILLION-DOLLAR IDEA TO ATTRACT IDEAS

IN CHAPTER 7, IN SETTINGS as varied as the rehearsal hall of a renowned chamber ensemble, the research labs of a world- class technology giant, and the "stock market for ideas" at a fast-growing software developer, I explored the power of surfacing the hidden genius inside organizations as a way to challenge the top-down, lone-genius style of leadership that has left so many companies short of ideas and so many executives short of breath. But it's important to recognize, as the search for the USS *Grunion* demonstrates, that this new leader- ship mind-set applies to brainpower *outside* the organization as well as inside, and to the no-nonsense business of actually getting things done as well as to the blue-sky excitement of generating ideas. Think of it as (hidden) genius at work: a virtual collection of shared minds can produce a real-world outpouring of helping hands.

John Abele puts it well. The opportunity for leaders, he argues, is not just to recognize the virtues of collective intelligence. It is, as he said, to build a platform for "collective capability"—creating the conditions in which diverse and dispersed groups of people can rally around a cause, sort through a problem, and make tangible progress on difficult-to-achieve goals. "So many people ended up working with each other without ever meeting each other," he says of the search for his father's long-lost vessel and the relatives of its crewmen. "Even within specific parts of the search, leadership roles changed hands depending on the task at hand. The volunteers who tracked down the families were different from the volunteers who organized the memorial service with those families. People had such different skills and experiences."

Indeed, in an era of huge dislocations and scarce resources, fewer and fewer companies are in a position to hire lots of new people or devote big budgets to new projects as a way of moving forward. But most companies are surrounded by customers, suppliers, fans, advocates, and interested parties of all kinds who are passionate about what they do, bursting with ideas, and eager to be more involved. Why not invite them to demonstrate their creativity to you, share their best ideas with you, and collaborate to solve your toughest problems or deliver on your most promising opportunities? Unlike, say, an orchestra, where the only people who can play are quite literally the musicians onstage, the performance of your organization can draw on talented "players" who may never work *for* you but are eager to work *with* you, especially if you, as a humbitious leader, work to keep them excited and engaged. It's a mind-set that challenges how most executives define their jobs, but that improves the odds that they will succeed in the job of making real progress in difficult circumstances.

Most companies are surrounded by customers, suppliers, fans, and advocates who are bursting with ideas and eager to be more involved. Why not invite them to share their best ideas with you?

It cost Reed Hastings, founder, president, and CEO of Netflix, Inc., the Internet-based movie-rental service, a cool one million dollars to experience this phenomenon firsthand—and it was arguably the smartest money he has spent in the history of his company. My colleague Polly LaBarre and I analyzed the growth of Netflix in our book, *Mavericks at Work*, and we made the case that its smash-hit success (which has gotten even bigger since *Mavericks* was published) was as much about the intelligence it delivered to its customers as about the DVDs it shipped in the mail or streamed over the Internet. Brick-and-mortar retailers like Blockbuster focus on *distribution*, looking to stuff as many DVDs, computer games, candy, and popcorn into as many homes as possible. But Netflix is an online innovator that aims to enhance the quality of *selection*—tapping the intelligence of millions of members to help individual members discover movies they wouldn't find otherwise.[5]

"It's possible to totally misunderstand Netflix," CEO Hastings explained. "Some people think of us just as a DVD-rental service. But the real problem we're trying to solve is, How do you transform movie selection so that consumers can find a steady stream of movies they love? It's a huge matching problem. We've got [more than 100,000] DVD titles over here. There are 300 million Americans over there. But most people can't tell you ten movies they're dying to see because they know they're going to be great. The way you solve the problem is to use the insights of other people to build a community effect. It is absolutely the key to customer satisfaction."

Over the years, the company's homegrown recommendation software, called Cinematch, did such a good job of suggesting movies for customers to see, given what movies they'd already seen, that Netflix grew like gangbusters. (Its customers make some 60 percent of their viewing choices based on what Cinematch recommends for them.) At the end of 2009, just ten years after the company began offering its rent-by-mail service, Netflix had annual revenues of more than $1.6 billion, a stock-market value of $3 billion, and a position of genuine influence in Hollywood. That's because it had some twelve million paying customers who had provided an astounding *two billion* movie ratings—a database of likes and dislikes that influences the movies customers want to see next, based on the movies they and other customers have already seen.

Think of it as the Netflix Effect. The list of the one hundred most popular movies in Netflix history bears little resemblance to the list of all-time Hollywood favorites—in part, of course, because movie enthusiasts still like to see blockbusters on the big screen, but in larger measure because the experience of being a Netflix customer exposes you to a wider range of genres and titles than you would normally see, driven by recommendations from customers who tend to like what you like. "What we are trying to do is open up people's tastes," the CEO told us. "We give everyone a platform to broaden their tastes in movies."

What Reed Hastings *didn't* tell us was that as the company's collection of titles got bigger and bigger, and its customer base got more and more diverse, it was becoming harder and harder for Cinematch to improve its performance—to predict more and more accurately which titles customers would like to see. It was a vexing technical limitation that threatened to become a real business limitation, especially for a company whose success was built on a loyal and passionate following of customers who felt like Netflix had an uncanny knack for identifying movies they would enjoy. "If we knew how to do it, we'd have already done it," Hastings told one reporter about the challenge of making recommendations more effective. "And we're pretty darn good at this now. We've been doing it a long time."[6]

If Hastings were more of a conventional leader, he would have made all the familiar, conventional moves—put even more pressure on his programmers and engineers to tweak the software, hire more programmers and engineers in an effort to throw big resources at a big headache. Instead, he took the decidedly unconventional step of inviting the rest of the world to address Netflix's challenge. Just as John Abele created a platform in which smart people could help with his all-consuming search for the *Grunion*, Reed Hastings created a platform in which smart people could help him search for ways to improve his all-important Cinematch software.

The proposal was simple—and alluring. Hastings opened a database for outsiders to work on that included more than a hundred million ratings of nearly eighteen thousand movies by more than 480,000 customers, the largest such database ever published. He then announced that he would pay $1 million to anyone, anywhere in the world, who could improve the performance of Cinematch by 10 percent—that is, make it 10 percent more likely that a specific customer would enjoy (and thus rate highly) a specific movie that Cinematch predicted he or she would enjoy. It would be a small improvement in performance that would pay huge dividends for the company in terms of customer satisfaction.

Hastings called the program the Netflix Prize, and he unveiled it on Monday, October 2, 2006 (the very day *Mavericks at Work* was published, coincidentally enough). News of the prize took the technology world by storm. What a vast database! What a tough mathematical challenge! What a huge reward! On Monday, September 21, 2009, precisely 1,082 days after the challenge was unveiled, Reed Hastings declared a winner. A seven-person team of software and electrical engineers, statisticians, and machine-learning researchers from Austria, Canada, Israel, and the United States submitted an algorithm that improved the performance of Cinematch by just more than 10 percent. Hastings presented a check to the winners at an event at the Four Seasons Hotel in New York City—the first time all seven members of the group had been in the same place at once.

Already, the Netflix Prize has achieved iconic status in geek circles. *Fortune* declared it "the Internet era's most visible example of user-generated innovation" (although, in fact, tens of thousands of the rank-and-file participants weren't "users" of Netflix since the service is only available in the United States.) The award "should serve as a model for other tech companies working on hard problems," argued Farhad Manjoo, the influential technology columnist at Slate.com, who calculated that Netflix "would have had to shell out more than \$3 million for just one year of the top performers' time"—and that assumes, of course, that the company "could have sussed out who the top performers were going to be." Manjoo went on to urge Microsoft, a company that does not exactly suffer from a shortage of ambitious, talented programmers, to come up with its own version of the Netflix Prize to help it compete with Google in the search-engine wars.[7]

These tech-centric accolades are certainly well deserved. But I'd argue that the Netflix Prize deserves iconic status in leadership circles as well as in software circles. Just as the cofounder of Boston Scientific demonstrated with his successful quest to locate a missing submarine, the founder of Netflix showed that the best way to work on hard-to-solve challenges is to challenge conventional ideas about what kinds of people can work with you to solve them. The real genius of leadership today is knowing how to move forward when you and your senior colleagues don't have all the answers—devising ways to uncover the most powerful ideas in the most unexpected places, even if those ideas come from outside the organization.

What are some of the nitty-gritty takeaways for leaders from the success of the Netflix Prize? One is the sheer scale and scope of the hidden genius at your disposal—if only you can figure out ways to invite it in to your organization. All told, the Netflix competition attracted entries from more than fifty thousand individuals or teams in 186 countries. The participants included people from all backgrounds and walks of life. In the middle of the competition, *Wired* profiled one participant, Gavin Potter, whose entries had rocketed to the top of the charts. He lived in London and was a retired management consultant who'd worked for PricewaterhouseCoopers, Shell, and IBM. He left IBM in the hopes of pursuing a PhD in machine learning. "When he read about the Netflix Prize he decided to give it a shot," the profile reported. "What better way to find out just how serious about the topic he really was?" About six months later, the *New York Times Magazine* published a feature that highlighted Len Bertoni, a "semiretired" computer scientist outside of Pittsburgh who swapped ideas with his twelve- and thirteen-year-old kids and was also high on the performance charts. A company named Opera Solutions, based in New York City, actually assigned several of its researchers to work on the prize for two years. (The CEO of Opera estimated that his company had generated $10 million worth of insights for its own business by virtue of its work on the Netflix project.)[8]

What's even more interesting, though, is that these individual brainiacs didn't just think on their own. Netflix was smart enough to keep the competition for the prize open, transparent, and dynamic. It maintained a "leaderboard" that tracked the progress of the top contenders, and it created an online forum where people could interact and exchange ideas. Very quickly, to the surprise of the company, the Netflix Prize morphed from a worldwide competition into a global community. And that's another big takeaway for leaders.

"We had no idea the extent to which people would collaborate with each other," James Bennett, vice president for recommendation systems, told *Wired*. Indeed, many participants shared their smartest thinking on the open forums and went so far as to supply their best code for all to see. "Competitors frequently help one another out," the *New York Times Magazine* noted, "discussing algorithms they've tried and publicly brainstorming new ways to improve their work, sometimes even posting reams of computer code for anyone to use. When someone makes a breakthrough, pretty soon every other team is aware of it and starts using it too."

Netflix showed that the way to work on hard-to-solve challenges is to challenge conventional ideas about what kinds of people can solve them. The real genius of leadership today is knowing how to move forward when you don't have all the answers.

Toward the end of the nearly three-year process, as the leaderboard showed that a bunch of teams and individuals were nearing the prize-winning threshold, the spirit of collaboration turned into one of flat-out mergers and acquisitions, as far-flung groups threw in together to cross the finish line. The winning team (called Bellkor's Pragmatic Chaos) was a merger of three different teams that decided to pool their ideas. The second-place finishers (whose algorithm matched the performance of the winning group, but was submitted twenty-four minutes later) was a worldwide coalition of thirty participants, who combined into a team called The Ensemble.

"We had a bona fide race to the very end," CEO Reed Hastings marveled on the day Netflix named a winner. "Teams that had previously battled it out independently joined forces to surpass the 10 percent barrier." Just as with the *Grunion*, collective intelligence turned into collective capability—shared minds produced an outpouring of helping hands that delivered tangible results.

THE SOLE OF COLLABORATION—JOHN FLUEVOG'S GENIUS BY DESIGN

I'LL BE THE FIRST TO admit that as compelling as the case studies in this chapter have been, they can also come off as somewhat intimidating. It's wonderful that John Abele and his worldwide team of volunteers worked together to locate a submarine that had been missing for more than sixty-five years. But their collective effort drew on a truly eclectic group of contributors with highly specialized knowledge and skills. It's impressive that Reed Hastings rallied tens of thousands of people from 186 different countries to address one of his company's most pressing technical challenges. But the Netflix Prize does feel a bit like "geeks gone wild"—mathematicians, statisticians, philosophers, and software engineers vying to prove to themselves (and to each other) how smart they really are. Are there case studies and business models that are a bit more accessible, a bit less technological, and a lot more applicable to the problems and opportunities facing leaders in more traditional environments? Are there examples of group genius at work that the rest of us can put to work in our organizations?

One colorful answer to this pragmatic question involves the leadership journey of John Fluevog. For nearly forty years, this Canadian-born designer has been creating high-profile, high-fashion (and pretty high-priced) shoes that he sells in his own high-end boutiques in Boston, Toronto, Montreal, New York, Los Angeles, and several other cities across North America. With tongue in cheek, Fluevog calls himself the company's "sole proprietor"—and there's no question that when it comes to footwear, few designers have his flair or his following. Some of the word's biggest stars wear his shoes, from musicians to supermodels to Hollywood celebrities. In *Truth or Dare*, the behind-the-scenes documentary of her "Blond Ambition" tour, Madonna flaunts her hot-pink Fluevogs (along with much else) before the cameras. The Black Eyed Peas are big Fluevog fans and like to wear his shoes onstage when they perform. Absolut Vodka devoted one of its iconic advertisements to a silver shoe designed by Fluevog, and his enthusiasts around the world describe themselves as "Fluevogers." In other words, when it comes to creating shoes that are off the beaten path and on the cultural radar, John Fluevog is something of a genius.

In recent years, though, Fluevog hasn't just been presenting ideas about shoes and style to customers; he has also been soliciting ideas from them—encouraging enthusiasts to submit their own sketches for leather boots, high-heeled dress shoes, even sneakers with flair. He posts the submissions on his company's website, invites visitors to vote for their favorites, and then manufactures and sells the most promising designs. "Customers want to express themselves, to be involved with the brand," Fluevog told me when we visited in Boston, at his boutique on shopper-centric Newbury Street. "For so long, people would hand me a drawing of their personal design for a shoe or ask if I had considered an idea they liked. This program is a natural outgrowth of that desire for connection. People want to be involved with companies they care about. We want companies to hear us."[9]

Patricia Seybold, the influential technology analyst who chronicles the changing relationship between companies and their customers, has heard this message loud and clear. In a well-regarded book titled *Outside Innovation*, she offered a big-picture perspective on the sort of mind-set flip that Fluevog's invitation represents. "There's an underlying assumption that drives traditional innovation: 'our experts are smarter that our customers,'" Seybold writes. "While it is certainly true that your company probably has deep subject matter expertise in a certain domain—automobile design, financial derivatives structures, new drug discovery—it's also true that your customers are subject matter experts in their own right. In particular, your customers know more about their context, their desired outcomes, their needs, and their constraints than you can ever hope to learn." What's more, Seybold adds, what customers know and want will affect how they behave. "They will innovate—with or without your help—to create better ways to do things or to design products and services that meet their specific needs," she argues. "If you want to harness the power of customer's organic creativity, you need to support their creative processes with tools, with resources, and with imagination."[10]

That's precisely what John Fluevog has done, and the results have been dramatic. Since he invited his customers to share their ideas with him, literally thousands of sketches have flowed into headquarters in Vancouver. To date, nearly three hundred have been good enough to get posted as finalists on the website, and the company has introduced twelve shoes based on customer designs. When I visited with Fluevog, his Newbury Street store was selling five of the most popular customer-inspired models, including the Urban Angel Traffic, a walking shoe (retail price: $179) designed by Nastassia Pojidaeva, a screenwriter in Moscow, and the Fellowship Hi Merrilee, a vintage-style pump ($189) created by Merrilee Liddiard, a children's book illustrator and graphic designer who was based in Provo, Utah, when she submitted the design.

Importantly, Fluevog doesn't write his customers checks to reward them for their designs. Instead, he offers them something of greater psychological value than money—the right to *name* the shoe, and thus to see the name they chose (after themselves, such as with the Fellowship Hi Merrilee, or after a source of inspiration or even an inside joke) on the shelves of boutiques in some of the most fashionable shopping districts in the world. (Nastassia Pojidaeva, the only Fluevog customer to submit two ideas that were made into actual shoes, chose to name her other design, the Halo Anastassia, more or less after herself.) Meanwhile, the company's website features their photos, bios, and the stories of how their designs came to be and what happened after the shoes hit the stores—a real spotlight on their talent, since this has become one of the most popular sections of the much-visited Fluevog site.

"My mother always made my sisters and [me] wear saddle shoes when we were younger," Merrilee Liddiard explained in her entry on the site. "We wore them for everything—home, church, school, play. I even had to wear them to gym class while the other kids had sneakers. At the time I was reluctant to wear them over and over again but as I've grown they have become nostalgic—a reminder of a magical childhood. I took these memories as inspiration for my Merrilee Fluevogs. I wanted to create something that would be a modern, classy and feminine homage to my childhood worn out saddle shoes. Once I had the idea, the sketch came pretty quickly. It took me only a couple of days to put it down on paper. . . . To see this shoe design come to life has been amazing and exciting."[11]

No one would accuse me of being an expert when it comes to fashion ideas, but I know a great *business* idea when I see it—and this humbitious, outside-in approach to leadership and design certainly qualifies. John Fluevog walks the talk when it comes to identifying and unleashing hidden genius: he has figured out how to tap the skills, passions, and ideas of his most loyal customers as a way to refresh the brand, recharge himself, and challenge his own design thinking. "We are all one big, beautiful brain," he likes to say when describing his philosophy of creativity. This well-designed invitation to customers allows them to contribute a bit of their brainpower to him, and to turn their creative ideas into commercial products.

In fact, the more I got to know Fluevog and his colleagues, the more I wanted to get to know some of their design-minded custom-ers as well—people who were so enthusiastic about the brand, and so eager to share their ideas, that they had offered their skills to build someone else's business. The more of these customers I talked to, the more impressed I was by their intelligence, their talents, their knowl-edge, and the incredible dedication they brought to their submis-sions—just because the founder was smart enough to invite them into his company. Forget recharging John Fluevog; getting to know these remarkable characters recharged *me*.

The first Fluevoger I talked to was Samantha Zaza, a thirtysome-thing artist who designed a striking slip-on shoe for women with a wide strap, three large buttons, and a miniheel that makes it both fashionable and comfortable. (The shoe, called the Zaza, went on sale in February 2009 for $239.) Samantha, a graduate of the Rhode Island School of Design (RISD), now lives in Istanbul, Turkey, where she does a wide range of artistic work, largely in colored pencil and ink, inspired by her love of history and her eye for historical fashion. (Her wonderfully playful series "Les Petits Désirs" features a collec-tion of women in towering wigs and classic gowns talking on and fumbling with cell phones. Her fabulously expressive "Coup" series showcases pigeons in various Napoleonic military uniforms.)

Samantha told me she's always been a fan of "spats"—a shoe accessory that covers the instep and the ankle—of the sort that were worn by the well-to-do and by military officers in the nineteenth century. ("I have no idea why," she says, "I just find them appealing.") So her design for a shoe was a spats-inspired take on a classic Fluevog look. "I'd always wanted to design a shoe, I got this idea, and I submitted a sketch on a whim," she told me a few weeks after her design went on sale. "Actually, I doodled the original sketch on the back of an appliance manual before I went to bed one night. The next thing I knew, I got an e-mail from the company telling me that they were intrigued by what I'd submitted. The final design is pretty close to my original sketches, so the process was pretty easy."

Next I talked to Janet Erwin, who runs her own advertising agency outside of Winston-Salem, North Carolina, and designed a knee-high leather boot that represented her twist on one of her favorite Fluevog models. Janet is a horse enthusiast, and she tried to wear the company's Rosabelle boot when she rode in competition. But the Rosabelle just wasn't practical for riding—the zipper was on the inside, which meant it rubbed against the saddle, and the lack of snaps meant the zippers could slide down when the rider's leg is bent. So she created a boot that worked in the ring and looked good when you wore it to parties. The result was an elaborate sketch submitted back in 2006 of a leather boot with a full-length zipper in the back, straps over the laces, and snaps on top—all meant to respond to her hard-core equestrian concerns and make a fashion statement as well.

Unlike with Samantha Zaza, Erwin's design did not meet with instant acclaim from the staff. Her boot was attractive, the designers said, but awfully expensive to manufacture. But she persisted, complete with letters, poems, and loads of e-mail interactions making the case for her ideas and responding to suggestions from Fluevog's team. The result was a striking boot called the Nanette, which was part of

Fluevog's Fall 2007 line. "We went back and forth for more than a year," says Erwin, who exudes the personality of a woman on a mission. In fact, she chose the name Nanette based on the old movie *No, No Nanette*—since Fluevog said no to her so many times before it finally said yes. "There was nothing like seeing that actual, physical boot when it finally arrived," she told me. "My passion paid off."

A young biochemist by the name of Jessica Masarek, who works for Pfizer, the pharmaceutical giant, was the third Fluevoger I got to know. The shy and soft-spoken Masarek impressed me a lot—and also *depressed* me a little. While she spends her days visiting hospitals, evaluating reams of data, and otherwise performing left-brain scientific tasks in connection with clinical trials of promising new drugs, she spends her free time as a right-brain whirling dervish. She has a real eye for design—her Fluevog shoe, called the Mini Masarek, debuted in the Fall 2003 line and was a big seller. But she doesn't just design shoes. After winning the Fluevog competition (inspired, she jokes, by "my short-lived shoe fame"), she enrolled in classes at New York City's Fashion Institute of Technology, where she learned how to *make* her own shoes. Meanwhile, she is also a highly skilled knitter and actually has her own knitting blog, where she offers advice on everything from hand-dyeing yarn to firsthand reports from a sheep and wool festival, to a series of posts on "nerdy knitting."

You can see why I got depressed: How does one person manage to possess such a wide variety of talents? (If I was that good at just one activity outside of work, I'd be pleased.) More to the point, how crazy would it be not to tap into a few of those talents, as John Fluevog did? "People used to tell Kurt Vonnegut that he could never be a writer because he was trained as a mechanical engineer," Masarek told me with a wry tone in her voice. "And he didn't start really writing until he was in his twenties or thirties. I keep that in mind as I pursue my interests outside of work. I am always making things, and I love to write about what I'm doing. I don't know how all this will affect my career, but I do think my 'creative' side will become a more important part of what I do. The Fluevog shoe was a big step in that direction."

John Fluevog's open invitation to his customers was a big step for him as well. He and his company get a wide range of ideas and inspiration, from an ever-wider range of enthusiasts, than they have ever gotten before. His performance in the marketplace improves, even as the demands on him as a lone genius are reduced. "Some of the ideas from customers are striking, but impossible to make," he explained as he reflected on the thousands of shoe ideas he's received over the years. (What tends to work best, he said, are intriguing twists on design themes that he and his colleagues are already exploring.) "But even submissions we can't make contribute to the stimulation. Our customers get more involved, and we get insights into who they are and what they're doing. It's better for both of us. At the end of the day, my customers make me who I am."

And he keeps improving on his invitation to customers. In November 2009, for example, the company launched a program called FluevogCreative, in which customers are invited to design print ads for specific shoes. One of the first models chosen was the Zaza, and in just the first few weeks of the program, a stream of customer-designed ads for this customer-designed shoe started flowing into Vancouver. They were really quite striking: funny, colorful, lavish, wildly creative. To this untrained eye, some of the most appealing ads for the Zaza were submitted by none other than Janet Erwin, the equestrian and Fluevog enthusiast who had designed the knee-high leather boot. It was a virtuous circle—talented customers who had designed shoes were designing ads for shoes designed by other talented customers.

THE COMPANY AS COMMUNITY—HOW THREADLESS PUTS *EVERYONE* IN CHARGE

IT'S HARD NOT TO BE inspired by John Abele's volunteer-fueled search for his father's final resting place. It's hard not to be amazed by the mathematical prowess that Reed Hastings unleashed by presenting a vexing challenge to tens of thousands of brilliant people (and paying handsomely for the best answers). It's hard not to be impressed by the creative spirit and raw energy of the designers, marketers, even scientists who responded to John Fluevog's call for ideas to recharge his popular brand. In each case, smart, powerful, successful leaders challenged themselves to rethink the right way to solve a problem or break new ground—and, in the process, figured out how to apply the hidden genius of contributors who will never work for them but were eager to work with them. Suddenly, it wasn't so lonely at the top.

Still, in each case, these examples of humbition at work are largely one-off initiatives—specific (albeit clever) ways to address well-defined problems that didn't lend themselves to traditional problem-solving techniques. But perhaps the highest form of humbition is when leaders rethink and reimagine the very role of the organization itself. That is, when they blur, even erase, the distinctions between who does the work and who makes the decisions, who's an employee and who's a customer, who's on the "inside" and who's on the "outside"—in other words, who's in charge in the first place.

That's what makes Orpheus both mystifying and gratifying as a metaphor for a new leadership mind-set. In the words of James Traub, the conductorless orchestra has figured out how "to establish authority without establishing an authority figure." That's also one of many lessons to be learned from Threadless, a small company whose meteoric growth offers big ideas for how organizations and their leaders may work in the future.

Threadless is in a pretty old-fashioned business—selling T-shirts (and a few other clothing items). But the company, which has become a full-blown Internet sensation, approaches the business in a completely newfangled way. All of the designs in its online catalog come from its customers, who submit original artwork to the site. Threadless has more than a million registered members and adds more than twenty thousand members per month. It receives an average of 150–200 new designs *per day*—that's more than a thousand designs a week. Members rate the submissions on a zero-to-five scale, and the most popular submissions, as determined by visitors to the site, become candidates to be made into actual shirts. (A team of Threadless employees makes the final decisions, based on a variety of creative and commercial criteria.) The company selects seven new designs (and reprints two old designs) each week and sells the shirts for $15 to $17 each. The winning designers receive $2,000 in cash and $500 in store credit for their designs, plus an additional fee if their designs get reprinted later.

This is an organization where, in the words of a headline in *Inc.* magazine, which has spent three decades chronicling how lone-genius entrepreneurs experience the thrill of victory and the agony of defeat, "The Customer Is the Company." Threadless "churns out dozens of new items a month—with no advertising, no professional designers, [and] no sales force," the magazine marveled. "And it's never produced a flop." All told, Threadless sells more than a hundred thousand shirts per month—that's more than a million shirts a year—with just thirty-five employees. (It also sells "hoodies," children's shirts and onesies, and, most recently, it added user-generated art prints to its catalog.)[12]

The brand is as hot as can be—young people around the world know and embrace Threadless as a company, a sensibility, and an online community. Since its inception in November 2000, according to an elaborate, multimedia Harvard Business School case study (yes, this free-spirited Internet outfit has gained the imprimatur of the West Point of capitalism), Threadless has attracted nearly 150,000 submissions from 42,000 aspiring designers—with more than 80 *million* votes cast by members to express their preferences. The company has nearly 1.5 million followers on Twitter (almost as many as Tony Hsieh of Zappos) and has launched what it calls Twitter Tees, in which Threadless members nominate actual "tweets" to be turned into shirts, and other members vote on their favorites. Threadless turns the most popular tweets—"Ironic, self-aware narcissism is still narcissism," or "Note to self: Actually read notes"—into nicely designed shirts.[13]

I asked Jacob DeHart, one of the company's cofounders, what leadership principles he and his colleagues have developed to guide the company's growth—without interfering with the guidance provided by its one million members. "We've got four rules we follow," he said. "We let the community create the content. We let the community build itself—no advertising. We let the community help with the business; we add features based on user feedback. And we reward members of the community for participating." In other words, Threadless doesn't just attract ideas for shirts—it provides opportunities for people with all sorts of skills to engage the company and each other, and for good ideas to emerge from all this interaction. "Most of the energy comes from how fast the product line is changing," cofounder Jake Nickell explained to me. "There's something for users to do every day—see which new designs are out, score the latest submissions, post a blog entry. It's just a very active community."[14]

> The Threadless phenomenon shows that you don't need a huge staff to do big things—particularly if you create a community of fans and allies who are willing and eager to do a lot of the work for you.

So what are the here-and-now lessons for leaders from this fashion-forward Internet phenomenon? First, you don't need a huge staff to do big things—particularly if you create a community of deeply engaged fans and allies who are willing and eager to do a lot of the work for you. What traditional design department could possibly match the creativity and energy of thousands, even tens of thousands, of talented young designers submitting their best work, and of visitors casting millions of votes to react to those designs? And these designers, it should be said, love to strut their stuff. Indeed, a few of them are so good, and have won so many times, that they've become minicelebrities in their own right, complete with devoted fans and vocal supporters who tout the virtue of their work.

Glenn Jones, a thirty-five-year-old designer based in Auckland, New Zealand, is one of the all-time Threadless champions. He has submitted more than a hundred designs since 2004, of which twenty have been printed—a remarkable track record given the number of designs from which users can select their favorites. He's been the subject of profiles in newspapers and magazines around the world, and recently started his own shirt-design and greeting-card company by virtue of his talent and visibility on Threadless. Ross Zietz, a young designer who grew up in Baton Rouge, Louisiana, is one of the few artists whose work rivals that of Glenn Jones in terms of its popularity—and he, like Jones, has put his Threadless celebrity to good use. Zietz submitted his first design in the summer of 2003 and has had twenty-five of his designs printed since then. As a result of his visibility, he's designed T-shirts for Dashboard Confessional, Dave Matthews Band, Phish, and other big acts. What's more, he now works full time at Threadless as the company's art director. Talk about a virtuous leadership circle: one of the company's most prolific outside designers has become one of its most valuable executives.

There's another big lesson for leaders: different people with different talents can contribute to your organization in many different ways. At Threadless, individual members don't just get rewarded for their artistic prowess. The company offers a collection of Type Tees (a forerunner to Twitter Tees) in which members who are clever with words submit pithy slogans ("Rock Is Dead, and Paper Killed It" or "To Err Is Human, to Arr Is Pirate") that get voted on and made into shirts. Meanwhile, members with a flair for marketing earn points (good for store credit) for referring new buyers and for submitting photos of themselves wearing Threadless shirts, evidence of their commitment to viral promotion. And since Threadless produces fixed amounts of each shirt, and does not add to the print run even if a particular design or slogan surges in popularity, members as a whole conduct a form of shared inventory control. One neat feature of the site is the constantly updated inventory bar, which shows how many shirts remain available in each size for each design—a warning for indecisive buyers to place an order before the supply runs out. Members can also vote to reprint a shirt that has gone out of stock as a Threadless classic.

Why doesn't the company sell unlimited quantities of its most popular offerings? "We're not like a traditional company that says, 'Oh this is selling really well, let's make it our meal ticket until people don't want to buy it anymore," answers cofounder Jake Nickell. "That doesn't do anything for the artist, and it doesn't do anything for our community. We've set the guidelines for how the company is going to run, and by staying within those guidelines, we foster and maintain trust with the people who participate. Trust is a very fragile thing. The most overlooked element of our company is how protective we are of our community, and how much we value having its trust."

Finally, it's worth emphasizing that these new ways of building and leading an organization don't just apply to the virtual world of the Internet. In September 2007, Threadless opened its first-ever physical store on the North Side of Chicago. The store stocks just twenty different T-shirt designs at a time, and no shirt stays on sale for more than two weeks—ways to evoke the sense of creative excitement and fast-changing selection that infuses the online catalog. But the real value of the store is not as a twenty-first-century version of the Gap. It is as a hangout, a community center, a social scene. The company and its members host art exhibits, run Photoshop seminars, and, in general, engage with and teach one another. They interact in the real world in the same spirit that they interact online—with a clear sense of grassroots participation and a commitment to distributed leadership.

Why does such a vibrant online enterprise need a physical manifestation of its brand, in the form of a store? (The company has since opened a second location in Chicago, this one focused on children's clothing.) "We wanted to have a physical place where people could learn about Threadless," says Jake Nickell. "We wanted to do in a brick-and-mortar space everything you could do on the site. That's why we don't think of it just as a store. It's an ever-evolving gallery space that shows what's new with our company and our members. Like everything else we do, we're putting everything in the hands of our customers."

CHAPTER NINE

RADICALLY PRACTICAL (III)—
FIVE HABITS OF HIGHLY
HUMBITIOUS LEADERS

MY AIM IN THE LAST two chapters was to show
how a wide range of high-powered executives
embraced a new leadership mind-set to meet a wide range of high-
stakes challenges—from the bright lights of classical music to the
secretive world of military software, from a quest to discover a long-
lost submarine to the search for ways to improve movie choices or attract fashion designs. For all of the variety in the stories and settings,
though, my aim was also to deliver a consistent message for executives, entrepreneurs, and innovators of all stripes who face the responsibility (and burden) of generating breakthrough ideas and delivering
outsized results. That message: you can't do new and exciting things
with your organization, especially under difficult conditions, with the
same old assumptions about what it means to lead.

Think back to that *Economist* essay I referenced in Chapter 7. Its
fondness for old-school titans of industry and larger-than-life moguls
was yet another expression of the Great Man theory of history. The
essay trumpeted the virtues of geniuses such as Bill Gates, Steve Jobs,
and Jack Welch (there were no women among its roster of heroes),
and then generalized from these (and earlier) movers and shakers:

"Henry Ford was as close as you can get to being deranged without losing your liberty. John Patterson, the founder of National Cash Register and one of the greatest businessmen of the gilded age, once notified an employee that he was being sacked by setting fire to his desk. Thomas Watson, one of Patterson's protégés, and the founder of IBM, turned his company into a cult and himself into the object of collective worship."[1]

Is this truly the face of leadership at its best? "The best ambassadors for business," the magazine insisted, "are the outsized figures who have changed the world and who feel no need to apologise for themselves or their calling." I'm sorry, but I don't think so. The best executives and entrepreneurs I've met understand that there is a vast difference between championing ambitious goals—aspiring to change the game in your company or your field—and assuming that you know best how to achieve those goals. Fierce personal confidence, a sense of infallibility as a leader, used to be a calling card of success. Today it is a warning sign of failure, whether from bad judgment, low morale among disillusioned colleagues, or burnout from the pressures of always having to be right.

There's a reason Bethany McLean and Peter Elkind titled their bestseller on the Enron disaster *The Smartest Guys in the Room,* and it goes beyond the arrogance, hubris, and criminality those deeply flawed executives displayed. That phrase captures the mind-set that too many of us expect even our most honest leaders to display—the assumption that being "in charge" means having all the answers. It may be lonely at the top, but executives who insist on solving problems or devising strategies on their own have no one but themselves to blame when they don't look so smart after all.[2]

Don't get the wrong idea: I'm not making the case that leaders are better off aiming low or being dull. That's a false choice as well as a ridiculous reading of history. Yes, game-changing executives champion new ideas and disruptive points of view—they have a compelling vision for the future. But that doesn't mean they have to (or expect to) see the future by themselves. Instead, they understand how to solve problems and make things happen in a world where no one—*not even them*—can expect to have all the answers. What follows, then, is a set of attributes to encourage you to challenge your own ideas and assumptions about what it means to lead. Or, as I like to think of them, the five habits of highly humbitious executives.

I. REAL BUSINESS GENIUSES DON'T PRETEND TO KNOW EVERYTHING.

INSTEAD, THEY RECOGNIZE THAT IN an interconnected world bursting with smart, well-trained, enthusiastic people, the most powerful ideas often come from the most unexpected places: the quiet genius locked deep inside the organization, the collective genius that surrounds the organization, the hidden genius of customers, suppliers, and other constituencies who would be happy to share what they know if they were asked. That's the mind-set of executives who figure out how to get killer results without killing themselves— and the difference, in the favorite phrase of longtime IBMer Jane Harper, between raw ambition and open-minded humbition.

The deeper I got invested in the stock market for ideas at Rite-Solutions, and the closer I studied the outpouring of brainpower unleashed by the Netflix Prize, the more I realized how little so many leaders (and organizations) ask of their employees, customers, and various outside partners. Not in terms of hard work, long hours, or loyalty—we may ask too much in that regard. But all too often, we barely scratch the surface of what the people we work with are capable of contributing to us, of what the people we sell to are capable of teaching us, of what the people we come into contact with are capable of sharing with us—if only we would look beyond their résumé, formal training, or official place in the hierarchy. As a leader, you never know what people are capable of doing until you invite them to show you what they can do. As Harriet Rubin has said, "Power is about what you can control. Freedom is about what you can unleash."

That's what made the Netflix Prize such a powerful phenomenon. Sure, the scale of the global creativity it unleashed was impressive—fifty thousand individuals or teams from 186 countries took part. But it was the wide-ranging diversity and surprising backgrounds of so many of the participants that made the competition so remarkable—and their ideas so original. Of course the Netflix Prize caught the fancy of mathematicians, database gurus, and software programmers. But management consultants, philosophers, and psychologists too? Over the course of the 1,082 days for which the competition was open to ideas, talented people from fields that, at first blush, have little to do with solving hard-core problems in collaborative filtering wound up making major contributions to the cause—mainly because Netflix CEO Reed Hastings gave them the opportunity to surprise him (and their fellow competitors). It's hard to know in advance who's got the answers you so desperately need.

The founders of Rite-Solutions have seen this same phenomenon play out in their company's Mutual Fun stock market. Employees aren't encouraged to limit proposals to technologies, business ideas, or cost-savings techniques in their field of expertise. Quite the contrary. Time and again, employees see possibilities for the company that have little or nothing to do with their function or department—and everything to do with the unpredictable nature of how and when fresh insights materialize. Since the stock market allows these grassroots innovators to post their ideas, and then enables colleagues with the necessary skills and experiences to invest in and work on the ideas, founders Jim Lavoie and Joe Marino get the benefit of both blue-sky thinking and roll-up-the-sleeves execution.

2. THE MOST CREATIVE LEADERS DON'T JUST TAP THE POWER OF HIDDEN GENIUS TO ATTRACT NEW IDEAS. THEY LEVERAGE THE VIRTUES OF COLLECTIVE GENIUS TO EVALUATE THE IDEAS THEY ATTRACT.

THERE IS A REASON SO many of the initiatives I described in Chapters 7 and 8 encouraged participants not just to contribute ideas, but also to vote on ideas submitted by others. As hard as it is to unleash a wave of fresh thinking about a tough problem or a big opportunity, it's just as hard to make sense of all the creativity you encounter. Is John Fluevog the only arbiter of good taste in the shoe designs submitted by his customers? Of course not. Is the gang at Threadless best qualified to judge, completely on its own, what illustrations or turns of phrase will most appeal to its million-plus members? Hardly. As creativity guru Keith Sawyer notes, "The real challenge to creativity isn't only quantity; many managers are fond of saying that 'ideas are cheap.' Just as important is that, eventually, someone has to pick the best ideas."

Which is why, in both cases, humbitious leaders don't just encourage lots of different people to become part of the idea-generation process—they give them a voice in the *decision-making* process as well. At Fluevog, the evaluation methodology is simple and straightforward. Customers submit designs to the website, and other visitors vote on whether or not they like them. It's not majority rule; John Fluevog and a team of professional designers, sourcing executives, and manufacturing experts express their opinions about which sketches look best, which are most feasible in terms of materials and costs, and which are simply impossible to make. But the voice of the customer does matter—after all, they're the ones expected to buy the shoes.

The idea-evaluation process at Threadless is far more elaborate—and puts even more authority and influence in the hands of the community. Sure, members have cast millions of votes over the years about which illustrations they like and dislike, a process Threadless calls "scoring." But Threadless is more than just a huge virtual ballot box. There are blogs, discussion groups, interviews with designers, videos submitted by members to support artists they believe in, tools for artists to promote their own designs—all sorts of ways not just to express thumbs-up or thumbs-down opinions about a shirt, but to shape the overall sense of style on the site.

Ultimately, Threadless is more than a never-ending design competition. It is an ongoing design *conversation* that invites hundreds of thousands of people to participate in ways that play to their strengths and talents. "There are lots of people on Threadless who never submit a design, but score a ton of designs," cofounder Jake Nickell told me. "They have great opinions about stuff, and those opinions matter— to us, to the community, certainly to the artists. Reading what other people think about your work has an effect on how you design, whether or not a particular design gets printed. All of the commentary and feedback helps good designers become better designers, and helps us make better decisions for the brand as a whole."

3. NOT ALL NEW IDEAS ARE GOOD IDEAS. SO LEADERS WHO ASK FOR LOTS OF IDEAS HAVE TO GET GOOD AT REJECTING THE BAD ONES WITHOUT DEMORALIZING THE PEOPLE WHO CONTRIBUTED THEM.

I'LL BE THE FIRST TO admit that when I study leaders who have challenged themselves to stop acting like lone geniuses and have worked to tap the hidden genius inside and outside their organizations, I zero in on the success stories—the far-flung team of engineers, statisticians, and machine-learning researchers who pooled their efforts and won the million-dollar Netflix Prize; the charming artists, marketers, and biochemists who took time away from their daily routines and designed shoes that captured the imagination of

John Fluevog and his customers. That's what's engaging, exciting, instructive, and fun to write about.

Of course, for every one of these boffo ideas, there are hundreds, thousands, even tens of thousands of bozo ideas—algorithms that don't advance the state of the art in collaborative filtering, shoe designs that fall flat. So a big challenge for leaders who want to get the best ideas from the most people is to figure out what to do with all the ones that aren't so great. How do you turn down bad ideas without creating bad blood among the people who came up with them?

There's no foolproof answer to this sensitive question, but the experiences of leaders such as Netflix CEO Reed Hastings, the senior team at IBM (which plays such a big role in its Innovation Jams), and Rite-Solutions cofounders Jim Lavoie and Joe Marino suggest a few hints about what works. Above all else, they suggest that it is vital for leaders to demonstrate that everyone's ideas got a fair shake, that there was nothing arbitrary or capricious about whose sketches, algorithms, or business plans turned into products or ventures. If you want to maintain a healthy flow of energy and ideas, you've got to keep information flowing about how and why certain ideas rise to the top.

That was fairly easy for Reed Hastings—the competition for the Netflix Prize was literally a math problem, so his company could publish a frequently updated leaderboard that showed the top-ranked entrants, when their solutions were submitted, and how well their algorithms performed against the 10-percent-improvement target. Participants always knew where they stood, because Netflix was always keeping score and posting the results.

IBM's much-chronicled 2006 Innovation Jam was more subjective than the Netflix Prize, which meant that senior executives had to be more creative about how they maintained morale. CEO Sam Palmisano and his colleagues didn't abdicate responsibility for figuring out how to turn advanced technology into successful businesses. Instead, they redefined their responsibility—and kept the process open for all to see. The company "developed a carefully thought-out process that it used after each phase of the Jam to harvest ideas," the *Sloan Management Review* explained. "Senior executives and others spent weeks sifting through tens of thousands of postings—gigabytes of often aimless Jam conversation. Working through the static enabled the leaders to extract ideas they thought were key, put them together into coherent business concepts and link them with people who could make them work. . . . Leaders found themselves taking a different role than in the past. Their new role was about nurturing and identifying a good idea as it was built by the organization. But they were still drivers of the process."[3]

The stock market for ideas at Rite-Solutions is like a clever blend of the Netflix Prize and IBM's Innovation Jam. On the one hand, there's no objective way to decide whether one "expect-us" idea is better than another, no precise formula for entering a new business or adopting a proposal to save costs. At the same time, there is an objective "score"—the price of each stock based on the investment choices of the company's employees. But here's the important part, at least from the perspective of morale: while every stock enters the market at $10 per share, prices only go up from there. Lavoie and Marino worried that it would be too embarrassing for rank-and-file employees to watch their $10 stocks drop to $1 or $2 per share, so they use this simple design feature to take some of the sting out of rejection.

"There's no management 'disapproval loop' here, no gauntlet people have to run if they want to propose new ideas," explains Joe Marino. "But there are pretty clear signals from the stock market about which ideas get the organization as a whole excited. We don't want people to feel like an idea got 'shot down' by their colleagues or by us. That's not the message. All you did was float an idea and see if people could get invested in it. If not, well, try again. It was nothing personal."

4. LEADERS WHO ARE EAGER FOR OUTSIDERS TO SHARE IDEAS WITH THEM HAVE TO BE EAGER TO SHARE THEIR IDEAS WITH OUTSIDERS.

EVER SINCE THE PUBLICATION, NEARLY two decades ago, of Peter Senge's monumental bestseller *The Fifth Discipline*, we've been in the age of the "learning organization." Smart leaders have come to understand that for their organizations to stay ahead of the competition, they and their people have to learn more (and more quickly) than the competition: new skills, new takes on emerging technologies, new ways to do old things, from manufacturing to marketing to R&D. It's hard to argue with this love of learning: that's precisely what makes humbition such an important leadership quality.[4]

But one thing I've learned is that the most humbitious leaders and organizations—those most eager to learn from others—also tend to be the best *teachers*, those most eager to *share* with others. Both IBM and Rite-Solutions have developed powerful techniques for harvesting great ideas from unexpected places—a big source of competitive advantage. So you'd think they'd want to keep these techniques to themselves. In fact, leaders at both companies are eager to share their techniques with other leaders who want to learn from them.

As I explained in Chapter 7, IBM has turned its Innovation Jams into a business—offering to do for other big companies what it's done inside its own company. When I first explored the Rite-Solutions stock market, one of the highest-priced stocks on Mutual Fun was *the stock market itself*—rank-and-file employees collectively saw the value, from the point of view of business leadership and thought leadership, of licensing their technology to other companies and showing them how to use it. Since then Jim Lavoie and Joe Marino have written white papers, delivered presentations, and visited companies to explain what they've learned about where good ideas come from—in part to drum up business, but more importantly to beat the drum for a smarter and more humane approach to leadership.

If you think back to earlier chapters, you begin to appreciate how many companies and leaders with an open-minded commitment to learning have a genuine commitment to teaching as well. Dr. Gary Kaplan and his colleagues at the Virginia Mason Medical Center, who learned so much from the Toyota Production System, have established an institute to train other hospitals and health-care executives in the quality-improvement techniques they've mastered. CEO Tony Hsieh and his colleagues at Zappos, who are voracious consumers of ideas about strategy, branding, and culture, have created a Web-based service called Zappos Insights that teaches subscribers the intricacies of how the company does business, and holds two-day, on-site boot camps that immerse participants in the Zappos culture. Why share the company's business tactics and people practices? Because "sharing," Hsieh told *BusinessWeek*, "is how we spread our brand."

The same spirit of sharing animates the founders of 37signals, the fast-growing software company I wrote about in Chapter 4. CEO Jason Fried and his colleagues have developed a truly original set of ideas about strategy, marketing, and the organization of work—ideas that have fueled their success. But they don't keep those ideas to themselves. Through a series of conferences (called Seed), a fabulously instructive blog (called Signal vs. Noise), and even a free e-book on the Web (called *Getting Real*), they share their ideas with anyone who wants to learn from them. Their approach to business, they like to say, is not to outmarket the competition, but to outteach the competition.

Why? Because teaching creates a different kind of presence in the marketplace and a higher sense of loyalty among those who learn from you. And it helps the company to create not just customers for its products but also an audience for its ideas—an audience that, in turn, is eager to share its ideas with the company. Collaboration is a two-way street: leaders who are eager for outsiders to share ideas with them have to be willing to share their ideas with outsiders.

5. HUMBITION CAN BE MORE THAN AN INDIVIDUAL STYLE OF LEADERSHIP. IT CAN BE AN ORGANIZATIONAL WAY OF LIFE.

As I noted in Chapter 8, most of my case studies of humbition at work were onetime experiments or extraordinary initiatives—well-designed responses to clearly defined problems. But the highest form of humbition is when executives rethink and reimagine the role of the organization itself, when they ask searching questions not just about how to charge up their supply of ideas, but about who's in charge in the first place. If you agree (as I do) with creativity guru Keith Sawyer that "innovation can't be planned, it can't be predicted; it has to be allowed to emerge," then you should also agree that the ultimate opportunity for leaders is to allow as many participants as possible to emerge as leaders.

That's the key lesson behind the long-term success of the Orpheus Chamber Orchestra. It would be a neat trick for a group of accomplished musicians to come together once or twice and delight an audience at Carnegie Hall by performing without a conductor. But for a conductorless organization to maintain a track record of excellence for more than thirty-five years, to tour the world, to release more than seventy recordings, to win Grammys and countless other awards—well, that's pretty clear evidence that something powerful is at work. As Professor Richard Hackman points out, the real genius of Orpheus is not that it has figured out how to play without a conductor as the all-knowing leader. It's that it has turned so many frontline players into real leaders and devised a system of "rotational leadership" that allows just the right people to exercise leadership at just the right time.

That's also the key ingredient behind the meteoric growth of Threadless. Most observers of this funky online fashion company (me included) get smitten by the miraculous creativity it has unleashed— tens of thousands of artists and illustrators whose work gets scored by hundreds of thousands of members. But the real reason Threadless has thrived as a business is that it has put so many elements of the business in the hands of its members—not just the process of design, but day-to-day, operating decisions that are traditionally the purview of serious, full-time executives. Harvard Business School professor Karim Lakhani, coauthor of a multimedia case on the company, explains it this way: "Threadless completely blurs the line of who is a producer and who is a consumer. The customers end up playing a critical role across all its operations: idea generation, marketing, sales forecasting. All that has been distributed."[5]

PRACTICALLY RADICAL WORKBOOK—EXERCISES TO RESHAPE YOUR COMPANY AND RECHARGE YOURSELF

SINCE THE PUBLICATION OF *Practically Radical*, I've had the chance to share its themes, advice, and case studies with audiences of executives, technologists, and entrepreneurs from around the world. What a long, strange, wonderful trip it's been—from urging on hundreds of Russian entrepreneurs in a movie theater in Moscow, to swapping ideas and business plans with advertising hotshots and startup founders on a rooftop in Berlin, to addressing thousands of human-resource professionals in a vast convention center in Toronto, to being grilled by engineers and technologists from one of the world's leading aerospace companies—literally an auditorium filled with rocket scientists.

Indeed, perhaps the greatest reward for having spent months and years honing the messages for this book is the chance to then spend months and years interacting with people who are interested in those messages. Over time, though, I've sensed a change in what these change agents want to hear about—or, more precisely, what they want to talk about. Increasingly, I'm being asked not just to present my ideas and themes, but also to help leaders at every level figure out how those ideas and themes apply to their problems—that is, how to put the ideas in *Practically Radical* to work inside their organizations and in their careers.

Hence, I've assembled this all-new *Practically Radical* Workbook—questions that define the core challenges of change for leaders in any field, along with exercises to meet those challenges and do the hard work of making long-lasting progress in fast-moving times. I've always thought that the value of a book aimed at leaders who want to make a difference has less to do with the precision of the arguments it makes than with the energy of the conversations it unleashes and the originality of the answers it inspires. Here's hoping these questions and exercises unleash energy and inspire answers for you and your colleagues.

QUESTION: WHAT IDEAS SEPARATE YOU FROM EVERYONE ELSE?

IF THERE'S A CORE THEME at the heart of this book, it's that the most successful organizations don't just offer competitive products and services, they stand for important ideas—ideas that shape the competitive landscape of their field, ideas that reshape the sense of what's possible for customers, employees, and investors. For so long, we lived in a world where the strong took from the weak. If you had the biggest factories, the deepest pockets, the most established brands, you won just by virtue of showing up.

That world is finished. Today, *the smart take from the strong.* The most successful organizations don't just work to outcompete their rivals. They aspire to redefine the terms of competition by embracing one-of-a-kind ideas in a world filled with me-too thinking. What are the ideas that define your company and its offerings? How are those ideas shaping how you do business? How do you, as a leader, personify those ideas?

EXERCISE: CONDUCT A "WHY SHOULD I DO BUSINESS WITH YOU?" AUDIT OF YOUR ORGANIZATION.

IN CHAPTER 4, I DESCRIBED a gathering of dispirited bankers who were complaining about turmoil in the financial markets, brutal competition from powerful competitors, customers who seemed impossible to please. Then those bankers heard from a renowned market-research guru, who described how his "mystery shoppers" visit bank locations across the country and ask employees they encounter a simple question: As a customer, why should I do business with you, as opposed to the bank across the street or around the corner? Two-thirds of the time, he reported, front-line employees have no good answer to that question—which is a questionable situation indeed for banks that want to stand out from the crowd and stand for something special in the marketplace.

You don't need to hire that market researcher to conduct a version of his eye-opening exercise at your company. Choose a small team of people to serve as your research brigade. Encourage them to interact with lots of their colleagues at every level of the organization, from senior marketers to mid-level finance executives to front-line service personnel. Have the team ask those people to explain as crisply and persuasively as they can why customers should do business with your company.

Then ask yourself: Do your people as a group have something clear and compelling to say? Do they as individuals more or less say the same thing—is there a shared understanding about what your organization is trying to achieve? Is what they say meaningfully different from what their counterparts at your two or three toughest competitors would say?

In other words, what do you promise that no one else can promise? What do you deliver that no one else can deliver? If your colleagues *don't* have compelling answers to those make-or-break questions, what does that say about the ideas your company stands for, and why you expect to win?

QUESTION: DO YOU AND YOUR PEOPLE CARE MORE THAN EVERYONE ELSE?

EVEN THE MOST CREATIVE AND disruptive leaders recognize that strategy and performance are not just about thinking differently from other companies. They are also about *caring more* than other companies—about customers, about colleagues, about how the organization conducts itself in a world with endless opportunities to cut corners and compromise on values. Sure, new business models allow innovators to transform the sense of what's possible in their industries. But sustaining performance is as much about cultivating a spirit of grassroots energy, enthusiasm, and engagement as it is about unleashing a set of game-changing ideas.

In other words, you can't be special, distinctive, and compelling in the marketplace unless you create something special, distinctive, and compelling in the workplace. As an organization or as a team, your strategy *is* your culture, your culture *is* your strategy. The most successful companies work as distinctively as they compete. Does yours?

EXERCISE: CREATE A "CULTURE BOOK" THAT CAPTURES HOW YOU WORK AND WIN.

ORGANIZATIONS OF ALL SHAPES AND sizes routinely create artifacts to explain themselves to the outside world, from annual reports to shareholders to slick marketing collateral for customers. But leaders who want their colleagues to work as distinctively as they compete also create artifacts that explain the organization to itself—language and rituals and materials that capture what it means to be part of something special and communicate the kinds of commitments that people make to one another.

Perhaps the most compelling workplace artifact I've come across is the annual *Zappos Culture Book* published by the fast-growing online fashion retailer. It's an amazingly creative and energetic document that runs to hundreds of pages, and serves as a platform for rank-and-file employees to explain what makes them tick as people, what makes Zappos tick as an organization, and how their personal values are in sync with the value proposition around which Zappos has built its business.

The ten "core values" that define life at Zappos are a touch off-beat—"create fun and a little weirdness" or "be adventurous, creative, and open-minded." The *Zappos Culture Book*, which gets bigger and weirder every year, is truly off-the-charts—a blend of art, poetry, photography, and assorted riffs and rants that describes how Zappos people work and live. CEO Tony Hsieh works hard to get the most heartfelt and outsized contributions from his colleagues, in part by vowing that he will not tone down or edit what they write—and that he will make the book available to any job candidate, customer, or supplier who asks for it.

What would a "culture book" at your company look like? How would people at every level explain why they have signed on to be part of the organization and why they could not imagine working with any other organization? How would they express the sense of camaraderie that holds them together, the sense of identity that connects how the company behaves in the marketplace with how they operate in the workplace? You don't have to make your "culture book" available to the outside world. But what if it became everybody's favorite read *inside* the company, a shared expression of what it means to be part of something meaningful and do something important?

QUESTION: DO YOU HAVE CUSTOMERS WHO CAN'T LIVE WITHOUT YOU?

THIS IS AN URGENT QUESTION for companies in every industry, because every industry has customers with a vast array of products and brands from which to choose. Remember, in a world defined by unlimited choice and sensory overload, if you have customers who can live without you, eventually they will. Harvard Business School Professor Youngme Moon, author of the must-read marketing treatise *Different*, likes to say that for companies, products, and brands, breakaway success requires "a commitment to the unprecedented."

That's why it's not enough to satisfy customers rationally. You have to engage them *emotionally*, to conduct yourself in ways that are unusual and unforgettable. At Umpqua Bank, Ray Davis and his colleagues have devised a retail experience that appeals to all five human senses. Their goal: "We don't want the experience of banking here to feel like banking anywhere else." At Life Time Fitness, a "healthy way of life" company that has reimagined how the health-club business works, leaders say their goal is "operating to artistry"—devising a blend of well-chosen offerings, high-energy spaces, and thoroughly engaged staffers that leads to a deeply felt level of engagement with customers. One of the make-or-break challenges for any organization is to become irreplaceable in the eyes of its customers.

EXERCISE: WRITE YOUR COMPANY'S "OBITUARY" AND BE HONEST ABOUT HOW MANY CUSTOMERS WOULD BE SAD TO READ IT.

IF YOU'VE SPENT ANY AMOUNT of time in executive retreats or offsites, you've probably been asked to participate in a familiar evaluation of your career and impact. "Take twenty minutes," the facilitator will say, "and write your leadership obituary. What legacy did you leave? What contribution did you make? What might your colleagues remember about you?"

At one level, it's a strange (and slightly morbid) exercise. At another level, it serves a worthwhile purpose—encouraging leaders to see themselves the way their colleagues see them, to evaluate their impact from the perspective of the people who feel that impact. I'd suggest that what goes for individuals goes for organizations too. Take some time (probably much longer than twenty minutes) and write your *company's* obituary. What legacy did your company leave? What contributions did your company make to its industry? What might your customers remember about the company and its products and services?

It's a simple exercise that grows out of a powerful question I heard many years ago from advertising legend Roy Spence, who says he got it from Jim Collins of *Good to Great* fame. Whatever the original source, it's worth taking seriously as a guide to what matters in terms of marketplace success. When Spence visits a client, he says, he makes it a point to ask them: "If your company went out of business tomorrow, who would miss you and why?"

Why might a company be missed? Because its products and services are so distinctive, because its culture is so unique, because its mission is so compelling, that other organizations can't come close to duplicating them. Precious few organizations meet *any* of these criteria, which may be why so many companies feel like they're on the verge of going out of business. Write an unblinking "obituary" for your organization, wrestle with its observations and implications, and perhaps you can avoid the real thing by crafting connections with customers that make it hard for them to live without you.

QUESTION: DO YOU HAVE NEW IDEAS ABOUT WHERE TO LOOK FOR NEW IDEAS?

INNOVATION IS ALL ABOUT IDEAS, so new models of innovation demand new answers to the question of where ideas come from in the first place. My simple answer is that new ideas for your organization can come from any organization in the world, in any field you can think of, if you as a leader are open-minded enough to look for them. Leaders at Lexus identified all sorts of new ideas to re-shape the market for luxury cars by searching for clues at brands such as Four Seasons and Apple—companies that were great at what they did, even though what they did had nothing to do with automobiles. Physicians and administrators from London's Great Ormond Street Hospital for Children redesigned many of their surgical procedures by studying how Ferrari's Formula One racing team handled pit stops.

Sure, there's always a place for R&D as research & development. But there's also a place for R&D as rip-off and duplicate: Ideas that are routine in one industry can be revolutionary when they migrate to another industry, especially when they challenge the prevailing assumptions and conventional wisdom that have come to define so many industries.

EXERCISE: ORGANIZE INNOVATION FIELD TRIPS TO FIND IDEAS THAT ARE WORKING IN AREAS OUTSIDE OF THOSE IN WHICH YOU AND YOUR COLLEAGUES WORK.

ONE WAY TO LOOK AT problems and opportunities as if you're seeing them for the first time is to survey a wide array of fields for ideas that have been working for a long time. That's what

Gary Kaplan and his colleagues from Virginia Mason Medical Center (VMMC) realized when wave after wave of doctors, nurses, and administrators left their comfortable surroundings in Seattle not just to study the Toyota Production System but also to work and live it themselves, spending a week on factory floors in Japan to master the techniques through which Toyota mastered the challenges of quality, efficiency, and productivity. VMMC's field trips, which have gone on for years, didn't just allow hospital personnel to import techniques and practices from Toyota; they also inspired a new mindset about what was possible in Seattle and unleashed far-reaching transformations.

You don't have to travel to Asia to organize mind-stretching exercises for you and your colleagues to get beyond traditional modes of thinking. Maxine Clark, founder and CEO of Build-a-Bear Workshop, and Kip Tindell, cofounder and CEO of the Container Store, spent time working on the front lines of each other's operations—and discovered all kinds of practices they transferred back to their organizations. All of your employees have companies they love to do business with, brands that make a huge impression on them, services that are a big part of their lives. Ask them to identify companies from far outside your field whose ideas and practices might reshape your field—and then encourage them to find ways to spend time inside those companies, switch jobs for a day with their counterparts at those companies, and otherwise get exposed to techniques that are working well in an unrelated field, and challenge the established order in your field.

Your job as a leader, in the words of PepsiCo CEO Indra Nooyi, is to "lift and shift" those ideas out of the arena in which they took shape and apply them to your company and industry. What better way to fuel your imagination than to look for inspiration beyond your field?

QUESTION: ARE YOU LEARNING AS FAST AS THE WORLD IS CHANGING?

I FIRST HEARD THIS QUESTION from strategy guru Gary Hamel, the world-renowned innovation expert, and it remains the ultimate challenge for any executive determined to unleash big change in difficult circumstances. In a world that never stops changing, great leaders never stop learning. The challenge for leaders at every level is no longer just to out-hustle, out-muscle, and out-maneuver the competition. It is to out-think the competition in ways big and small, to develop a unique point of view about the future and help the organization get there before anyone else.

IDEO's Tom Kelly likes to quote French novelist Marcel Proust, who famously said, "The real act of discovery consists not in finding new lands but in seeing with new eyes." What goes for novelists goes for leaders searching to discover a novel game plan for the future. If you believe that what you see shapes how you change, then the challenge for leaders is to see opportunities that other leaders don't see. But remember: You don't have to look all by yourself. These days, the most powerful insights often come from the most unexpected places—the hidden genius inside your company, the collective genius of customers, suppliers, and other smart people who surround your company. Tapping this genius requires a new leadership mindset— enough ambition to address tough problems, enough humility to know you don't have all the answers.

EXERCISE: HOLD A DISRUPTION DAY TO CHALLENGE CONVENTIONAL WISDOM INSIDE YOUR ORGANIZATION AND WITHIN YOURSELF.

BACK IN CHAPTER 1, I described how the brilliant marketers at TBWA, the global advertising agency behind game-changing brands such as Apple, Adidas, and Absolut, help clients develop new lines of sight into the future—by challenging obsolete visions from the past. They call the methodology "Disruption Days"— wide-open, freewheeling, yet highly structured examinations of the assumptions and behaviors that stand in the way of progress for a brand, a company, or an industry.

TBWA's methodology has evolved over the years. But certain

techniques remain central to the process. For example, the agency has developed a rich list of what-if questions to reframe strategic rethinking. What if we stop focusing on the traditional competitors and focus instead on the source of business (often indirect competition)? What if we reconsider using strategies usually considered unsuccessful (or taboo) for this category? What if, instead of differentiating the brand, we redefine the category experience? What if we reverse the logic of things?

Moreover, Disruption Days invite participants to rummage through their "brand attic" and reinterpret what's come before with a company or a product as a way to develop a line of sight into what comes next. Seeing the future with fresh eyes doesn't mean turning a blind eye to history. Sometimes, the very act of rediscovering the past creates the clarity and confidence necessary to craft a distinctive game plan for the future.

TBWA's specific questions and techniques, of course, are less important than the general spirit of the exercise, which is to challenge received wisdom. So why not organize a Disruption Day of your own to help "see with new eyes"—whether that applies to the organization as a whole or you as an individual leader? As Jean-Marie Dru, the agency's chairman, puts it, the point of the exercise is "questioning the way things are, of breaking with what has been done or seen before, of rejecting the conventional." That's how you keep learning as fast as the world is changing.

Acknowledgments

THIS IS, MUCH TO MY amazement, the fifth book I have written in the last twenty-five years. It is also the first I have written without a coauthor. But that in no way implies that *Practically Radical* is a "solo" venture. Everything about this book, from the core ideas to the case-study material to the simple fact of its existence, reflects contributions from friends, colleagues, supporters, and tormentors who have been a part of my personal and professional life for more years than I care to count. Writing can be lonely at times, but in all my years of thinking about what matters in business, and why business matters to the world, I have never felt alone. So please indulge me as I thank my friends, colleagues, and fellow travelers.

Richard Pine of Inkwell Management has been my literary agent for the last two decades. He's been invaluable as a guide to the confusing (and delightful) world of book publishing, but he's been indispensable as a friend, counselor, and yes, one of those tormentors who keeps challenging me to think bigger and push harder. I can't imagine writing books without Richard urging me on.

The editing and marketing team at William Morrow has been an endless source of smarts, energy, enthusiasm, and patience. I meet lots of fellow authors in my travels, and many of them like nothing more than to whine about their publisher. I listen quietly, nod sympathetically, and think to myself: I must be the luckiest guy in the world, because I can't imagine publishing this book without the world-class talents at William Morrow. Thanks to my supremely supportive editor,

David Highfill, publisher Liate Stehlik, Jean Marie Kelly, Lynn Grady, Andy Dodds, and all of their colleagues. What a crew!

One reason *Practically Radical* was fun to write is that I had an online platform to play with the ideas and showcase some of the characters as I was writing. That platform was courtesy of the editors at *Harvard Business Review* Online, the digital arm of *HBR* and Harvard Business School Publishing (www.hbr.org). Thanks to Josh Macht, Eric Hellweg, Jimmy Guterman, Paul Michelman, Sarah Green, Cathy Olofson, and so many others who embraced my work and welcomed me with open arms and open minds.

A big part of the experience of publishing this sort of book is getting the chance to talk about it at meetings, conferences, and gatherings around the world. The irrepressible spirits at the Washington Speakers Bureau have kept me piling up frequent-flier miles on the lecture circuit and interacting with all kinds of companies and audiences. I always learn something from these events, and I enjoy the wide variety of talks. What I enjoy even more is working with Tony D'Amelio, Christine Lancman, Kristin Downey, and all the WSB folks who make them possible. They are true professionals.

Now, for a few new nods to some old friends. Alan Webber and I started *Fast Company* back in the early 1990s. We live in different cities today, we don't see each other nearly as much as we used to, and the magazine itself has moved in new directions. But *Fast Company* remains a highlight of my professional life, and Alan has had a profound impact on how I do whatever it is that I do. Polly LaBarre, who was one of the first souls brave enough to sign on with us at *Fast Company*, and who then was crazy enough to write *Mavericks at Work* with me, has been a go-to colleague and source of energy for fifteen years. To Bill Breen, Elizabeth Busch, Charles Fishman, Gina Imperato, Pat Mitchell, Anna Muoio, Nate Nickerson, Curtis Sittenfeld, and the rest of the *Fast Company* alumni club: we're still together in spirit, even if we no longer laugh and argue together at the 'rang. To Eric Albert, Steve Ferzoco, Carl Mayer, Carlos Ramos, and Eliot Spitzer—thanks for the friendship, laughter, and (occasionally sincere) words of encouragement.

To all of the organizations that opened their doors to me as I researched this book, and to all of the leaders who shared their ideas and strategies with me, thank you for your time, your enthusiasm, and your intellectual honesty. I have been amazed by—and grateful for— the willingness of so many people, doing such important work, to make room for me to listen in, poke and prod, and follow up—again and again. For me, the great joy and inspiration is not what I get to write but whom I get to meet—remarkable people doing extraordinary things.

And speaking of remarkable people. . . . Everything I do, professionally and personally, is inspired by the love, energy, and laughter I get from Chloe, Paige, and Grace. I spend lots of time thinking, writing, and lecturing about change, but you three are perfect just the way you are. To Johnny (the cat formerly known as Johnny Damon), who sat on the sofa in my office and stared at me as I stared at my computer screen—thanks for the companionship. As for Livvie the dog, well, your bark is worse than your bite. (Note to appalled readers: my children insisted that I acknowledge the pets.) No one could ask for a more supportive or fun-loving family. For me, that never changes.

As I stated in the introduction, I read widely and deeply about business and change. But the way I truly *learn* about change is to see it for myself. So most of the material in this book is the direct result of company visits, personal interviews, and first-person observation. Still, I drew on plenty of secondary sources for context, perspective, background, and statistics. These notes identify the material I found most valuable during the research and writing of *Practically Radical*.

Introduction:
A Game Plan for Game Changers

1. Tom Friedman has an unrivaled ear for clever quips and intriguing one-liners. I first saw the Paul Romer reference in Friedman's column, "Kicking Over the Chessboard," *New York Times*, April 18, 2004. The quote from the "unknown Texas genius" is also from a Friedman column, "9/11 and 4/11," *New York Times*, July 20, 2008. For more on Paul Romer, see "The Economics of Ideas," by Kevin Kelly, *Wired*, June 1996.

2. See *Reset: How This Crisis Can Restore Our Values and Renew America*, by Kurt Andersen, Random House, 2009.

3. The Charlie Rose interview with Warren Buffett aired on October 1, 2008. www.charlierose.com/view/interview/9284.

4. The explanation of "animal spirits" comes from the master's masterwork, *The General Theory of Employment, Interest, and Money*,

by John Maynard Keynes, first published in 1936. The latest hard-cover edition is available from BN Publishing, July 2008. A more recent statement of the basics of behavioral economics is *Animal Spirits: How Human Psychology Drives the Economy, and Why It Matters for Global Capitalism*, by George A. Akerlof and Robert J. Shiller, Princeton University Press, 2009.

5. "Design Loves a Depression," by Michael Cannell, *New York Times*, January 3, 2009.

6. Russel Wright has special significance for me, as coauthor of *Mavericks at Work*, because he was an enthusiastic participant in a crazy event called the Maverick Festival, an annual summer gathering of artists, musicians, and dancers near Woodstock, New York, that made the "other" Woodstock look tame by comparison.

7. The Library of Congress has a wonderful collection devoted to "The Work of Charles and Ray Eames: A Legacy of Invention." See it on the Web (www.loc.gov/exhibits/eames).

8. "Downtime Opportunity," by Bradley Johnson, *Advertising Age* White Paper, December 2008.

9. "Hanging Tough," by James Surowiecki, *The New Yorker*, April 20, 2009, is a short essay that packs a big punch. See also "Missing the Boat and Sinking the Boat: A Conceptual Model of Entrepreneurial Risk," by Peter R. Dickson and Joseph J. Giglierano, *Journal of Marketing*, July 1986.

CHAPTER 1:
WHAT YOU SEE SHAPES
HOW YOU CHANGE—THE VIRTUES OF VUJA DÉ

1. For an overview of the trials and tribulations facing Rhode Island and its capital city, see the following articles: "Smallest State Grapples with Oversize Problems," *New York Times*, March 1, 2009; "Now Free to Speak Its Mind, an Ex-Mayor Is Doing So,"

New York Times, April 28, 2008; "Providence Gangs' Feud Festering Since Last Fall," *Providence Journal*, March 29, 2009.

2. See "Providence Murder Rate Spikes in 2009," by W. Zachary Malinowski, *Providence Journal*, December 21, 2009.

3. See "Clean Slate," by Jim Taricani, *Rhode Island Monthly*, September 2007.

4. The best article I've read on the history of community policing and the work of Dean Esserman is "Bratton's Brigade," by Rob Gurwitt, *Governing*, August 2007. It was a vital resource for this chapter.

5. In addition to meeting him in person, I read two excellent profiles of Teny Gross. See, "The Reluctant Warrior," by Denise Dowling, *Rhode Island Monthly*, April 2006, and "Taking It to the Streets," by Nell Porter Brown, *Harvard Magazine*, Jan.–Feb. 2009.

6. Crime statistics provided by the Providence Police Department in its report, "A Return to the Neighborhoods: 2003–2008." See also "A Gathering Storm—Violent Crime in America," Police Executive Research Forum, October 2006.

7. John Kotter has literally written the book (and lots of essays) on change. For some of his most influential work, see *Leading Change*, Harvard Business Press, 1996; *A Sense of Urgency*, Harvard Business Press, 2008; and "Leading Change—Why Transformation Efforts Fail," *Harvard Business Review*, March–April 1995.

8. For a brief history of vuja dé, see the following sources: *The Ten Faces of Innovation*, by Tom Kelley, Currency Doubleday, 2005; *Weird Ideas That Work*, by Robert Sutton, The Free Press, 2002; "The Collapse of Sensemaking in Organizations: The Mann Gulch Disaster," by Karl E. Weick, *Administrative Sciences Quarterly*, December 1993. Thanks again to Tom and Bob for introducing me to this language.

9. For an overview of TBWA's thinking on disruption, see the following books: *Disruption*, by Jean-Marie Dru, Wiley, 1996; *Beyond Disruption*, by Jean-Marie Dru, Wiley, 2002; and *How Disruption Brought Order*, by Jean-Marie Dru, Palgrave Macmillan, 2007.

10. There are several excellent accounts of Pedigree's transformation. See *Disruption Stories,* by Warren Berger with Jean-Marie Dru and Lee Clow, published by TBWA, 2005; "By Design, A Company's Culture Goes to the Dogs," by Warren Berger, *one. a magazine,* Design Issue 1.3; "Must Love Dogs: On TV and Online, in Print and at Retail, Pedigree's Brand Is Puppy-Powered," by Eleftheria Parpis, *Adweek,* February 18, 2008

11. "Dog-Food Ad to Try a New Trick," by Suzanne Vranica, *Wall Street Journal,* December 22, 2008.

12. "The Man Who Invented Management," by John Byrne, *BusinessWeek,* November 28, 2005.

13. To get a sense of Dean Esserman's incorrigible critics, see "After Department Drug Sting, Providence Police Chief Blasted, Hailed," by Amanda Milkovits, *Providence Journal,* March 15, 2010.

14. The quote comes from "The Birth of the Swatch," by Youngme Moon, Harvard Business School Case Study 9-504-096, 2004; see also "Nicolas G. Hayek," by Dominik E. D. Zehnder, Harvard Business School Case Study 9-495-005, 1994.

15. In addition to telephone conversations with Nicolas Hayek conducted in February 2009, my material on the transformation of Swatch Group draws heavily on my interview with Hayek published in *HBR.* See, "Message and Muscle—An Interview with Swatch Titan Nicolas Hayek," *Harvard Business Review,* March—April 1993. The story of Omega and the JFK ad relies on an article in the *New York Times,* "Omega's Reminder: JFK Wore One," by Andrew Adam Newman, August 3, 2009.

16. You can watch a video of Irving Wladawsky-Berger's discussion of IBM and its near-death experience at http://tinyurl.com/c9wev5.

17. "Girl Scouts Shake Up the Recipe," by Irene Sege, *Boston Globe,* March 21, 2009; "Blogs In, Badges Out as Girl Scouts Modernize," by Megan Greenwell, *Washington Post,* March 2, 2009.

18. "The Girl Scouts: Uncharted Territory," by Lissette Rodriguez,

The NonProfit Quarterly, Fall 2007. By far the most insightful article on Kathy Cloninger and the transformation of the Girl Scouts is "How Do You Transform a 95-Year-Old Organization? Ask the Girls," by Polly LaBarre, *360° The Merrill Lynch Leadership Magazine,* November–December 2006.

19. *How Girls Can Help Their Country: Handbook for Girl Scouts,* reprinted by Applewood Books, 2001.

CHAPTER 2:
WHERE YOU LOOK SHAPES WHAT YOU SEE—
OF BIG DOTS, PIT STOPS, AND HOT SPOTS

1. "The Bell Curve," by Atul Gawande, *The New Yorker,* December 6, 2004.

2. For an insightful history of IHI and its work, see "Institute for Healthcare Improvement: The Campaign to Save 100,000 Lives," Stanford Graduate School of Business Case L-13, by David Hoyt, January 21, 2008.

3. Donald Berwick's quote also comes from the Stanford case.

4. Polly LaBarre and I wrote extensively about Commerce Bank in *Mavericks at Work: Why the Most Original Minds in Business Win,* William Morrow, 2006.

5. *Benchmarking for Best Practices: Winning Through Innovative Adaptation,* by Christopher E. Bogan and Michael J. English, McGraw-Hill, 1994.

6. Two articles describe the unusual collaboration between doctors and pit crews: "Ferrari Pit Stop Saves Alexander's Life," by William Greaves, *The Telegraph,* August 29, 2006; and "A Hospital Races to Learn Lessons of Ferrari Pit Stop," by Gautam Naik, *Wall Street Journal,* November 14, 2006.

7. "CEO Swap: Two Best Companies Chiefs Trade Places," by Paul Keegan, *Fortune,* February 8, 2010.

8. Thanks to Polly LaBarre for sharing this quote. See John Dewey, *The Quest for Certainty: A Study of the Relation of Knowledge and Action*, first published by Minton, Balch & Co., 1929.

9. The description of Interpol's old approach to red notices comes from a fabulous profile of Ron Noble. See "Terrorists Strike Fast . . . Interpol Has to Move Faster. . . . Ron Noble Is on the Case," by Chuck Salter, *Fast Company*, September 2002. For another great profile of Noble's career and work, see "The World's Top Cop," by Maggie Paine, *UNH Magazine*, Winter 2002.

10. "The Man from Interpol," *60 Minutes*, October 7, 2007. A transcript of the segment is available at cbsnews.com.

11. Harvard Business School has published an in-depth case study of the work of Gary Kaplan and his colleagues. See "Virginia Mason Medical Center," by Richard M. J. Bohmer and Erika M. Ferlins, HBS Case 9-606-044, October 3, 2008. It was an important resource for this chapter.

12. "Hospital on Cost-Cutting Mission Adds Trip to Japan," by Lisa Heyamoto, *Seattle Times*, June 6, 2002; "To Build a Better Hospital, Virginia Mason Takes Lessons from Toyota Plants," by Cherrie Black, *Seattle Post-Intelligencer*, March 15, 2008.

13. This vignette comes from a Harvard Business School case study by Richard M. J. Bohmer and Erika M. Ferlins.

14. Charles Kenney's book was a crucial resource for me to understand IHI, Virginia Mason, and health-care innovation in general. I owe this work a huge debt of gratitude. See *The Best Practice: How the New Quality Movement Is Transforming Medicine*, by Charles Kenney, Public Affairs, 2008.

15. "President of Toyota Apologizes," by Hiroko Tabuchi and Micheline Maynard, *New York Times*, October 3, 2009.

16. The *Wall Street Journal* has done an especially good job of covering the rise of Lexus and the ideas behind its success. See, for example, "To Woo Wealthy, Lexus Attempts an Image Makeover," by Gina Chon, *Wall Street Journal*, March 24, 2007. See also

"Luxury-Car Sellers Put on the Ritz," by Neal E. Boudette, *Wall Street Journal*, December 18, 2007.

17. "Selling the Special Touch," by Jennifer Saranow, *Wall Street Journal*, July 18, 2008.

18. *The Innovation Killer: How What We Know Limits What We Can Imagine—and What Smart Companies Are Doing About It*, by Cynthia Barton Rabe, American Management Association, 2006.

19. There is no shortage of material on hard times in the Motor City. See, for example, "Detroit's Outlook Falls Along with Home Prices," by Tim Jones, *Chicago Tribune*, January 29, 2009; and "Nonprofit Hospitals Leave the City for Greener Pastures," by Barbara Martinez, *Wall Street Journal*, October 14, 2008.

20. "Restaurant Chef Matt Prentice Embarks on a Quest to Reinvent Hospital Food," by Kate Lawson, *Detroit News*, January 27, 2009.

CHAPTER 3:
RADICALLY PRACTICAL (I)—FIVE TRUTHS OF
CORPORATE TRANSFORMATION

1. This quote comes from my *Harvard Business Review* interview with Nicolas Hayek, March–April 1993.

2. Jean-Marie Dru describes the "Wear a Different Hat" exercise in *Beyond Disruption*, Wiley, 2002.

3. These quotes come from an interview I did with Laurel Richie. For more on how the organization is rethinking its brand, see "Girl Scouts Seek an Image Makeover," by Ellen Byron, *Wall Street Journal*, March 25, 2008.

4. Once again, I tip my cap to Charles Kenney's book, *The Best Practice*, in which he writes extensively about the Esther Project. It was at an event celebrating the book's publication that I heard the panel discussion with Göran Henriks.

Chapter 4:
Are You the Most of Anything?
Why Being Different Makes All the Difference

1. My insights on Zappos are based largely on conversations with CEO Tony Hsieh and his colleagues, and in-person visits to the company's headquarters and its fulfillment center in Kentucky. But three articles provided important background. See, "The Zappos Way of Managing," by Max Chafkin, *Inc.*, May 2009; "Zappos Knows How to Kick It," by Jeffrey M. O'Brien, *Fortune*, January 22, 2009; and "Happy Feet," by Alexandra Jacobs, *The New Yorker*, September 4, 2009.

2. Tony Hsieh's essay appears on his blog, http://tinyurl.com/dgsh4a.

3. See "Happy Feet," by Alexandra Jacobs, *The New Yorker*, September 4, 2009.

4. Tony Hsieh has written a terrific book about the story of Zappos. See *Delivering Happiness*, by Tony Hsieh, Business Plus, 2010.

5. In addition to my interviews with Umpqua Bank CEO Ray Davis, his book provided a valuable history of the bank's growth strategy. See *Leading for Growth: How Umpqua Bank Got Cool and Created a Culture of Greatness*, by Ray Davis with Alan Shrader, Jossey-Bass, 2007.

6. For a case study of Umpqua's approach to design, see "Umpqua Bank: Managing the Culture and Implementing the Brand," by Dr. Karen J. Freeze, Design Management Institute, February 2005.

7. "A Downturn Wraps a City in Hesitance," by Peter S. Goodman, *New York Times*, March 27, 2009.

8. *Different—Escaping the Competitive Herd*, by Youngme Moon, Crown Business, 2010.

9. For the basics of the Ryanair story, see "No Apologies from the Boss of a No-Frill Airline," by Sarah Lyall, *New York Times*,

August 1, 2009; "My Stupid Business," The Weekend Interview with Michael O'Leary, by Kyle Wingfield, *Wall Street Journal*, September 15–16, 2007; "Snarling All the Way to the Bank," *The Economist*, August 23, 2007; "The Guardian Profile: Michael O'Leary," by Andrew Clark, *The Guardian*, June 24, 2005; and "Big Worry for No-Frills Ryanair: Has It Gone as Low as It Can Go?" by Keith Johnson and Daniel Michaels, *Wall Street Journal*, July 1, 2004.

10. From "The Guardian Profile: Michael O'Leary," by Andrew Clark, *The Guardian*, June 24, 2005.

11. "No Apologies from the Boss of a No-Frill Airline," by Sarah Lyall, *New York Times*, August 1, 2009.

12. "The Brash Boys at 37Signals Will Tell You: Keep It Simple, Stupid," by Andrew Park, *Wired*, March 2008.

13. *Getting Real* is available online (https://gettingreal.37signals .com). See also *Rework*, by Jason Fried and David Heinemeier Hansson, Crown Publishing, 2010.

14. *Drive: The Surprising Truth About What Motivates Us*, by Daniel H. Pink, Riverhead Books, 2010.

15. See *3:59.4—The Quest to Break the 4 Minute Mile*, by John Bryant, Hutchinson, 2004.

16. *The Power of Impossible Thinking*, by Yoram (Jerry) Wind and Colin Crook, with Robert Gunther, Wharton School Publishing, 2005.

17. Robert MacDonald told me he borrowed the term "reminiscing about the future" from the legendary journalist Murray Kempton, who used it to describe the visionary talents of Walter Reuther, the great labor leader. For more on MacDonald's business philosophy, see *Beat the System: 11 Secrets to Building an Entrepreneurial Culture in a Bureaucratic World*, by Robert W. MacDonald, John Wiley & Sons, 2008. See also "LifeUSA's Number-One Policy— Speed," by Kate A. Kane, *Fast Company*, August–September 1996.

18. Thanks to Oscar Motomura and Marco Pellegatti of Amana-Key for their insights on Magazine Luiza. In addition to my interview with Frederico Trajano Rodrigues, I relied on two important sources. See "Courting the Poor, a Retailer Rise to No. 3 in Brazil," by Todd Benson, *New York Times*, July 14, 2004; and "Magazine Luiza: Building a Retail Model of 'Courting the Poor,'" by Frances X. Frei and Ricardo Reisen De Pinho, HBS Case 9-606-048, December 12, 2006. The material on the Liquidação Fantástica comes from this HBS case.

19. For more information on the Humana Innovation Center, visit http://crumpleitup.com.

20. My discussion of Gamal Aziz's "working backward" methodology is based largely on interviews with him and visits to the MGM Grand. However, one important additional resource was "From Good to Grand," by Paul Kaihla, *Business 2.0*, July 2006. For an in-depth analysis of the "culture of engagement" at MGM Grand, see *Closing the Engagement Gap: How Great Companies Unlock Employee Potential for Superior Results*, by Julie Gebauer and Don Lowman, Portfolio, 2008.

CHAPTER 5:
DIFFERENT ON PURPOSE—MOTIVATION, INSPIRATION, AND THE HEART OF INNOVATION

1 "The Choice: Years on Dialysis Brought Joe Mole to a Crossroads," by Michael J. McCarthy, *Wall Street Journal*, November 3, 2005.

2. "The Dialysis Business: Fair Treatment?" by Andrew Pollack, *New York Times*, September 16, 2007.

3. The Stanford case study is a fabulous source of ideas, history, and data on DaVita, and I relied on it extensively. It is where I found the Davita Academy graduation proclamation and where I first learned about "Reality 101." See "Kent Thiry and DaVita: Leadership Challenges in Building and Growing a Great Company," by Jeffrey Pfef-

fer, Stanford Graduate School of Business, February 23, 2006.

4. *Rules of Thumb: 52 Truths for Winning at Business Without Losing Your Self,* by Alan M. Webber, HarperBusiness, 2009.

5. The Lombardi biography is a truly inspiring and insightful study of leadership. See, *When Pride Still Mattered: A Life of Vince Lombardi,* by David Maraniss, Touchstone, 1999.

6. See *Drive: The Surprising Truth About What Motivates Us,* by Daniel H. Pink, Riverhead Books, 2010. See also, "The 'Pronoun Test' for Success," by Robert B. Reich, *Washington Post,* July 28, 1993.

7. *Love Is the Killer App: How to Win Business and Influence Friends,* by Tim Sanders, Three Rivers Press, 2002.

8. "Steeling their Courage," by Michael Levenson, *Boston Globe,* February 21, 2009.

9. *It's Not What You Sell, It's What You Stand For: Why Every Extraordinary Business Is Driven by Purpose,* by Roy M. Spence Jr., with Haley Rushing, Portfolio, 2009.

10. "Companies and the Customers Who Hate Them," by Gail McGovern and Youngme Moon, *Harvard Business Review,* June 2007.

11. Thanks to Roy Spence and Haley Rushing, in *It's Not What You Sell . . .* , for alerting me to Arnold Glasow.

12. Two excellent resources capture the findings of the Gallup project. For a book-length treatment, see *Human Sigma: Managing the Employee-Customer Encounter,* by John H. Fleming and Jim Asplund, Gallup Press, 2007. For a more concise look, see "Manage Your Human Sigma," by John H. Fleming, Curt Coffman, and James K. Harter, *Harvard Business Review,* July–August 2005.

13. London Drugs is a privately held company that releases little detailed financial information, but it generously opened its doors to me in the course of two eye-opening visits.

Chapter 6:
Radically Practical (II)—Five New
Rules for Starting Something New

1. Professor Sarasvathy's fascinating research on entrepreneurship appears in a wide range of formats. See *Effectuation: Elements of Entrepreneurial Experience*, by Saras D. Sarasvathy, Edward Elgar Publishing, 2008; see also, "What Makes Entrepreneurs Entrepreneurial?" (available at www.effectuation.org) and "The Affordable Loss Principle," Darden Business Publishing, 2006.

2. *Rework*, by Jason Fried & David Heinemeier Hansson, Crown Publishing, 2010.

3. See "The Guardian Profile: Michael O'Leary," by Andrew Clark, *The Guardian*, June 24, 2005.

4. For more on London Air Services, see "Air Drugstore," by Eve Lazarus, *Marketing*, September 10, 2001; and "Star on Rise for Airline of Rich and Famous," by Michelle Hopkins, *Richmond News*, April 3, 2009.

5. See "Manage Your Human Sigma," by John H. Fleming, Curt Coffman, and James K. Harter, *Harvard Business Review*, July–August 2005.

6. This much-discussed blog entry appeared on www.zazlamarr .com.

Chapter 7:
Leadership Without All the
Answers—Ambition, Humbition, and the
Power of Hidden Genius

1. Thanks to the Orpheus Chamber Orchestra for allowing me to sit in on its rehearsal of January 23, 2009. The account that opens this chapter is based on my personal observations, as well as a wonderful behind-the-scenes documentary created by filmmakers

Chris and Alex Browne. Some of the quotations, including the observations about the orchestra by Anoushka Shankar, come from this documentary. It is available on the Web at www.orpheusraga.com/ragasaga.html.

2. "The Orpheus Mystique (and Myths)," by Barbara Jepson, *New York Times*, October 6, 2002.

3. "Orpheus: The Conductorless Orchestra Turns 35," by Joe Lazar and Lindsay Grimm, University of California Berkeley, Haas School of Business, Case Study 001, September 30, 2007.

4. "Passing the Baton," by James Traub, *The New Yorker*, August 26, 1996.

5. "It's Lonely at the Top," by Rachel Donadio, *The Atlantic*, November 2004.

6. See "The Cult of the Faceless Boss," *The Economist*, November 14, 2009, and "The Decade of Steve," by Adam Lashinsky, *Fortune*, November 5, 2009.

7. "Killer Results Without Killing Yourself," by Michael S. Malone, *Fast Company*, Premiere Issue, 1995.

8. The manifesto is called "Staying Extreme: How to Make a Difference in Any IBM Environment." Jane Harper and several of her colleagues contributed ideas to the manifesto, which was written by a then-IBMer named John Wolpert.

9. *Group Genius: The Creative Power of Collaboration*, by Keith Sawyer, Basic Books, 2007.

10. Harriet Rubin is the founder of Doubleday Currency, a much-admired business-book imprint, and the author of a bestseller called *The Princessa: Machiavelli for Women*, Doubleday Business, 1997. I first heard her insights about freedom and power at a *Fast Company* gathering. See "The Fast Pack," *Fast Company*, January 1998.

11. For a thorough analysis of the 2006 event, see "An Inside View of IBM's Innovation Jam," by Osvald M. Bjelland and Robert Chapman Wood, *Sloan Management Review*, Fall 2008.

12. The quotes on Orpheus are taken from *Leading Teams: Setting*

the Stage for Great Performances, by J. Richard Hackman, Harvard Business School Press, 2002.

13. My analysis of the Rite-Solutions culture, as well as the Mutual Fun stock market for ideas, is based largely on in-depth conversations with founders Jim Lavoie and Joe Marino. However, I also drew on two other important sources. See "Rite-Solutions: Mavericks Unleashing the Quiet Genius of Employees," by David Hoyt, Stanford Graduate School of Business, Case Study HR-27, September 2006. See also, "The Innovation Engine at Rite-Solutions: Lessons from the CEO," by Jim Lavoie, *The Journal of Prediction Markets,* Issue 3, 2009.

Chapter 8:
Hidden Genius at Work—From Shared Minds to Helping Hands

1. John Abele is the best source of information on the remarkable quest to locate the USS *Grunion.* I first learned about this story when I attended a presentation he gave at the fourth annual summit of the Business Innovation Factory on October 15, 2008. You can view it on the Web at http://tinyurl.com/ydsmrda. After seeing that presentation, I conducted an in-depth interview that provided more details. There have been some superb articles about the search as well, and I relied on two of them for my account. See "Mystery at Sea," by Donovan Webster, *Reader's Digest,* January 2008; and "Flowers on the Water," by Rand Richards Cooper, *Amherst Magazine,* Spring 2009.

2. The excerpts from the *Kano Maru's* log appeared in the *Reader's Digest* article by Donovan Webster, who accompanied John Abele and his crew on the voyage to identify the lost sub.

3. See "Sub Ladies Uncover Tale of Lost Crew," by Craig Wilson, *USA Today,* October 22, 2008.

4. I must once again recognize the value of the Rand Richards Cooper

article in *Amherst Magazine,* which is a fabulous piece of work. Readers interested in reading the "Jim Book" prepared by Bruce Abele can download it on the Web (http://tinyurl.com/yhbcpvh).

5. See *Mavericks at Work: Why the Most Original Minds in Business Win,* by William C. Taylor and Polly LaBarre, William Morrow, 2006.

6. "And If You Liked the Movie, a Netflix Contest May Reward You Handsomely," by Katie Hafner, *The New York Times,* October 2, 2006.

7. See "Tapping Tech's Beautiful Minds," by Michael V. Copeland, *Fortune,* October 12, 2009, and "The Netflix Prize Was Brilliant," by Farhad Manjoo, Slate.com, September 22, 2009.

8. See "This Psychologist Might Outsmart the Math Brains Competing for the Netflix Prize," by Jordan Ellenberg, *Wired,* March 2008 and "If You Like This, You're Sure to Love That," by Clive Thompson, *The New York Times Magazine,* November 23, 2008.

9. I first wrote about John Fluevog and his new approach to design in "To Charge Up Customers, Put Customers in Charge," *The New York Times,* June 18, 2006.

10. *Outside Innovation: How Your Customers Will Co-Design Your Company's Future,* by Patricia B. Seybold, HarperBusiness, 2006.

11. To explore the wide range of designs submitted to Fluevog, and to read about the winners of the competition, visit the Web (http://www.fluevog.com/files_2/os-1.html).

12. "The Customer Is the Company," by Max Chafkin, *Inc.,* June 2008.

13. "Threadless: The Business of Community," by Karim Lakhani and Zahra Kanji, Harvard Business School Case Study 608-707, May 2008.

14. I conducted two sets of interviews with the leadership of Threadless—a phone conversation in June 2006 and a personal visit to the company's office-and-warehouse complex in August 2008.

CHAPTER 9:
RADICALLY PRACTICAL (III) — FIVE HABITS OF
HIGHLY HUMBITIOUS LEADERS

1. "The Cult of the Faceless Boss," *The Economist*, November 14, 2009.
2. *The Smartest Guys in the Room: The Amazing Rise and Scandalous Fall of Enron*, by Bethany McLean and Peter Elkind, Portfolio, 2003.
3. "An Inside View of IBM's Innovation Jam," by Osvald M. Bjelland and Robert Chapman Wood, *Sloan Management Review*, Fall 2008.
4. *The Fifth Disciple: The Art & Practice of the Learning Organization*, by Peter M. Senge, Doubleday Currency, 1990.
5. Karim Lakhani is quoted in "The Customer Is the Company," by Max Chafkin, *Inc.*, June 2008.

INDEX